NATALIE BRAMBLE

WIN THE GRANT WITH THE GRANT WRITING SYSTEM

A practical step-by-step guide to
WRITING A WINNING GRANT

'After being unsuccessful in nine consecutive applications, we had a few mentoring sessions with Natalie, and we secured over $100,000! Thank you, Natalie.'

Val Watson

Home Start National

'I've been writing successful grants for more than 20 years. This is a resource that I wish I'd had before I wrote my very first grant, but it's also a resource I recommend to experienced grant writers in the spirit of "sharpening the saw". The system covers all the essential elements of successful grant writing, including project development, logic models and language.'

Megan Dixon

CEO

Regional Development Australia Orana

'I attended a half-day workshop. Natalie's presentation was excellent. I am pleased to say that I wrote an application for a small grant and was successful – I am 100% positive that if I had not attended the workshop the result would have been different – I learnt so much and would recommend this system to anyone wanting to gain or improve grant writing skills.'

Trish Evans

Training participant

'The hundreds of tips and tools Natalie has provided in her grant writing sessions have now been consolidated into this book about The Grant Writing System. These have assisted me to win over $5.3 million of funding over the last five years for local community groups focused on aged care, seniors, veterans, and the vulnerable in our community; as well as local chapters of service clubs and charities, various festivals and events, museums, sporting clubs, showgrounds, community halls, meeting spaces and our local business chamber.'

Nicholas Pyers

Grants Officer

Junee Community Network

'As a Grant Coordinator working to increase regional investment, I can honestly say this Grant Writing System is a game changer for helping businesses and community groups to succeed. After many years of experience, Natalie has developed a system and used it as a best practice benchmark to upskill grant writers and develop a network of professional grant and tender service providers for our region, so we know it works! This system has even won an innovation award. I love it, and you will too.'

Cindy Baker

Grants Coordinator

GW3, Greater Whitsundays

‘I harnessed Natalie’s tips and wrote a proposal for a research grant for an internal funding application at a university. I did it for practice and you might already have guessed the result ... YES, we were awarded the grant, and I was offered a post-doctoral position to manage the project. It’s a short-term intensive project, but the School will be using the funds very wisely to secure longer term projects.’

Dr Karyne Ang

‘Natalie has written the golden formula to accessing capital, grants, and investments for Not for Profits. Understanding your organisation’s Why and doing the project planning is key to being able to articulate your investment’s impact. The Grant Writing System breaks down the components of developing your proposal, practically demonstrating how to craft and answer the questions. Natalie’s system ensures you understand your outcomes and how these align to the grant’s selection criteria so that you are competitive through the assessment process. A critical tool for Not for Profits to add to their toolkit, especially those wanting to win that grant!’

Allison Mudford

Former Grant Program Manager

‘After attending a few of Natalie’s grant writing workshops, I received my first grant – after many unsuccessful applications. Natalie’s presentations and tools are always clear, coherent, and logical. This system gave me all the information I needed to make a good application.’

Val Clark

Author, writer and festival organiser

'I was lucky enough to secure a place on the Grant and Tender Writing Business Program. Natalie used The Grant Writing System throughout this program. Having previously submitted grant applications with no particular system, the framework provided is outstanding, providing a very clear path, with a host of tools to help including the Grant Application Tool and Grant Answer Map. Having the tools brings clarity to guidelines and outcomes all in one place and shows areas which are lacking.'

Heather Batrick

Business Solutions

'Grant research and writing will never be the same again. The Grant Writing System is *a must* if you want to deliver a successful grant submission.'

Michael Tame

Community and business grant writer

'The mentoring and guidance that Natalie has provided around the grant writing process and approach to grant writing has been invaluable. There have been many "light bulb" moments and I've seen an increase in successfully winning grants since implementing Natalie's grant writing concepts and approach.'

Jordana Morrison

Grants writer

First published in 2023 by Natalie Bramble

A catalogue entry for this book is available from the
National Library of Australia.

ISBN: 978-1-923007-26-0

Project management and text design by Publish Central
Cover design by Pipeline Design, Jishan Design and Danny Media

Disclaimer
The material in this publication is of the nature of general comment only, and does not represent professional advice. It is not intended to provide specific guidance for particular circumstances and it should not be relied on as the basis for any decision to take action or not take action on any matter which it covers. Readers should obtain professional advice where appropriate, before making any such decision. To the maximum extent permitted by law, the author and associated entities and publisher disclaim all responsibility and liability to any person, arising directly or indirectly from any person taking or not taking action based on the information in this publication.

Contents

Acknowledgements

I acknowledge and extend my respect to Elders past, present and emerging across Australia and express my deep thanks for Elders and Aboriginal and Torres Strait Islander people who I have worked with, and those I work with today. Thank you for generously sharing your lived experience, knowledge and cultural intelligence with me. Yindyamarra (Respect).

I live on the lands of the traditional owners, the Tubba-Gah and Wilay peoples of the Wiradjuri Nation in Dubbo NSW.

When I started in business, one of my first contracts was the secretariat for the Dubbo Aboriginal Community Working Party. The experience was life-changing for me. The resilience, knowledge and wisdom shared with me by the Elders and working party members helped me understand what authentic community engagement and self-determination is. I learnt firsthand how important it was to support people when they were ready, not to do it for them. I also developed a deep appreciation for how critical it is to involve the people who will be affected by a project in its development. I learnt how vital it was to understand the environment, opportunities and constraints for those engaged in projects, and how to design inclusion into everything, from language to physical assets.

My time with the secretariat raised my level of knowledge on the barriers and constraints some people face, why it's so important to understand systems and processes, and how understanding helps us to work around, under and over these barriers. I've embedded these lessons in the way I work and train every single day. I thank them deeply for sharing their cultural and lived experience with me. They have had a significant impact across the communities I work with, as I share these same lessons with others and work with communities across Australia and the Pacific. Mandaang Guwu (Thank you).

I also want to acknowledge and thank all the wonderful volunteers and community-minded people who strive to build better communities.

Every day I work with amazing people who are doing wonderful things in our communities, and I'm forever grateful for those I've spent time with and the passion and motivation they've shared with me that makes our world a better place.

You inspire me. You're amazing – please keep doing great work!

Thanks to a crew of supporters who helped to bring this book to life. Thanks to Cindy Baker, Megan Dixon and Lisa Griffiths for highlighting the uniqueness of the system I'd created! Thanks to Cindy and Megan for being my critical friends, assisting me to shape The Grant Writing System. Cindy, an extra special shout-out to you. You gals rock x. Lisa, your interpretations, learning design and critical feedback are on point. I just know what I do. Your eye to spot and interpret the process or framework I use has been magic! Love your work.

Thanks to Kellie Jennar for always keeping me grounded, acting as my sounding board to name and refine tools, and for being a research goddess. You're a gem. Thanks to the wonderful Andrew Griffiths for his sound advice on bringing this book to life and to Michael Hanrahan for his endless patience with me over four years! And thanks to Charlotte, for your wise editing work. A big thanks to my wonderful beta readers who gave me such valuable feedback.

The most important acknowledgement I've left until last, and it would take reams of paper to truly recognise the deep appreciation I have for my husband, my partner in business and life, Glen Dunkley. Glen, you've believed in me from day one, never wavering in your absolute support of everything I do. You've travelled the sometimes-bumpy road of business with me, supported my risks and backed me 200%. You help me to slow down and remember to take care of myself when I'm working to the bone and supporting others. You lighten my life with your humour and quick wit and are my compass and rock. I'm so thankful I get to do life and work with you.

Acknowledgements

Preface

The stillness for a split second when my heart stopped. I'd just received exciting news. As I took a deep breath and my brain processed what I'd just heard, my heart started beating double time, and I felt giddy. The overall reaction was clear, I'm sure, from the growing grin on my face.

I had won the first grant I applied for. In fact, it was the first grant our youth group, Rotaract, had ever applied for. Thanks to the Foundation for Young Australians and the advice of then Dubbo City Council Grants Officer Damien Duffy, we had received the green light to start a project to support youth in the community. The grant was for a professional development program, which included workshops on personal finance, credit management, understanding employment contracts, career development and learning job-ready and leadership skills.

Our club was pleased. We received amazing press and media support for the program, and it increased our profile as a club that got things done. The biggest satisfaction, though, was for the people who took part in the program (and I was one of them). The skills we learnt at these workshops set us up for our jobs and helped us avoid common financial mistakes – such as signing our life away because we didn't understand the fine print on contracts!

I've experienced the same euphoria over the years, winning grants for community organisations and businesses, and hearing success stories of those I've trained. These grants have gone towards building new houses for people who are displaced, giving them shelter, food and, above all, safety and somewhere to call home. Businesses have been able to grow their workforce and deliver services to communities who had previously missed out. They've developed innovative new products and been able to get them to market and grow their products and services. Communities have been able to implement hygiene and food programs, supporting families and getting children ready to learn. People who are in vulnerable and at-risk situations have been able to remove themselves from the situation and access support to lead the life they choose. Pre-schoolers can now read, thanks to volunteer in-home reading programs. People have finished their weekends with unforgettable memories of events and festivals. Communities have improved medical services, and developed new tourism products and recreational facilities that have brought more money to the community, supporting more local businesses and organisations, and created more jobs.

This is the magic grants offer communities. They provide opportunities for community organisations and businesses to apply for funds that can change businesses, lives and communities for the better.

This impact drives me every day to improve people's skills and knowledge so they can Win the Grant they're applying for. I want you to achieve the same, so I'm open with what I've learnt. That's why I'm here to share my system and tools to guide you on your journey to Win the Grant.

About me

I have a success rate of over 80% (some years it's around 82%, others 100%). I've raised millions of dollars directly and I've raised even more through the grants I've written, which clients have re-used in other applications. I've trained thousands of people over the years, many succeeding soon after the training, and they've gone on to win millions of dollars for their organisations and communities. People have developed skills and knowledge to improve their careers and their income, some even launching their own successful grant writing businesses.

The system and tools I provide through this book, do work. And you can start using them straightaway.

The knowledge in this book is a culmination of my work as a grant and tender writer, chair of assessment and judging panels, trainer, and consultant to funders planning their funding programs, guidelines and application forms. I'm curious about how others decide, so I'm always seeking to understand what decision-makers are thinking, and what led assessors and funders to decide the outcome for an applicant, win or lose.

Of course, I haven't always had such a high grant writing success rate. This deep curiosity to understand the world of grants began when I lost my first grant, the fourth one I had applied for. I couldn't believe it. The crushing disappointment hit first and then, of course, the blame - as we all often do when something goes wrong. We internalise things and self-blame: 'What did I do wrong?', 'Why didn't they like what I'd written?', 'Why didn't they like the project?' Next came the anger: 'Well, they don't know what they're doing, do they?!'

When I settled down, I asked myself a more useful question: 'How can I improve to Win the Grant?' This question led me to research the whole process more deeply, and ask everyone I could about grants. Unfortunately, this was before the days of the online information age. (Well, for most people, anyway. The only people I knew who were online were in government, in business, and in chat rooms.) Library research and talking to people were the only ways I could find out information about grants. No workshops or training options were offered in the region, and a trip to the city with accommodation added to the workshop fees was out of my budget. So, most of what I learnt was by trial and error. I had to filter out the relevant information in the books I was reading and work out how to implement the many tips I learned.

My question 'How can I improve to Win the Grant?' created a questioning, curious mindset. I wanted to learn everything I could. I knew I would make mistakes – I'd already lost out on one grant. Importantly, I wanted to learn from those mistakes. So, for every grant, regardless of whether it won or lost, I analysed the guidelines, the funders and grant applications a few months after I'd submitted them. I analysed the applications to understand what I thought worked and what didn't. I asked every funder for feedback (most provided feedback back then!) and guidance on where I could improve in future submissions. Because I was doing this for each grant, I started noticing changes and trends coming through in funder guidelines and grant applications.

The information I would have shared with you 10 years ago differs from the information I am sharing with you now. Over the years, I've developed training to respond to trends influencing the world of grant writing. Many of the things I'm sharing here, I would once have only talked about in the advanced workshops. What was once expected of larger grants of above $100,000 is now expected of smaller grants. Even smaller grants from local councils are nowadays more strategic. Heck, their plans align with the United Nations' Sustainable Development Goals, and guess what? The projects you want funded by your local council assist them to report on these UN goals. So, they invest in things to achieve this (international) strategy, aligned with their community strategic plans and other government strategies and plans.

You need to work out if the grant you're reviewing is worth the time and energy you'll need to give it. Some organisations won't look at any grants under a certain limit – for example, $10,000. For them, they don't feel the work is worth the potential return. Sometimes you'll feel like you're asked to do a lot of work for only a small amount of money, and then you have additional reporting obligations to meet if you're successful. When I sat on the other side of the table as an assessor and advisor on grant programs, I began to understand why they ask so many questions, particularly for larger grants. Funders and program managers know how difficult it is to manage organisations and how easy it is for projects to fail if something is missed. They can have staff and volunteer turnover and conflicts; financial concerns and other situations can put them in varying positions of risk. They can appear to be solid, and then 12 months later can have changed so much that now getting involved with these organisations is a major risk.

So, over my years of experience, I have learnt there are things we can change, things we can advocate for, and things we choose to accept. For now, we must accept grant application processes are just that, a process – similar to a job application process. So, while we can advocate for simpler application processes, doing your groundwork is essential to guide organisational project plans. These plans deliver the impacts of the projects we're seeking funding for – and that's what this book is all about.

Who this book is for

This book is for anyone who wants to improve their grant writing skills and success rate, no matter their level of experience. However, it's not a 101-grant writing book – there's a free download on www.winthegrant.com if you'd like that. It's for people who have tried in the past and not been successful, and those who have had some success but want to improve their knowledge. Even experts have taken away insights and adopted tools into their business and approach to grant writing. I share stories of business and community organisations, from interest-based projects to business-development programs through to services and infrastructure. Each project requires different components. It doesn't matter what type of organisation you are. It's what you want to achieve and what the outcomes (benefits) are that can change the approach you take. I share those approaches as we progress through the book.

The world of grants can feel complex and confusing because every funder has different goals, processes and applications. I've been applying for and assessing grants for over 20 years and there's always something changing. Every funder has a different approach, and nearly every funding round has different guidelines, questions and assessors. Because of this, grants can feel complex with a variety of approaches and factors to consider.

Many people think grants are about simply writing answers to the questions in the application. But that's not how it works. Sure, one aspect is learning how to write better answers - and I do share my tips on this through this book - but this shouldn't be your focus. Let me share one irrefutable truth.

> *Grants are about strategy. They're 80% planning and thinking and 20% writing.*

The good news is you don't need a university degree, or to study strategy. Sure, this kind of formal study helps, but we all learn to think strategically at an early age. Have you ever played a game where someone hides, and you have to search for them? That's what thinking strategically is like. Hide and seek. When you seek, you use your brain to think strategically. Where did I last hear a noise? What's big enough for my friend to hide behind?

You can think strategically to put your project and your organisation in the best position to Win the Grant.

So, your focus shouldn't only be about 'How do I answer this question?' It's about putting yourself in the shoes of the funder with the assessor's hat on. The funder's looking to see if you understand why they're providing grants in the first place, what they want to achieve and how your project assists them. Your answers should make this clear. If you don't understand grants, the funder and the process, you won't give the assessor the information they want. This will drastically reduce your points at the assessment stage. For many, this means they don't even make the short list.

If I'm going to put my time and effort into an application, I like to know there's a bit of certainty, and I've done as much as I can to Win the Grant. While I was writing and assessing grants, I was also mentoring and training others. While for me it had become second nature, I knew there was a better way to teach others to learn how to be more successful with their grant applications. So, I set about developing an approach and tools to give people direction and I created a system. I call this The Grant Writing System.

About The Grant Writing System

Over the years, I've learnt that systems save me energy, time and stress - and I love them. I don't enjoy reinventing the wheel. If someone has a useful approach or tool, I'll use it and adapt it to my needs. And throughout this book, I do refer to some of these, because they work.

However, I couldn't simply adopt an existing grant writing system - because there wasn't one out there. Personally, I felt that made the grant world so much harder to navigate than it should have been. With food products, manufacturers use different ingredients and different amounts to create their unique offerings. To guide us, the food industry created a food labelling system to compare the same foods to make the best decision. However, understanding guidelines and preparing applications wasn't easy – so I developed a system myself.

The Grant Writing System follows a 7-Stage Grant Writing Cycle. Each stage contains steps, and I provide a total of 12 tools. This overall system provides structure and directions to guide you, no matter what grant you're applying for. I've even used some of these tools in my process when applying for things other than grants, including award applications, tenders and sponsorship, with similar success rates.

Understanding The Grant Writing System

This book outlines my Grant Writing System – a practical step-by-step guide to writing a strong application. Because there are so many variables, of course, I can't guarantee you'll then win any grant you're applying for, but I can promise you, if you follow these steps, you'll learn strategies to develop a stronger project and write a stronger grant application. I know this system works. I use this, and I've taught others this system and they've gone on to win more grants than they have before. One person attended a recent workshop and then won eight of the 10 grants they applied for, on behalf of their clients.

As a grant writer, you go through a predictable cycle – from planning to reporting, to using those reports and outcomes to market the results and developing your planning for the next grant. While this isn't always a sequential process, understanding the stages involved can make the whole process easier. This is why The Grant Writing System is structured around The 7-Stage Grant Writing Cycle.

The seven stages in The Grant Writing System are as follows:

1. **Plan:** Plan to get grant ready!
2. **Find:** Find grants and choose the right one.
3. **Align:** Align to the funder's goals.

4. **Write:** Write a strong application.
5. **Submit:** Submit without regret!
6. **Manage:** Manage the outcome, win or lose.
7. **Report:** Report and leverage data for more funding!

These stages are also outlined in the following figure.

The 7-Stage Grant Writing Cycle

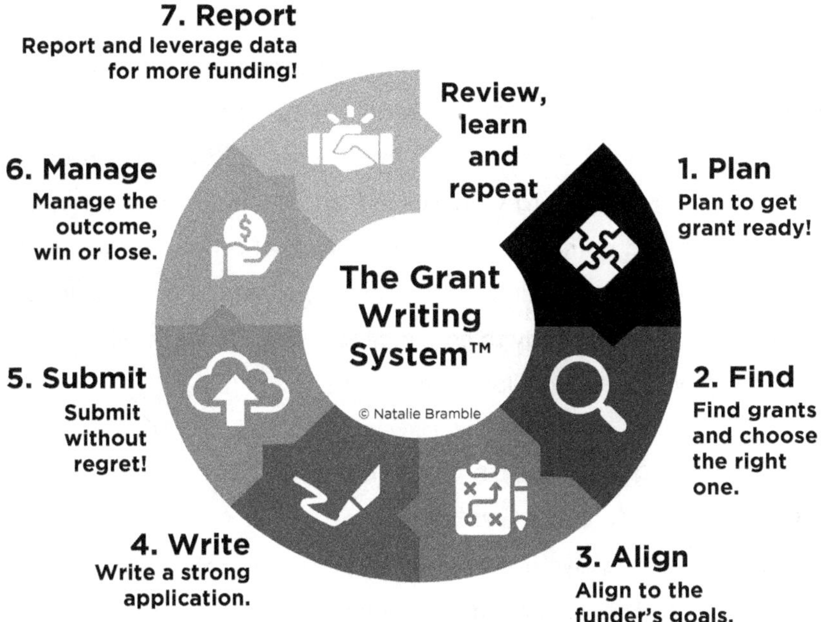

The structure of this book aligns with these seven stages, with each part focusing on one stage in The Grant Writing System. In each stage, you'll explore steps and tools to guide you through The Grant Writing System.

As mentioned, while I follow The 7-Stage Grant Writing Cycle in this book, the stages are not always sequential. You may go through different stages of The 7-Stage Grant Writing Cycle at different times. For example, if you haven't done the planning stage when a grant's announced, you might work on your planning at the same time as drafting your application.

In an ideal world, you'd get your project plan ready and use insights from the planning stage to write your application. Often, however, the steps outlined in stage 1 ('Plan to get grant ready') through to stage 4 ('Write a strong application') happen in a short time frame or simultaneously.

Some people even find the grant first, and then plan what they're going to deliver. Now, I live in the real world, and I understand why this happens. I get it. The opportunity is there, so why wouldn't you decide to apply even though you aren't quite ready?

However, having to do the minimum you need in this process – from planning through to writing – in a short amount of time means more stress and commitment. Getting started on the stages in the process as early as possible can support you and your organisation to get grant ready – ready to convince funders you know what you're doing and you're an excellent investment.

Introducing the steps and tools in The Grant Writing System

The Grant Writing System breaks down The 7-Stage Grant Writing Cycle even further, outlining the separate steps within each stage and highlighting the 12 tools I've developed across the seven stages. These tools represent my process and guide you through the grant writing world to save you time and stress.

The figure on the opposite page shows The Grant Writing System in full.

As with any new process, working through The Grant Writing System will take focus; however, once you're used to the system, it will become second nature and you may not need to do each of the steps, or use each of the tools every time. No matter how experienced

The Grant Writing System™

Stages in The Grant Writing System™	1. Plan	2. Find	3. Align	4. Write	5. Submit	6. Manage	7. Report
Steps in each stage	**Plan to get grant ready!** a. Get yourself and your organisation grant ready. b. Get your idea grant ready. c. Get your project grant ready.	**Find grants and choose the right one.** a. Search, pitch and attract funds. b. Decide if it's the right grant to apply for.	**Align to the funder's goals!** a. Understand the funder. b. Think like an assessor. c. Analyse the application documents.	**Write a strong application.** a. Understand the question. b. Communicate strategically. c. Refine your answer.	**Submit without regret!** a. Review and edit. b. Avoid submission mistakes.	**Manage the outcome, win or lose.** a. Manage the project. b. Monitor and evaluate outcomes.	**Report and leverage data for more funding!** a. Share good news and manage challenges. b. Use reports and outcomes as marketing tools.
Tools to guide you	i. The Grant Ready Checklist™ ii. The Grant Ready Kit™ iii. The Grant RICE Score™ iv. The Grant NDOIS Pitch™ v. The Grant Project Plan™	vi. The Grant Calendar™ vii. The Grant Go/No-Go Decision Checklist™	viii. The Grant Application Tool™	ix. The Grant Answer Map™	x. The Grant Submission Checklist™	xi. The Grant Evaluation Plan™	xii. The Grant Acquittal Report™

you become (or already are), the steps and tools I provide in this book are always a good back-up - even I go back and check them from time to time to verify I'm not missing something, in the lead up to deadline.

I use the tools for different reasons and in different ways. When I'm working with a new organisation, I use **The Grant Ready Checklist** and **The Grant Ready Kit** (covered in step 1a of this book). If we're deciding which project we should focus on to find funding, or which solution best meets a need I'll use the **The Grant RICE Score** (step 1b). If we're working to secure partnerships, persuade influencers and attract diverse areas of funding and support I'll use **The Grant NDOIS Pitch** (step 1b).

If a project needs work, I use **The Grant Project Plan** (see step 1c). When I'm searching for grants I'll use the **The Grant Calendar** (step 2a) to keep on track of announcements and closing dates. Where I've assessed a grant using **The Grant Go/No Go Decision Checklist** (step 2b) and know it's a simple one I want to apply for, I go straight to using **The Grant Answer Map** (stage 4, steps 4a to 4c). For more complex grants, I'll use **The Grant Application Tool** (step 3c).

I always check through **The Grant Submission Checklist** (step 5b) during editing and before I submit. When I receive the funding, I use **The Grant Evaluation Plan** (see step 6b) and if I don't receive a template report from the funder, I'll use **The Grant Acquittal Report** (step 7b).

How to use this book

I've written this book so you can either start from the beginning and read through, or you can choose any step that interests you most or that you're working on right now. It's been designed to be a resource you can dip in and out of, getting those tips and approaches to help you in your work, right now. To be this resource you need in the step you've chosen to read and work through, you'll see references to other stages and steps of The Grant Writing System. I've done this because I don't want you to miss information from other stages and steps that can help you Win the Grant.

But I know learning any new approach or system can be a little overwhelming. So, if you asked me what are just two things you can do right now to improve your chances to Win the Grant, I'd say it depends on the complexity of the grant. **For a simple grant, use The Grant Go/No-Go Decision Checklist** (step 2b) **and The Grant Answer Map** (stage 4, steps 4a to 4c). **For more complex grants, complete The Grant Application Tool** (step 3c) **and The Grant Answer Map** (stage 4). Then, when you've understood those, reflect on other stages in The Grant Writing System and where you can improve.

The Grant Writing System and the tools within it can assist you to maximise your points at the assessment stage and give the assessors the information they need – to say, 'Yes! You did Win the Grant.'

You can write a successful grant, particularly a small one, without going through every single step I share in this book. Even if a few steps and tools are enough for right now, you will no doubt reach a point where you just can't seem to get any more funding. You'll notice your success rate isn't as high, and you'll notice you can't seem to get any more money than perhaps the few thousand dollars in a local grant program. Perhaps your regular funder is having conversations with you about being self-sustainable. Maybe they're suggesting you need to look elsewhere for financial support, or you should seek sponsorship to make your event viable. Or you might find if you're trying to increase the amount of money you attract, funders want more information and evidence from you. Making use of the full Grant Writing System assists to overcome these tensions.

If you're fairly new to grant writing, I'd recommend starting at the beginning. You'll find gems of information and knowledge in the first part of the book. Some terms and concepts might be new if you've never written a grant before. So, focus on the areas you'd like to learn more about. As you improve in those areas and feel confident, continue to delve further into the details.

What tools should I use right now?

	You have a lot of ideas and aren't sure where to start	You found a grant and want to know quickly if it is suitable for your project	You want to get grant ready	You're not sure how to work out the benefits of your idea
1. The Grant Ready Checklist™			✓	
2. The Grant Ready Kit™			✓	
3. The Grant RICE Score™	✓			
4. The Grant NDOIS Pitch™				✓
5. The Grant Project Plan™	✓		✓	✓
6. The Grant Calendar™				
7. The Grant Go/No-Go Decision Checklist™		✓		
8. The Grant Application Tool™				
9. The Grant Answer Map™		✓		
10. The Grant Submission Checklist™				
11. The Grant Evaluation Plan™				
12. The Grant Acquittal Report™				

Grant is due tomorrow, and you need to write your answers	You need to promote your idea and get support	Writing a small grant (under $10,000)	Writing a medium-size grant $10,000 to $100,000	Writing a large grant $100,000 +	You've received a grant and need to manage and acquit it
	✓				
	✓				
✓		✓	✓	✓	
			✓	✓	
✓		✓	✓	✓	
		✓	✓	✓	
					✓
					✓

If you have written a grant before, start wherever you'd like to improve your grant writing. Just don't make the mistake of thinking it's only about writing!

Regardless of your experience, you can do the self-assessment in the last step of the book or reflect on the table in the appendix to identify areas for improvement.

Even if you feel you're more advanced, the beginning of the book is still of value because everyone has unique experiences and reflects on the same subject differently and learns different lessons. You'll also learn how to use The Grant Writing System tools as you progress. Once you've grasped the concepts, choose the steps and tools to guide you as you improve your grant applications and grant writing skills.

Throughout the book I've also provided example answers to reinforce the key points and improve your understanding of how this strengthens grant applications and answers.

Because there are a lot of different situations I'm trying to guide you through, this book contains the main tools I have developed and use for different grants. I don't use all the tools at once. Sometimes all you'll need is two key tools, other times you'll need a few more. However, it can feel overwhelming not knowing what tools would work at a minimum for different situations. On the previous pages is a quick reference guide on the tools in The Grant Writing System.

'I'm in a community organisation. Is the book useful for me?'

Absolutely! I work with charities, not-for-profits and social enterprises. All the information provided here is going to assist you. You'll need to gather and provide more information than a business that deals with products and services. You must think about outcomes and impact, and how your resources and workforce needs differ.

We'll dive into these areas in the book and if you want to dig deeper into more of the 'how to' I provide more resources in the online kit and the training resources at iClick2Learn. Just find the corresponding stage and step from the book to find what you're looking for.

'I work in government. Is the book useful for me?'

Government departments, like any organisation, must justify spending money on projects. If you work within government, sometimes you're pitching to other departments for financing or grants to support your work. I've had people in local and state government tell me The Grant Writing System has assisted them understand how to write a sound proposal to get their work, or even their grant program, funded.

If you work within government and are supporting organisations applying - for example, as a local council grants, community or sports development officer or a grant program manager for state or federal government - you'll be able to share your insights and information on how to access The Grant Writing System. You can also join our licensing program to share The Grant Writing System in your organisation and with businesses and groups in your community.

'I'm in a business. Is the book useful for me?'

Yes, it certainly is. I've been using The Grant Writing System to secure grants for businesses, including our social enterprise, for many years. Unless I include a specific mention of a business, in this book I use the term 'organisation' to incorporate all types of organisations to reflect what I'm saying applies to all. I share examples of business grants throughout this book. However, unapologetically, this book leans more into businesses and organisations that deliver benefits and projects to people. This is because these organisations need to do more, and outline more complex matters on services and community, to Win the Grant.

Most business grants are based on an organisation's logical, strategic decisions, which are easily demonstrable - for example, designing a website, or expanding manufacturing of a product, creating jobs or upgrading buildings. These are about business growth, products and infrastructure. So, while you'll need to access tools to calculate these, the application is logical. Community development is more human-focused and, therefore, story-based, requiring community consultation and data sourcing from various sources. While assessors still make logical, strategic decisions, they also consider the element of social and human impact, which is less tangible. So, this means a little more work and a little more strategy.

Even though some approaches tend to focus more on community development, the steps and tools in The Grant Writing System are transferrable to your business. One manufacturing business owner attended a community workshop out of interest and rang me a few months later to say he thought he'd apply for an innovation grant using the knowledge I shared. And he did Win the Grant! He was so excited. I get similar feedback from other business owners and staff who are so amazed when they realise they can apply the learning to their business.

If you're a business applying for these types of grants, you'll learn from this process. Decision-makers want to know their funding is making a difference to your business, your team, your industry and your community.

'I'm an individual achiever, researcher, athlete or artist. Is the book useful for me?'

Yes, you'll pick up a lot of ideas and useful approaches you can apply to what you're doing. These apply to many individual grants, including sports sponsorship, creative pitches, writing a book, applying for a bursary or seeking funding to produce work. While I don't cover specific areas, such as artist statements or coach references, you'll still learn many useful tips and tools to guide you when thinking about your application.

As an example, one researcher who attended my two-hour grant writing training session picked up some valuable tips to understand how to apply for a grant. Shortly after, Jing-Li applied for her first academic university research grant – and did indeed Win the Grant! I teach these same tips and much, much more in this book. It's like doing an intensive grant writing masterclass!

If you work with organisations that either support your work or seek you out to work on a project together, this book is for you. Using these tools will assist you to think strategically. You'll be able to think like the funder and understand the grant assessment process.

I'm not in Australia; does this information translate to grant processes in my country?

While I don't have personal experience applying for grants in other countries, I've helped a few people who have attended my grant workshop Q&As who have applied for international grants. I've also guided others who live in another country and are applying for grants (they've been dedicated joining us in their time zone!). I've also researched a few grant programs across Commonwealth and European countries and found many similarities in the processes.

Fundamentally, if you have to do any or all of these things:

- ✓ design a project to address something that you, your clients or your community needs
- ✓ decide which idea has more merit than others
- ✓ work out the benefits of your idea
- ✓ plan what you're doing and how you're going to achieve it
- ✓ find funding and pitch your project
- ✓ an application process with rules about what you can and can't do
- ✓ submit or complete a form with questions
- ✓ negotiate or sign a contract or agreement, or
- ✓ comply with requirements and report on achievements ...

... then absolutely YES, the strategic approaches and tools in The Grant Writing System will be of value to you.

Other support you can access

I want you to use the information I'm sharing and bring in money to achieve your goals. **You can access further learning and support in five ways:**

1. Join our newsletter at www.winthegrant.com and access the free grant writing Q&As we run every four to six weeks.

2. Check out our online kit at www.winthegrant.com/online-kit. This kit includes videos, interviews and tools shared in this book. (You'll need a coupon to access all the resources. When you sign up use this coupon code W1nTh3gR@nT to access this for free.)
3. If you're in regional Australia, you can access a free grant writing introduction course, thanks to the innovate with nbn® education innovation award and grant we won. This was delivered by NBN Co, in partnership with the Regional Australia Institute. Find out more at www.winthegrant.com.
4. Talk to me about speaking, training or mentoring. My email is natalie@winthegrant.com.
5. Consider licensing the content. If you're a grant writer, trainer, funder, or a government grant, community or sport and recreation development officer and want to use The Grant Writing System, we have a licensing and train-the-trainer program. This way you can use my system and tools with my permission. Don't risk a breach of copyright. (Gosh, I hate having to remind people about intellectual property rights and copyright. I've had to talk with other grant writers and trainers about passing off my content as theirs. Let's all do the right thing by each other.) Contact me or find out more here: www.winthegrant.com/licensing.

I'm not going to wish you good luck, because grants are a game of strategy and it's not luck that wins. Instead, what helps you win is putting what I share in this book into practice, and continuing to ask yourself, 'How can I improve to Win the Grant?' This will assist you in writing stronger applications.

Improve one skill at a time. Keep practising, and keep learning, and keep picking yourself up if you are unsuccessful! You've got so many ideas and plans to start!

Overview of grants

While this book focuses on supporting you to improve your grant writing, I recognise some new grant writers may not have the same experience with funders. For example, you may have written a successful local council grant or two and are now approaching a state-government grant. The requirements will be different, and you need to improve your understanding.

So, before we jump into The Grant Writing System in full, I'll first run through the fundamentals about grants. In this introduction, I cover what grants are, where the money comes from, why funders give out grants and what type of grants are out there. I also list what makes a strong grant application.

For some extra support if you have never written a grant before, you can also download my book *Win the Grant 101: An introduction to Grant Writing* at www.winthegrant.com/grants101.

What are grants?

My dad used to say any tool I borrowed from him was 'on permanent loan, just take care of it'. I think of grants in the same way. The funder has something you need - money and support - and they're happy for you to use it on permanent loan; you just need to do the right thing and take care of it. Another way to think of grants is they're like payment-free loans. You'll have to contribute something to the project, and perhaps even share the risk with a financial co-contribution yourself. Ultimately, if you're successful, the funder gives you the rest of the money.

You don't have to pay anything if you do the right thing, but the funder has an interest in what you do. Often, this interest extends beyond the funding period, which is why I talk about grants in terms of permanent and payment-free loans. (I cover this in more detail throughout the book, particularly when I discuss funding contracts.)

The key thing to recognise is grants are not free money. You commit to delivering a project and achieving outcomes for the funder's investment by signing a funding contract. If you don't do what you say, you may have to pay the grant money back, in full. If you breach a clause in the contract, you may have to pay the grant money back, in full. So, the grant has to be taken seriously.

Grants have the following features:

- ✓ Grants can fund you, your organisation (business, not-for-profit or social enterprise) or your community to achieve positive outcomes.
- ✓ They can fund the delivery of a specific product, helping you improve or grow your business or deliver a project or service. For example, they can fund the delivery of activities, works and exhibitions, events, scholarships or infrastructure such as a new building or upgraded facilities.
- ✓ They are time limited. Funders commit to funding for outcomes to be delivered by a set date, with the majority having 12-month timelines. Some funding is multi-year, dependent on a successful outcome being achieved.
- ✓ They are aligned to the funding body's objectives to address challenges and opportunities identified by the funder.
- ✓ They have to meet one, more than one, or all of the outcomes the funder wants to achieve with the grant program.

Your role is to demonstrate:

✓ the need and justification for your idea

✓ a sound understanding of the funder's objectives and outcomes

✓ the best way to achieve the desired outcome

✓ you know what you're doing and have the skills and resources to deliver

✓ you have the support of the people you're working with, and who are benefiting from the grant

✓ you have partnerships in place and are collaborating with appropriate organisations and individuals.

Why do funders provide grants?

Funders provide funding for tangible and intangible outcomes. For example, they might fund a new product you're developing in your business, or a building upgrade (a tangible outcome). Or they may fund a mental health program or youth leadership development workshop (intangible outcome).

In my experience, funders desire to improve our businesses and communities through any or all of the four lenses covered in the following sections. The funder you're reviewing may have one or all of the following goals in mind when they developed their funding program. In the program, they'll have objectives that need to be met, and this may differ from other funding programs they offer.

Systems change for improved outcomes

In this situation, funders want to improve communities and industries at a strategic level. This requires investment into programs that haven't been tested in the industry or area they work in. Sometimes, they fund an innovation, like technology or product development; other times, they fund a change in systems based on evidence-informed approaches.

Whatever the motivation, this type of funding requires a risk appetite for failure because they're exploring alternative approaches to solve challenges. You'll generally find this type of funder in the philanthropic space, or in emerging areas such as industry or systems change funding, which can also be through government to meet their strategic or future-proofing plans.

Funding gaps in different areas of society

These funders recognise specific sections in society need support, primarily in human services areas. For example, staff retention and recruitment or industry upskilling. Existing community health centres might need to increase their focus on an emerging population group, so they launch targeted funding programs. While they make strategic decisions and their giving is part of their overall strategy, they'll target those areas they've identified as a gap.

Some funders have multiple programs with very different focus areas. For example, one program is children's education while another one might be addressing the housing crisis.

Investing in stronger, sustainable businesses and communities

Business and community expectation can drive funding demand, such as responding to a crisis like fire and flood, or embracing a new trend like innovative technology. The funder targets areas where they see a need. This could include investing into volunteer training or delivering tender writing training for businesses. It could also include investing in events, such as a caravan and camping show. Funders using this lens care about individual and collective community, environmental and economic impacts.

Stick to their niche and continue to support and fund those areas they believe are working

Some funders stick to their area of expertise, but the focus here is not simply rolling out the same old, same old. They'll want you to test what's working and to outline ways to improve those areas that aren't, and to design a model that delivers maximum impact. They're looking for innovation but may not have the risk appetite to fund something completely out-of-the-box.

The bottom line is funders don't give out money randomly. Even if you convince them with an emotional ask, you still need to meet their strategic objectives. I talk more about aligning to the funders' goals in stage 3.

Understanding grant funding models

Grant funders use different funding models to deliver their strategic objectives. Understanding these models is useful because they provide potential opportunities for you. Some of these approaches are open to any eligible applicant, while others are only offered to pre-selected organisations and individuals.

Grant-funded programs

This is the primary funding model covered in this book. This can be based on either output, such as numbers of new full-time jobs created, or outcome, such as increased health and wellbeing, or a mix of both.

Commissioned or results-based programs

This is where the funder commissions someone to deliver a service or program, based on an agreed scope of who, how and when. This makes the model similar to a service contract – for example, you pay your house painter a deposit and stagger payments until they finish the work to the standard you've agreed on.

Some funders pay 'in arrears' – that is, you only get paid when milestones and results are achieved and reported on. This funding model is more like a tender process. The Grant Writing System will guide you through your application because much of the information is transferable. The Tender Writing System I developed and use with a success rate of over 85% is very similar to The Grant Writing System.

Other names for this funding model include 'social benefit bond' or 'social impact investment'.

Looking at the types of grants available

The four types of grants you're most likely to experience are:

1. competitive
2. demand-driven
3. responsive-limited
4. discretionary.

Competitive

Competitive grants are where you compete with other applicants to Win the Grant, and include open or closed competitive grants. Most grants will be 'open competitive', which means they're open to anyone who meets the eligibility criteria and aligns to the objectives of the grant. You'll apply in a competitive pool with other applicants.

Funders use a selection process to determine who they believe has the best project and is best placed to deliver it. Assessors use a set of criteria to score your application and rank your application by the score. The higher your application ranks, the more likely your project will receive funding. This type of funding is the more common type of funding approach. An example would be a local council community event grant open to businesses or communities. I cover the assessment process in much more detail in stage 3.

The other type of competitive funding is 'closed competitive', or 'invitation only'. This means an organisation has either passed an expression of interest process, the funder has identified a suitable organisation they want to invite, or the funder has organisations they have funded previously and want to support again. In 'closed competitive' or 'invitation only' programs, an expression of interest process generally applies first. This creates a group of eligible organisations who can apply for competitive funding, with the funding only open to those who were pre-approved or to a certain type of organisation. An example would be funding that is only available to domestic violence services, and not to organisations that run programs for people who have experienced domestic violence. It might only seem like a slight difference, but the difference is important.

Demand-driven

This type of grant launches in response to advocacy or consumer trends. Research may have shown increasing demand from community and media to commit to funding to address a specific need. An example of this would be the funding of women in tech programs and multicultural entrepreneur investment grants. These were launched to address identified barriers for these target groups to access commercial investment opportunities.

A community-based example is the grant program that replaced the Small Volunteer Equipment Grants. This program has been renamed the Volunteer Grants program and you now must submit an expression of interest to your federal member of parliament, who chooses organisations from these expressions of interest. Only invited organisations will then receive the grant application form to apply for funding. I've included this example in the demand-driven type of grant, because to be invited, your member of parliament will need to have an awareness of you and your project through your advocacy. This advocacy demonstrates demand.

Responsive-limited

This type of funding responds to limited situations, industries or organisations. An example of this might be a round of flood or fire recovery or prevention funding during flood or fire, where the industry supply or food chains are affected.

As another example, this type of funding occurred during the pandemic, where governments of all levels announced funding to meet business and community needs around mental health, staffing shortages and business recovery.

When the grant is responsive and limited to an industry or organisation, it will only be open to a specific industry with specific requirements, such as accreditation or a geographical area, or it will list the organisations that are eligible to apply.

Discretionary

The final type of funding is discretionary. Funders have budgets with 'discretionary funding'. This means certain roles in the funding organisation have the discretion and budget to spend up to a certain amount before you're required to go through a competitive grants program. This amount could be $2,000. For others, it's $5,000 or sometimes, if it's political incentivised funding, it can be thousands or millions.

Discretionary funding doesn't mean cutting corners, though. You'll still need to provide information for funders to justify their decision.

You can access this funding in three ways. The first is if you're asked to put in a proposal, the second is pitch at a collective giving event and the third is to identify the influencer or organisation and pitch to them.

If you're asked to put in a proposal with an offer, or to a set amount, it's fairly certain that, with a bit of negotiation, you can come to an agreement for funding.

Being able to ask for funds when you need them, without a long wait for the funds to be in your bank, certainly makes life easier. An existing relationship with the funder is a significant benefit, and you need to have different projects or parts of projects they can support for these amounts of funding. Often you won't need to complete complex forms for this. In many cases the project plan you developed with actual costs will replace an application form - although, you may have to rework your project and costs to fit the discretionary amount.

Sometimes these discretionary funds aren't only from an organisation with a budget. Individuals may also offer funding via collective giving. People pitch their ideas at collective giving events, and those individuals invest in the idea that connects with them. Some organisations can walk away with a few thousand, others with over $50,000.

As an example of the importance of pitching when looking at discretionary funding and influences, I had a call from a Volunteer Rescue Squad captain telling me they needed funding for a new shed. They wanted to apply for community project funding. I knew that the grant allocation was per electorate, meaning the state member would influence it. I mean, it's obvious, right? Also, I was in a decision room once and was told by another state member that they had a 60% weighting on that grant fund. Hearing that at the time confirmed what I'd assumed anyway! Though it was nice to get confirmation.

So, I told the Volunteer Rescue Squad to put together a few pages of information, in the NDOIS format (see step 2a), and have a meeting with the state member. I gave them a plan of what to do and said, 'If the state member says to apply for the grant and you need me, I'm happy to support you, but try approaching them directly first.'

I didn't hear back from them. (Sadly, I sometimes don't, and I love to know the outcome from assisting people. Please let me know if this book has made a difference to your work.)

Anyway, I read a big announcement online about eight weeks later - of $750,000 being awarded to the Volunteer Rescue Squad. It was not a grant announcement. This was discretionary political funds. It was one project announced in a group of projects of around $10 million.

So, you never know what discussions are happening, or who has discretionary amounts of money, unless you share your project with influencers - and I don't mean just political funds. We get calls before the end of financial year from organisations needing to spend their discretionary amounts of funding and we get these calls because they're aware of what we do and how we can support them achieve their goals.

What skills do grant writers need?

Most people will say you need writing skills to be a successful grant writer. In fact, at iClick2Learn*, we recently assessed 150 advertised grant writing positions across Australia, the United States and the United Kingdom and found 85% listed grant writing skills as the top priority, followed by research skills at 57% and communication skills at 23%.

Now, depending on your role, this might sound right to you - particularly if you have a team around you who does the strategic

---

* iClick2Learn is an education social enterprise, co-founded by Natalie Bramble and Glen Dunkley. See more at www.iclick2learn.com.au.

thinking and partnership development. However, if you're a small team or the only lonely grant writer, it's not your writing skills that are a priority. It's the way you think and the way you identify opportunities. It's how you find different ways to approach challenges and go around, under or over them.

Don't think I'm saying grant writing is an academic exercise, or that it's difficult. You only need an academic writing level for academic grants. When I started grant writing, I'd only completed year 10. While I did go on to complete academic qualifications later, I still wrote many successful grants before the degree. You don't need to have a degree; you don't need to be a perfect writer. Passion, determination and a curious mind is your gold. You'll learn what you need to know, because you want to! Otherwise, you wouldn't have picked up this book.

What makes the difference is the way you think about the grant writing process. It's a mindset of strategy and how you develop this is through The Grant Writing System. This is one thing you'll learn. It's a skill to analyse the information the funder cares about and decide how to communicate it. I mention the importance of strategy in the introduction to this book, and it's worth emphasising again here.

> *It's not writing, it's strategy that wins. Grants are 80% strategy and 20% writing.*

Writing a grant application requires you to do more than communicate the idea. It requires you to think like the funder and assessor, be critical about what you're trying to achieve and what information you're including, be competitive in your thinking so you can deliver a strong application and be open to the weak spots of the project that need fine-tuning before you hit submit.

When you're working with a team, you're required to be the project manager and collaborator who merges all the information and coordinates the resources and information needed. Sometimes you'll need to fill the gap and support the team to design the idea.

Grant writing requires attention to detail, time management and project management skills. Interestingly, these skills were at the bottom of the list for the job ads we researched, with only 12% of advertised positions asking for these skills. Yet, these are the most critical skills you can develop.

Of course, we can't all be perfect and have all the required skills as natural abilities. For some of us, these aren't and will never be our strengths. That's why it's useful to have others around you who have experience in application reviews, grant application management and team coordination - and to have standard systems, tools, and templates in place. This is where the steps and tools in The Grant Writing System guide your work.

You also need to be both the critic and the champion of the projects you're writing applications on. You need to find and highlight the valuable aspects of the project, and critically assess the project to test its weak spots. Being able to perform both roles means you can strengthen your information before you submit the application, rather than lose points at the assessment stage. Thinking like an assessor will be another skill you'll learn in stage 3.

What makes a strong grant application?

While funders can search for different things in an application, **a strong application will include some or all of the following:**

- ✓ meets all funder requirements
- ✓ shows how the funder's objectives and outcomes are met with project need and project outcomes

- ✓ shows awareness of the funder's strategies and alignment with those
- ✓ highlights how the project aligns to and supports the applicant's plans
- ✓ demonstrates and provides evidence of the need or opportunity the project addresses
- ✓ demonstrates a track record of existing experience, skills, knowledge and resources to deliver and implement the project, or in similar comparable projects
- ✓ shows collaboration and partnerships to support the project, increasing outcomes and reducing the funder's investment risk
- ✓ answers all parts of the question, and information applies to the question
- ✓ shows value for money (and I don't mean cheap!)
- ✓ demonstrates that project design, monitoring and evaluation engage with the target group appropriately
- ✓ shows how project outcomes through the funding period will be monitored and evaluated
- ✓ incorporates tangible and intangible outcomes
- ✓ considers sustainability of outcomes
- ✓ provides relevant supporting evidence
- ✓ demonstrates applicants are passionate, inspiring and motivated, and focused on their strengths
- ✓ demonstrates appropriate risk mitigation and for a range of strategic, operational and project risks, including how sustainability and retention of key people and partners will be managed
- ✓ includes a realistic budget that meets guidelines
- ✓ shows the project budget includes cash or other other contributions by applicant, partners and supporters
- ✓ The submitted application is compliant and follows all funder instructions.

Additionally, some applications should:

- ✓ include a Logic Model (for not-for-profits delivering intangible outcomes)
- ✓ include service model (for service-based organisations)
- ✓ demonstrate strong governance and operational compliant policies and processes to meet relevant industry and legal requirements - for example, child protection, cyber security, accreditation and/or Privacy Act.

Finally, your application should follow the 4Cs - concise, clear, consistent and confident.

How can I avoid common mistakes?

Assessors and funders are often as disappointed as you are, when they can't say 'Yes' to your application. We know the time and energy you've spent. However, our job is to choose the best applications who meet requirements. Seeing simple mistakes is frustrating - especially when we know those simple mistakes are easily avoided.

At the end of this book, I've included a troubleshooting guide, showing the common problems that occur consistently across grant applications. I've gathered these common mistakes over my many years working as a grant writer, and working with other grant writers and assessors. I've also incorporated learnings from discussions over the years with a range of funders across private, philanthropic and government, and from research on public feedback across 39 funding programs.

Artificial Intelligence for good, not evil

If you haven't heard, AI (Artificial Intelligence) is changing the way we work. Yes, there are ethical considerations and a host of other concerns about its misuse. Many people are concerned about their jobs, from marketers to grant writers. But one thing is certain. It's here to stay. So, how can you use AI for good?

The first thing to understand about AI is that it can't replicate a person's emotions or feelings. It doesn't have different lived experience, it can't use personal experiences and conversations with people to join the dots between stakeholders, clients and community. It won't be able to apply the same level of strategic thinking you'll need to write a strong application.

But that doesn't mean it doesn't have value. AI is good for a few things in the grant writing process. I've put it to the test and there have been grants secured by others just by using AI. I personally would never submit an AI-generated grant application and you'll understand a little of this here, in the examples in the online kit and even more so as you delve into The Grant Writing System.

I think of AI as Google on steroids. It's like an assistant. I started working in the typewriter days (gosh, I'm sounding old LOL!), when I'd type up my boss's letters and then they'd get the pen out and make a lot of corrections. I soon learnt what they liked and didn't like so each new letter would have less corrections than the last. We can train AI in a similar way, to know what it's doing that we like and what doesn't work. It can also be trained to 'replicate' your voice - sort of. So like AI, I could never write exactly what my boss would write because they'd often make a handwritten note when they signed the letter, to give it personal context and connection. So, I could never replace them 100%. I wasn't their writer; I was their assistant. This is how I'd like you to think about AI. I refer to AI throughout this book as your AI Assistant for this very reason.

It's also important to recognise that the AI Assistant uses data available to craft a response - but it doesn't have access to all of your data. Since it doesn't have access to all of your data, or similar information from other organisations, grant answers or grant programs, it's never going to be 100% right. It will likely miss out referencing any new terms, language or industry trends. While some AI writing programs enable you to provide the program with your statistics and evidence, it's still not going to be the right statistic or story to use in the response.

Even the founder of one of the newer grant writing AI programs, Phillip Dang from Grantable, has stated that AI won't do the job of a grant writer. But there is value.

So, what do I use my AI Assistant for?

In summary, I use it to develop a first draft of something, particularly when the 2 pm slump hits and I'm not feeling productive! Or I'm stuck for ideas and just need to get a head-start. Personally, I get my creative brain switched into gear when I start with a bit of an outline or content I can critique and build on, rather than having a blank canvas. I've developed a lot of templates over the years to help with these areas. This is where AI is now - a bit of a template. It's not perfect. I wouldn't use it as is for a grant application, and it definitely needs information from me, that context and connection, to finish it.

Your AI Assistant is helpful for:

✓ suggestions on content for logic models
✓ suggesting other similar programs and outcomes (although don't rely on its accuracy of information!)
✓ budget outlines
✓ delivery timelines
✓ ideas on how to address questions
✓ giving you ideas on different ways to phrase something

- ✓ suggesting different stakeholder stories you could use in an answer
- ✓ doing a spell and grammar check
- ✓ reducing word and character counts in answers
- ✓ even critiquing an example answer from an assessor's perspective (even its own draft answer, which I find so funny!). If you give it the assessment criteria that's where it can add a lot more value.

What it's not so great at:

- ✗ Strategically assessing the grant program documents using multiple approaches to uncover key messages and 'read between the lines'.
- ✗ Considering all your statistics and stories to determine which has greater impact to include.
- ✗ It's a bit random with reducing word and character counts. Sometimes it can do it, sometimes not.
- ✗ Relevant, accurate and quality research on your project, industry, target groups and funders.
- ✗ As a warning, it also has inherent bias in its answers and may use language that's not appropriate, current or respectful.

It does deliver a passable response, particularly for very simple, small grants. In the online kit I've included an example of three grant applications, one of these is written by the AI Assistant, one by a human and one I've written applying the strategies and tools from The Grant Writing System. If you do think that AI is the answer to solve your grant writing task, then think again. In the online kit I'll take you through these three examples to show you how it fails in a competitive environment against stronger answers.

One of the keys to guiding your AI Assistant is using prompts to 'train' it. Some key points are:

- **Be specific.** Tell AI Assistant who they are supposed to be replicating. E.g. 'You're an expert grant writer'. 'You're an assessor on a grant assessment panel'.
- **Check understanding.** Like active listening, check AI Assistant understands what you want by asking it if it understands. AI will then tell you what it understands.
- **Target specific areas in the response to improve.** For example, introduce new information and ask it to include it in specific areas. Select parts of the response and ask it to dig deeper or provide the same information in a different way.

To explore this further sign up or log in to the online kit. You'll find sample prompts to guide you. The instructions to access this are in the preface section.

Summary

You should now have a sound understanding of various types of funders and funding models. Once you get further into your grant writing journey, the common mistakes troubleshooting guide provided in the appendix will be useful for you to review. It's particularly useful to give you direction, if you know there's an area you need to strengthen.

What can you do now?

Here are a couple of actions to implement the learning so far:

- [ ] Review one of your applications against the 'What makes a strong grant application' checklist. What areas can you improve on?
- [ ] When you've identified areas you can improve on, head to the troubleshooting common grant mistakes guide in the appendix to guide you on how to improve.

Stage 1: Plan

The Grant Writing System™

1. Plan 2. Find 3. Align 4. Write 5. Submit 6. Manage 7. Report

Plan to get grant ready!

Welcome to the first stage in The 7-Stage Grant Writing Cycle - Plan, as shown in the following figure.

Plan: Stage 1 in The Grant Writing System

Plan to get grant ready!

1. Plan

Get Grant Ready!

Steps in this stage

a. Get yourself and your organisation grant ready.
b. Get your idea grant ready.
c. Get your project grant ready.

Tools to guide you

i. The Grant Ready Checklist™
ii. The Grant Ready Kit™
iii. The Grant RICE Score™
iv. The Grant NDOIS Pitch™
v. The Grant Project Plan™

In this stage, I guide you through how to get grant ready, explaining three key steps and five tools from The Grant Writing System and how they will increase your chances of winning your next grant. This stage is split into three steps, covering the following:

1. *How to get your organisation grant ready:* As part of your grant application, you'll be asked to provide information about your organisation such as insurances, policies and processes, your track record, resources, and operational and governance structures.

2. *How to get your idea grant ready:* You have a lot of ideas. In this step, we explore how you can identify the best one that meets your need and the funder's if you've already identified a grant. We also review the different plans you may need to consider.
3. *How to get your project grant ready:* A project plan is the most common document the majority of funders either ask for or expect you to have. And incorporating the Logic Model into your project plan really takes it to the next level. This tool answers many grant application questions.

Using The Grant Writing System throughout this stage, I outline what documents and information you need, and how storytelling boosts your application.

I show you how to use the first five tools in The Grant Writing System:

i. The Grant Ready Checklist
ii. The Grant Ready Kit
iii. The Grant RICE Score
iv. The Grant NDOIS Pitch
v. The Grant Project Plan

Step 1a

Get yourself and your organisation grant ready

The number one mistake made in grant applications is when people jump straight to answering the questions in the application, without understanding their organisation and the project they're trying to communicate. This is like going to the bank for a big loan without evidence of your income and ability to pay that loan. You wouldn't do it if you want them to say 'Yes'.

Ideally, you should do a lot more groundwork before getting to the answering questions stage - starting with understanding what funders need to know about you and your organisation.

Understanding why you need to get grant ready

The more money you're asking for, the more information you need to share, to persuade and influence funders to support you.

So, to achieve this, you need to understand and demonstrate:

- ✓ what you're doing
- ✓ why you're doing it
- ✓ how you know it will work
- ✓ what the benefits are
- ✓ who you're doing it for
- ✓ who your partners and supporters are.

No doubt one of the things you do when you find a funder is research the funder and the grant program. You discover what their motivation and interests are and what the objectives and outcomes are for the grant program. But your research and planning shouldn't end there. You also need to think about - to then be able to communicate - how your project's needs and outcomes align to what the funder wants to achieve. This is what I call The Grant Funding Sweet Spot, as shown in the following figure.

The Grant Funding Sweet Spot

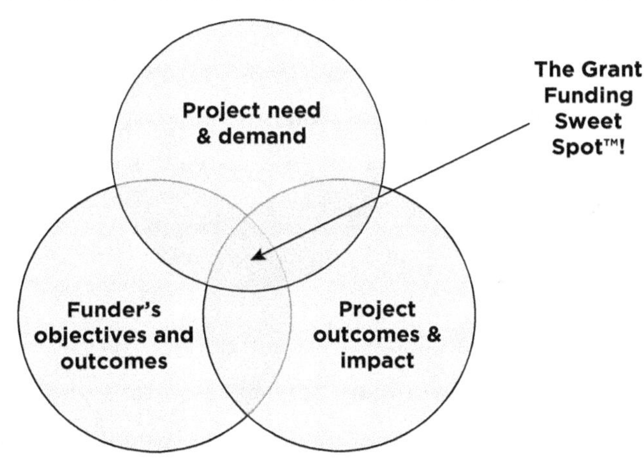

Quite frankly, you won't be able to write a strong answer until you understand the benefits and outcomes from your idea and match those with what the funder cares about. This is where the strength is - by understanding and demonstrating how your needs, activities and outcomes all align to achieve the funder's objectives.

You need to think about the difference you want to make over the long term, and how your project helps you on that journey. And you should have a written plan for this - either a one-page plan or a full detailed plan can be referred to and attached, if able to, to support your application.

Planning is such a fundamental element, but plenty of applicants are not doing it or not talking about it. I've had hundreds of conversations with funders and assessors about the issues they experience with applications during the assessment process. From these conversations, I estimate that around 70% of community applications and 40% of business applications indicate a planning weakness. Every grant writing training session I've delivered on behalf of funders – at any level, be it government or philanthropic – I'm always asked to include information on planning.

Here's an example of what assessors and funders often say:

> The application lacked depth and demonstrated a lack of planning. Applicants were not clear on why they want to do the project, how their outcomes achieve this objective, or how they'll implement the project.
>
> Grant Assessor's Feedback[*]

It's obvious when the planning hasn't been done to the depth it should be. Assessors and program managers have a good understanding of the activities and expenses required to implement projects. They don't want to be embarrassed funding something that didn't work out, and for their bosses to discover they funded it when the application had clear gaps.

Organisations that were successful with a grant and then couldn't deliver, or later realised they didn't have enough funds to complete what they planned, have had to give the grant money back. Buildings have been built that couldn't be used and didn't receive a certificate

---

* All example grant assessor feedback included through this book is based on my assessment experience, conversations with assessors, funders and program managers, and research analysis of feedback from 36 grant funding programs.

of occupancy because they lacked accessible design, resources and funds. Many of these mistakes could have been avoided or forecast if they'd been well-planned. It's also one of the reasons an approved Development Application and landholder approval is now required for most building grants.

What I have learnt and can say with full conviction is planning and preparation saves time, money and stress, and gives you the ability to find the gold in your project and communicate this strategically to influence assessors and funders

How grant ready do you need to be for your project?

In this and the following two steps, I cover what you should be doing to get your organisation, idea and project grant ready. The depth of planning required will differ. If it's a simple project or you're asking for a small amount of money, a one-page plan overview may be enough. The more complex the project, and the more money you're asking, the more detailed plans and information you'll need.

So you can understand the level of planning that may be required for your project, I've developed the matrix shown in the following table. This outlines the types of plans you might need based on the type of project you're proposing.

Don't worry if you're not sure what some of the elements I've included in the matrix are. After reading further through this and the following two steps, you should be able to make an informed decision about the depth of planning you need. (And you can always come along to one of my live Q&A sessions and ask if you're still not sure.)

Plans needed for projects

Plan / Project	Bursary/ scholarship	Crisis recovery/ resilience/ hardship	Event/ activity/ workshop	Research/ business case development
CV/bio/ artist statement	Essential	Not generally	Yes, if work is dependent on individual skills/ knowledge	Yes, if work is dependent on individual skills/ knowledge
Strategic plan	Not generally	May be required	May be required	May be required
Business plan	Not generally	May be required	Not generally	Not generally
Feasibility study	Not generally	Not generally	Not generally	May be required
Business case	Not generally	Not generally	Not generally	Possibly for some research projects
Project plan	May be required if project based	Not generally	Yes, and include event details or develop an event plan	Likely to be asked for or you need information from it to answer questions
Theory of change	Not generally	Not generally	May be required/will strengthen your application	May be required

Growth/ innovation/ manufacturing grant	Service delivery/ programs	Equipment	Infrastructure
Likely to be asked for business owner/ founder/key people	Yes, if work is dependent on individual skills/ knowledge	Not generally	Yes, if work is dependent on individual skills/ knowledge
Likely to be asked for	May be required	Not generally	Essential to be competitive and demonstrate alignment
Essential to be competitive or you'll need information from it	Not generally	May be required	Essential to be competitive and demonstrate alignment
Not generally	May be required if it's new	Not generally	May be required
May be required	May be required	May be required	Essential to be competitive or you'll need information from it
Likely to be asked for or you need information from it to answer questions	Likely to be asked for or you need information from it to answer questions	May be required	Likely to be asked for or you need information from it to answer questions
Not generally	May be required	Not generally	Not generally

Plan / Project	Bursary/ scholarship	Crisis recovery/ resilience/ hardship	Event/ activity/ workshop	Research/ business case development
Logic Model	Would assist to show outcomes	Not generally	May be required/will strengthen your application	May be required
Risk/WH&S plan	May be required if project based	Not generally	Essential to reference and include examples	May be required
Service model	Not generally	Not generally	If a service program, essential to be competitive	Not generally
Financial plan/ forecast financials	May be required if project based	Essential if showing financial impact scenario	May be required/will strengthen your application	May be required
Marketing plan	Would assist to show how learning will be shared	May be required for marketing/ growth focused recovery	May be required/will strengthen your application	Not generally
Stakeholder/ community engagement plan	May be required if project based	Not generally	Not generally however can strengthen your application	Not generally

Growth/ innovation/ manufacturing grant	Service delivery/ programs	Equipment	Infrastructure
Not generally	May be required/will strengthen your application	Not generally/ will strengthen your application	May be required/will strengthen your application
Likely to be asked for	Essential to reference and include examples	May be required	Essential to reference and include examples
Not generally	Essential to be competitive	Not generally	Not generally
Essential to show financial impact scenario/s	Essential to show financial viability of organisation	May be required	Essential to show financial impact scenario/s
Likely to be asked for	Not generally	Not generally	May be required
Not generally	May be required	Not generally	May be required

Step 1a: Get your organisation grant ready

As the following figure shows, we're now up to the first smaller step in the first stage.

Stage 1: Plan – Step 1a. Get your organisation grant ready

1. Plan

Get grant ready!

Step 1a. Get your organisation grant ready

Tools

i. The Grant Ready Checklist™

ii. The Grant Ready Kit™

Funders won't fund 'cash grabs'. They want to fund projects, programs and services aligned to their objectives and outcomes, which also support your organisation achieve its purpose and plans. Funders and assessors are often confused about certain organisations applying for funds when it doesn't seem to be a good 'fit'.

> *Applicants aren't clear on why they're doing the project with the target group and how it helps their cause.*
>
> Grant Assessor's Feedback

For example, imagine a photography club outlining that their members are 40+ years of age, but then applying for a youth grant for youth 18 years or less, without demonstrating how it engages with them and addresses a need identified by youth. This won't convince the funders it's an authentic project that delivers outcomes to youth. Also, funders would likely question why the youth council didn't apply in their name. It's a stronger position for the youth council to apply if they're eligible and have the photography club as their partner.

After you've submitted an application or have been identified for potential funding, funders may research you to understand your organisation's objectives, your impact goals and your plans. Some funders, such as foundations, have dedicated staff who research organisations before presenting a select few to their manager or board for potential funding. While it might seem a bit scary to think people are making decisions about potentially funding you based on research they've uncovered, knowing this gives you an advantage - you can put in the groundwork before your application to ensure everything is in alignment.

Regardless of the funder and the funding approach, they'll be assessing your organisation to determine if they think you're the ideal organisation for them to fund, based on the factors covered in the following section.

Outlining your organisation's objectives

It's not enough to know what your objectives and plans are; you need to document them for the funder.

As outlined in the previous section, the detail you need to provide depends on the project and level of funding you're applying for. **However, plans usually required for larger projects and organisations include:**

- strategic plans
- 12-month business plans
- operational plans, such as a risk management plans, financial plans and marketing plans.

You'll likely have heard about, or even have some or all of these types of plans. You'll likely also be required to provide some detail from some of these plans in your answers, so it's helpful to have them ready. I review risk management plans as they relate to project planning and your grant application in step 1c.

Some grants, such as business growth programs, may ask for very detailed information from your plan, or a full copy of your plan. Otherwise, your organisational plans don't need to be exhaustive for the purposes of your grant application – referencing the plan or including extracts in your answers will likely be enough. You could also include a one-page summary if relevant.

The focus of these plans is more about demonstrating you have clear objectives, structure and systems, and you plan your projects. Being clear about your organisation and what you do will assist you in addressing the questions and demonstrating evidence. One national community-focused funder has a standard question in the form for applicants to 'Describe your vision, goals and achievements'. It's a bit hard to address the first two without a plan.

I'm not going to go into further detail about the strategic and business plans. If you don't have any of these, you can check out the resources available to assist you develop them in the iClick2Learn library.

For organisations that deliver benefits to people and wish to prove they make a positive impact, **for larger projects and for projects that need to build more strength to align to a funder's framework, the following is useful:**

- Theory of Change framework (see the following section)
- Logic Model (see steps 1b and 1c).

Outlining your organisation's impacts and purpose with a Theory of Change framework

A Theory of Change framework describes your organisation's goals and purpose (also called your mission or objectives), your intended long-term results (impacts) and what you'll focus on to influence the change. So, it's big picture and shows the pathway to achieve your impact. It answers the questions, 'Why do we do what we do? What's the difference we want to make?' If you want to convince philanthropic funders or have a social enterprise, this is 101 for you. Unfortunately, however, I find regularly in grant writing workshops many who should have one and don't. (Sometimes they call this Logic Model or Program Logic, but technically they aren't the same thing.)

As an example, iClick2Learn's 'why' is to build inclusive, healthy and adaptive communities. Our pathway to achieving this impact is to build people's capacity. Our Theory of Change framework demonstrates how this focus drives our strategies to achieve our 'why'.

> *Your Theory of Change framework helps people understand your 'why' and the areas you're working on that achieve your 'why'.*

As mentioned, this Theory of Change framework can be confused with the Logic Model (or Program Logic), which I cover in detail in steps 1b and 1c. They both use the same visual framework to show what your organisation does. However, they are easily identifiable because the Logic Model focuses on the detail of one project, service or program whereas the Theory of Change framework asks you to focus on the big picture. Theory of Change is strategic, while the Logic Model is on the program or operational level.

Organisations that want to influence change set impact plans and goals (outlined in their Theory of Change), in addition to their strategic plans and goals for their organisation. These plans and goals influence each other. You shouldn't set a strategic direction that's inconsistent or doesn't help you achieve your impact goals.

Another way to understand the relationship between goals is to think about strategic goals represented with a dollar sign, and impact goals represented by a heart. When an organisation makes decisions on their direction, they need to consider the consequences to both the dollars and the heart.

When organisations are planning a new product, service or enterprise, they use different plans such as project plans. Impact-focused organisations should also use a Logic Model to demonstrate the investment and how activities achieve outcomes.

The following figure represents the relationship between these plans and your other organisational plans. It also highlights the relationship and influence impact goals have on your strategic direction. They come first. Without impact goals, your strategy might not support you in achieving your impact through planned outcomes.

The relationship between impact goals and strategic goals

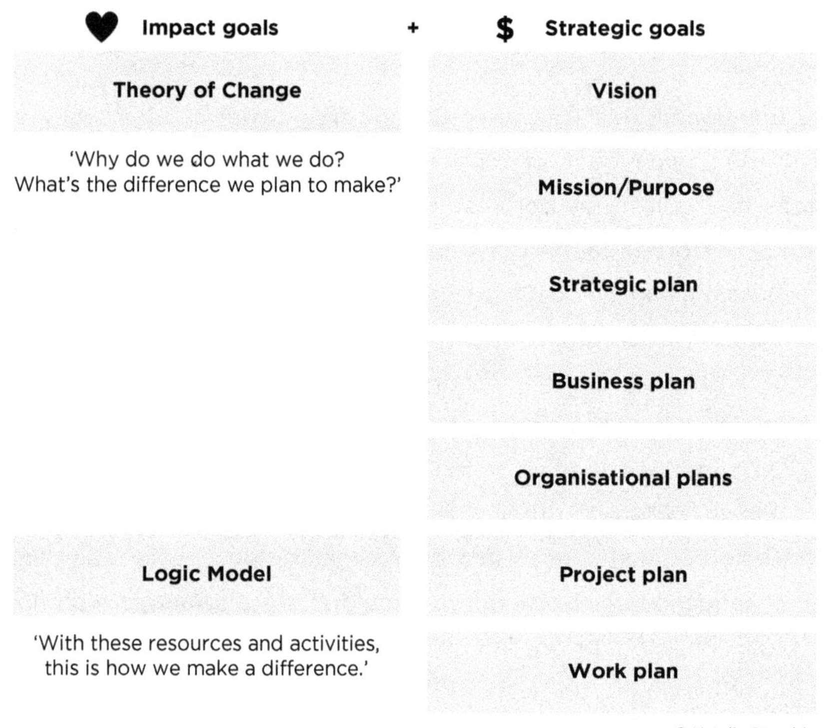

Bringing in The Grant Ready Kit

One of the easiest things you can do to get grant ready is to have all the information on your organisation, and its objectives, impacts, plans and ideas in a central place, accessible for all staff and volunteers. I call this The Grant Ready Kit. It's like your go-to filing system where you'll find all the information you need to apply for funding, to avoid feedback like the following:

> Applications did not provide detailed information and evidence, or the applicant did not provide the required plans, policies or systems.
>
> Grant Assessor's Feedback

I develop a kit for every organisation I work with. On many occasions, I've needed to access documents such as insurance details or statistics and stories to weave into an answer, and knowing I have all the information I need at my fingertips reduces my stress and increases my confidence of success.

To get you started on preparing your kit, let's go through The Grant Ready Checklist.

The Grant Writing System Tool: i. The Grant Ready Checklist

The full checklist is too long to include here, and some differences exist for each type of organisation, so I've provided a comprehensive checklist in your online kit. **As an example of what you'll need, your Grant Ready Kit at minimum should have the following information:**

- business name and trading name
- legal structure
- tax structure – for example, registered for GST or not, taxable charity status or deductible gift recipient status

- ABN/ACN/Incorporation number
- bank account details for depositing grants
- contact details for relevant office and key people
- years trading and average annual turnover
- equity and shareholder details for businesses and social enterprises - for example, 50% First Nations-owned business
- accreditation and certification - for example, accredited non-government school, certified social enterprise or Supply Nation certified
- organisational team - for example, number of staff and volunteers, organisational chart and your diversity indicators and goals
- strategic, business and risk plans - at minimum, a simple one-page plan
- a demonstration of your experience and track record, including case studies and testimonials, evidence of satisfaction, achievements and outcomes
- extracted and referenced key statistics (with links) relevant to your industry and target group/s
- key policies - for example, governance, financial management, cyber security, conflicts of interest, whistle-blowers, diversity and inclusion, working with children and risk management
- website and social page links
- annual reports and financials - up to the last three years
- community, membership, volunteer and client profiles - including statistics and geographic and demographic information
- certificate of currency documents for insurances such as workers compensation insurance and public liability.

You should also include a 100- to 150-word summary on key areas you'll be able to use in your application. These include:

- *Your organisation and what you do:* Think of this as a pitch. Anyone you give it to should understand the industry you're in, why you exist, what you offer, who you support and your impacts.
- *Your background and history:* Include key milestones such as when you delivered big projects, or grew your attendee, client base or service area.
- *Your purpose:* Some call this your mission. For community organisations, this must align to your statement of objectives in your constitution. Funders sometimes ask for your constitution or research it to check alignment.
- *Your activities:* Include a list of the types of activities you deliver, or services you offer. This should align to your constitutional objectives, theory of change and strategic plan.
- *Your impact:* These are the benefits that result from what you do.
- *Biographies of key people in the organisation:* Think about these from a governance and project perspective. Summarise their experience and knowledge as it relates to your organisation and your activities.
- *Previously funded projects:* Include a table listing information on what the project was, who the funds were from, how much the funding was, the total project value and the partners who were involved. This demonstrates you can manage grants. Include projects of a similar value to what you're seeking or wish to apply for. You can use The Grant Calendar for this (step 2a).

Ideally, for services, programs and workshops you should have:

- Your Theory of Change framework (covered in step 1a).
- Related Logic Model (see steps 1b and 1c).
- Your service model documented, ideally supported with a visual diagram.

- Evidence that the model and approach work in practice and are delivering results.
- A documented template plan for how you monitor, evaluate, review and improve your work. You may call this an evaluation plan; however, it should include all four areas. (I cover this in much more detail in stage 6).

Adding in statistics and stories

To build understanding, empathy and trust, you should weave statistics and stories into your application. You need to gather your own evidence and evidence from stakeholders. You'll update this when you've found a funder, because they'll have their own research and statistics that will relate to what you're doing. Use relevant statistics and stories to support the statements in your application.

You need to demonstrate your facts come from a process of evidence gathering, particularly when the funder has a focus on evidence-informed approaches, co-design or engagement. I've known some people try to find evidence after they've decided what the facts are! Trying to create evidence and facts to fit a story is much harder work than creating a story around the facts.

Your application needs to be supported with relevant statistics and stories that provide the evidence for your statements. Statements without supporting evidence are only opinions and are treated as such in the assessment rounds, which means you'll receive fewer points for your answers!

Statistics and stories support your statements. Anything else is just an opinion. And opinions don't win points.

In the steps in stage 4 ('Write a strong application'), I review some examples, showing you how to weave statistics and stories into your answers.

Connecting with decision-makers through statistics and stories

A grant writer's job is to connect with the decision-makers and influence them. You need to keep four influencing factors in mind. These factors include Aristotle's three modes of persuasion, with an extra one I've added. These four factors are shown in the following figure.

The four factors influencing decision-makers

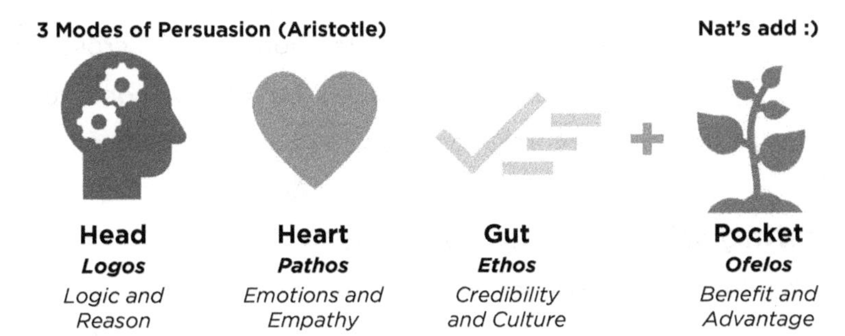

How these four factors influence decisions is as follows:

- *Logos (head):* People make decisions based on logic and reason, past experiences and bias.
- *Pathos (heart):* People made decisions based on emotional connection and the empathy they feel.
- *Ethos (gut):* People make decisions based on gut feelings that tell them the organisation is credible and they know what they're doing. Organisational culture influences practices and outcomes.
- *Ofelos (pocket):* People make decisions based on the project's benefits (and how this gives them a return on investment), which creates an advantage by furthering their achievements. (This one's my addition which recognises the funder.)

I often refer to this when I'm writing or speaking. I find chanting 'Head, heart, gut, pocket' is a great way to make sure I consider all areas. In applications, I used to lean towards the evidence side of things more than stories, so chanting the four factors helped remind me I have to balance statistics and facts with examples and stories. If you find you're more of a storyteller, this chant will remind you to include statistics and facts. Assessors really enjoy an application when they can sense the passion, but they need a balance of evidence to validate your statements.

Statistics build trust and stories build empathy

So, your statistics and stories influence decision-makers across these areas. They may make instinctive decisions, but they've come to that decision based on the information you've provided in the application.

Knowing when to gather evidence

You should gather evidence in the planning stage, before finding and applying for your grant. This will assist you to identify your community's needs, the goals of your organisation and the project or services required. For example, if your research demonstrates a funder has released a report about a particular area, it generally means they have an interest in supporting and funding projects to achieve their outcomes in this area. You could reach out and connect with the funder and pitch your project. I discuss this in more detail in step 2a.

The other time you'll need to gather evidence is when you've found a grant that meets your organisation's goals. Sometimes unplanned opportunities come up, so you might be developing your plans and application concurrently. While it's not ideal, we live in the real world, and this does happen.

In this case, check the grant guidelines and application form, because some funder requirements or questions may indicate other areas of research you need to do to complete your application.

Selecting your evidence

To generate statistics for your application, you first need to find the data. Some statistics may draw from multiple pieces of data that have been analysed to create the overall statistic.

Some useful websites are available to provide research (and we've included an updated list in the online kit). Some common ways of finding relevant and current research are through your membership with an industry body, which will notify you, or a search engine to find a document to support a statement you want to make.

Keep in mind the four Rs of research:

1. *Reason:* Why do you need this research? How does it support your project?
2. *Relevant:* How is the research you're doing relevant to your project, need and outcomes, or the funding program, the funder and the questions asked of you?
3. *Reputable:* Is the research from a reputable source? Would the funder consider it to be reputable?
4. *Relatable:* How you can make the research relatable? How can you bring your statistics and stories to life?

For now, let's look at the types of data you should focus on gathering. This is the data you'll use to demonstrate the need for the project and that it will work. (I delve more into research in step 1c, where I cover the need statement, and in step 4b, where I cover how to turn your evidence into a story and use data to support your statements.)

The two types of evidence you need to gather and show are quantitative and qualitative.

Quantitative data

Quantitative data, also called hard data, is anything that can be counted or measured; it refers to numerical data. For example, questions like, 'If we expanded our business and offered *x* service to you, would you use it?' are designed for a yes or no answer. The resulting statistic might be expressed as '97% of existing clients surveyed said they would use *x* service'.

Examples of hard data are:

- statistics describing your clients or community - for example, demographics
- hours of service, or units of product sales
- data on program participation and engagement
- evaluations, self-assessments or accreditation reports
- numbers of and types of referrals given and received
- economic impact analysis.

Qualitative data

Qualitative data, also called soft data, is descriptive, capturing things that can be observed but not measured numerically - such as colours or emotions. If you asked someone to expand on their answer with a written response expressing thoughts and feelings, this is qualitative data. The responses will be varied. They won't use the same words, and the words they use may not have the same meaning to everyone.

Turning this kind of data into a statistic takes a little work. You can use sentiment analysis, for example, but you need to assess statements and identify the sentiment as positive, neutral or negative - or use a system to do this for you. A useful way to use this data is for it to form part of the story in your application. This would be sharing the overall statistic and a quote or two from the survey.

Examples of qualitative or soft data sources include anecdotes, stories, testimony, quotes and letters. **Qualitative data also includes written and verbal feedback from:**

- stories of change, satisfaction or success from current and past members, clients and families
- testimonials from an organisation you're partnering with
- stories and conversations about lived experience and the need for a service or product.

Using primary and secondary research

To gather hard and soft data, you can use primary and secondary research methods. Primary research is research you've produced, and secondary research is research produced by others.

An example of primary research might be a client needs survey. You've developed the methods and the questions and undertaken the research to gather the data. You've turned this data into statistics, and you've used clients' words to share these statistics in a story.

The types of primary research you should be gathering includes information about your clients' current and future needs and how they're being met (or not met), and operational data such as expenses. You could also use impact analysis systems to quantify the economic return of any current projects – for example, the economic benefit your event brings to the region.

An example of secondary research is your industry's strategic plan, local council's strategic plan, community strategic plan or Community Needs Assessment. Many organisations have already invested funds to identify needs. Lucky you – you can access these reports with statistics and information you can use to support your case. For event applications, secondary economic research on the event impact would come from researching other similar events, or research demonstrating the industry average for economic spend per person at similar events.

Expand your secondary data to align to the outcomes you want to achieve. For example, if your business expansion project is connected to employment opportunities for Aboriginal and Torres Strait Islander youth employment, then unemployment data related to this target group is important.

Communicate and tell stories with your data that:

- *Describes places and things:* For example, when 'painting' a picture about your community, you could look for statistics that describe the community and demonstrate the circumstances of that community, such as access to health.
- *Describes people:* For example, you could include the age, economic status and education level of the people in your target group. This is also known as demographic and psychographic descriptors.
- *Compares one thing to another:* For example, you could compare the physical health of your target group to a national average, or the expected physical health benchmark for people in that target group.
- *Identifies trends:* For example, you could look at projected growth of a population, or demand for a service.
- *Analyses influencing factors:* You could use data to tell a story about environmental factors that may influence the project - for example, policy changes to prioritise funding of housing stock of one-bedroom units, which decreases housing opportunities for families, thereby creating a greater need for affordable family housing.
- *Justifies your position:* For example, you could include evidence demonstrating your local Crown Reserve is booked out and unable to accommodate the regular waitlist of caravan and camping bookings, justifying a need to develop more sites.

The Grant Writing System Tool: ii. The Grant Ready Kit

Now you've gathered all your information, you need to file it. The following figure provides an example of a file structure with a list of folders. The folder titles follow The Grant Ready Checklist. You can modify and change the wording as needed.

An example file structure for your toolkit

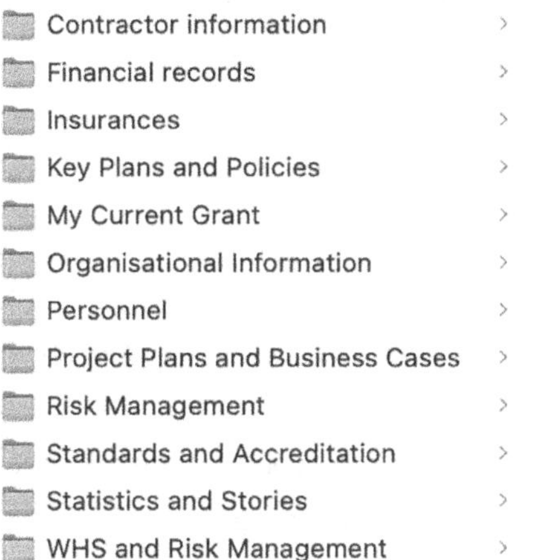

Make your folder sharable and file information so your team can access it when needed. Start gathering your information from The Grant Ready Checklist. Divide up the work so others are supporting you. Once you've gathered all your information, you can start getting your idea grant ready which is covered in the next step.

Summary

In step 1a, you learnt why it is so important to get your organisation grant ready and how it saves you a lot of time and stress in the intense lead-up to a grant deadline.

What can you do now?

Here are some actions to implement the learning from this step:

- ☐ Download The Grant Ready Checklist from the online kit. Use the suggested priority order or create your own and start gathering information.
- ☐ Download The Grant Ready Kit and install it in your filing structure.
- ☐ Work out where you should file your shared documents.
- ☐ Review any past grant applications to see what things you've been asked to provide in the past. Add these to the file.
- ☐ Diarise expiry dates of all documents, such as insurance or accreditation, so you remember to update these in your file when they renew. Place it in a shared calendar so others will know if you're away.
- ☐ Start gathering your stories of change and case studies.
- ☐ Review any past acquittal reports and add any success stories to your kit.
- ☐ If you're in a business or service-based organisation, talk with your team and develop a process to regularly gather stories and statistics on the difference you make. This will also make your reporting and acquittal so much easier.
- ☐ Find out what industry or target group statistics are relevant and sign up to any related newsletters so you find out about new research when it's released.
- ☐ Make sure your people are listed in an 'About' page. Funders do research your organisation, and most ask for a website address. This is your opportunity to add all the extra information about who you are, your skills and what you've achieved. Put in a timeline of successes. You simply don't have enough words in a grant application to say it all so use your website for this.

Step 1b

Get your idea grant ready

We come up with ideas to address challenges or opportunities. You need to document these ideas, ready for a grant application, and assess if they're the right idea to address the challenge or opportunity. So, it's now time to get your idea grant ready, as shown in the following figure.

Stage 1: Plan – Step 1b. Get your idea grant ready

1. Plan

Get grant ready!

Step 1b. Get your idea grant ready

Tools

iii. The Grant RICE Score™

iv. The Grant NDOIS Pitch™

In this step, I focus on developing your idea and understanding the kind of plan you need to provide.

The amount of work you need to do to get your idea grant ready will depend on how large and complex the idea is, and how much money you're applying for. Many simple grants for a few thousand dollars only require a completed application form. This form includes questions on the idea, why it's needed, the budget and some details about the difference it will make. For these grants, this step outlines my NDOIS tool for you to identify the key features of your idea and provides The Grant NDOIS Pitch framework to use as a pitching tool to gather support for what you plan to achieve.

For larger grants - for example, projects such as product development, programs, services or more complex projects such as buildings - a lot more information is needed. Hard evidence of the long-term need is essential, and relevant evidence will prove future potential.

You'll also have to demonstrate you've planned the idea in consultation with the people you're trying to support, or the market you're trying to sell to. When you get to the point where either the funder is asking for more information or the project is more complex, you'll need a plan. This could be a project plan, business plan or a feasibility study. The first step is often deciding which idea you should focus on first. This is where The Grant RICE Score will guide you.

Using RICE to decide which idea to work on

We are solution thinkers, most grant writers or project teams are. We see a need and jump right to the solution. The coffee is too hot - we'll add cold water or milk. If it happens enough, we'll find out why it's constantly too hot, which could mean putting the kettle on a different setting or replacing the coffee machine's thermostat.

However, we don't have the luxury of fixing things or trying different approaches when we're delivering projects. Funders want to fund projects that have some guarantee you're building on or replicating success you've already had. This means they rarely have appetite for you to make obvious mistakes over and over again in a project.

They also want to make sure you're working on the right idea that addresses the need you've identified. To guide you to focus on the right idea, you can use a RICE scoring system we developed at iClick-2Learn. We use this system when we're reflecting on ideas and which idea we should progress to planning. (Glen from our team designed our RICE score based on a technology decision matrix from Sean Ellis of GrowthHackers.)

RICE stands for relevance, impact, confidence and ease. Each of these contain two elements worth 5 points each for each person to score individually.

The Grant RICE Score

Here's how you rate your idea with The Grant RICE Score:

1. **Relevance.** How much will this idea achieve plans and goals of:
   a. your organisation? __/5
   b. your stakeholders, such as partners or funders? __/5
2. **Impact.** How much will this idea positively impact:
   a. your finances? __/5
   b. your target group (e.g. clients or beneficiaries)? __/5
3. **Confidence.** How confident are you of the project need, based on:
   a. what the data is showing you? __/5
   b. what people are telling you? __/5
4. **Ease.** How easy is the project to:
   a. implement with your existing resources? __/5
   b. deliver to other target groups or communities? __/5

Once everyone has rated each of these points out of 5, add up everyone's scores. To get an average, you divide that score by the number of people involved and then divide that average by 4 (being the total number of key areas in the RICE score). You'll then get a final score, for example:

- 55 total points, divide by 3 people, divide by 4 areas = 6
- 73 total points, divide by 3 people, divide by 4 areas = 8

Based on the final score for each idea you have, you can then prioritise them from the highest to lowest score.

You can also use the score to discuss ideas that either need more work or should be set aside. For example, we would disregard any idea that scores below 3 points, or review the idea to see what needs improving to shift the score. An idea that scores between 4 and 6 points could work if you strengthen the areas the idea scored low on; and ideas 7 points and above are viable and should be explored.

Once you've had discussions and determined which idea to move forward with, you'll need more information on it to start sharing with stakeholders and influencers.

Start with NDOIS

In this part of the book, I take you through being clear about your idea and the need for it. You'll develop a pitch you can use to communicate your plan and provide everyone with an overview of your idea and why you're doing it.

> *If you can't clearly communicate your idea, you won't convince others to support you.*

Whenever people talk with me about their ideas, I'll ask questions about their Need, Demand, Outcomes, Impact and Solution. These form my acronym NDOIS (as shown in the following figure) – but don't necessarily need to be discussed in that order. Depending on their approach, I might ask what the solution is and what they want to achieve and why it's needed. The amount of knowledge they have about their idea as it relates to these five areas indicates to me the level of planning and the type of plan they need to do.

Knowing the Need, Demand, Outcomes, Impact and Solution for your project

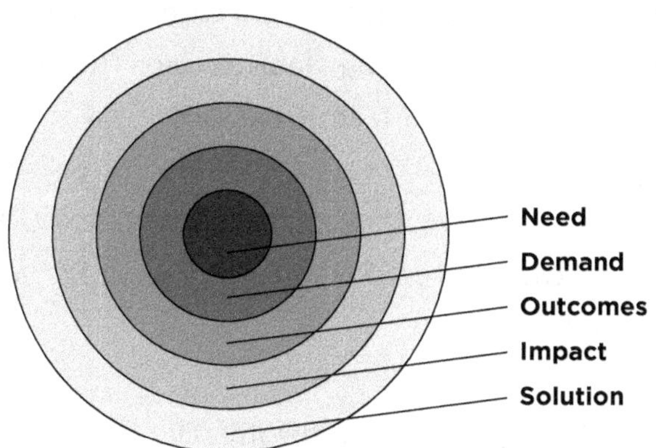

Here's how each of these areas influence your idea and your project:

1. *Need:* Need is often one of the first areas a funder will focus on, and one of the first questions asked in a grant application. They will ask something like, 'What's the need for your project?' They're basically asking you to justify why it has to happen. They want to know that you understand this reason and you understand your target group.
2. *Demand:* Demand is a numbers and percentage game. Funders want to know their grant funds have supported a number of people immediately and into the future. Consider demand in a few different ways, including current, future, unmet and urgent demand (see step 1c for more).
3. *Outcomes:* This is the difference you want to make with your project in the funding period. Think of them as short-term benefits. It's important to explore all of these outcomes for all stakeholders, because doing so expands your list of potential funders.
4. *Impact:* This is the long-term benefit your project contributes to. For funding purposes, it's beyond the funding period, usually 12 months. Likely, these are the reasons you exist. While you shouldn't

be including impact measures in grant applications unless it's a multi-year grant, you can use stories of impact. This builds a case for sustainability and strengthens the case for investment.

5. *Solution:* This is the idea you want funded. The solution should address the previous four factors (NDOI).

> *Knowing your NDOIS will increase the number of grants you can apply for, giving you more chances of funding!*

NDOIS is the starting point of understanding how much you need to document and the depth of research and evidence you need to support your funding ask. Understanding your NDOIS means that you can start identifying grants and funders who want to invest in the types of outcomes and impacts you create.

If you want to increase your chances of funding and support from other sources, which also strengthens your grant submission, it all starts with taking your NDOIS and developing a clear statement you can use to pitch for support.

Using The Grant NDOIS Pitch

You can go through your NDOIS from the previous section and write down points, and then use aspects of this to develop a scope statement or pitch. Try to keep this pitch to 120 words or less. That will give you a one-minute pitch with enough space for pauses and emphasis.

In the different frameworks, you'll find something called a 'call to action', or CTA as it's commonly known. This is a statement you have to finish with, that tells funders what you want from them. Sometimes it's better to state this up front – for example, 'I'm here today to talk with you about supporting ...' Other times it's better at the end of the pitch – 'You can support us by …' Move your CTA to where it makes sense to you. Just make sure you give your call to action a sense of urgency by providing a deadline for them to respond, or a deadline for when it should be funded. Just think of the TV shopping channel – what do they need to do to invest in you and by when? (Keep in mind 'right now' might be a big ask but indicating their interest to you within a few weeks may be reasonable.)

Let's look at the different frameworks in The Grant NDOIS Pitch you can select for different approaches and different stakeholders. Just don't forget to include the CTA at the beginning or the end:

- **Solution-focused framework:** In this framework, you focus on the solution. For example, 'We will *[solution]* to address *[need]*. It's important that *[share relevant outcomes to beneficiaries]*. One of our *[include a story of need from community or client]*. We know they aren't alone and *[include statistics of demand]*. Long term this will result in *[impact]*. You can support by *[call to action]*.'
- **Strategic alignment framework:** In this framework, you focus on their strategy. This is what they invest in achieving. 'Like us, you care about *[impact]*. Your strategy *[demonstrate alignment to their strategy and goals]*. The situation in our community is *[need and demand]*. Our *[solution]* will deliver *[outcomes]* to achieve the *[impact]* together. You can support by *[call to action]*.'
- **Empathy/story-focused framework:** Here, you focus first on the story and establishing empathy. For example, 'One of our *[include a story of need from community or client]*. We know they aren't alone and *[include statistics of demand]*. This is why we will *[solution]* to address *[need]*. I'm sure you can see why it's important that *[share relevant outcomes to beneficiaries]*. Others in our community would also benefit from *[impact]*. You can support by *[call to action]*.'

- **Aspirational-focused framework:** This framework focuses on the aspirations of the project. For example, 'Everyone deserves *[share relevant outcomes to beneficiaries]*. One of our *[target market]* experienced *[need]* and accessed *[solution]*. They were able to *[outcomes]*, which meant they achieved *[impact]*. We know they aren't alone and *[include statistics of demand]*. This is why we will *[solution]*. You can support by *[call to action]*.'

Once you're clear on this, you can use the information to develop a need statement for your project plan and grant application. I look at this in more detail in step 1c. Once you start talking with stakeholders, you'll add and change information in the framework to respond to other factors they may raise.

Developing a sound idea

A sound idea will get support when it is deemed viable, supported by your market, demonstrates need and demand and shows an expected positive result. You can start promoting your idea to attract additional support or funding. If people in your team are good at influencing and persuading, get them to start pitching using The Grant NDOIS frameworks we reviewed earlier in this step. Any support, financial or non-financial, you receive generally leads to more support from other stakeholders. (I guide you through this in more detail when I discuss budgets in step 1c.)

You need people who can communicate well, both verbally and in writing, to succeed. Some of us aren't strong in both of these areas. For example, Alice attended my fundraising and grant writing training in Byron Bay some years ago. Alice told me, 'I'm not good at writing, but I can pitch'. We worked on her pitching skills in the workshop and, shortly after, Alice secured $20,000 to run a project for her organisation. That motivated Alice to look for more funding.

Since then, Alice has continued to develop grant writing skills and has written many grant applications, raising hundreds of thousands for her organisation. Alice now sits on state grant assessment panels as well. I was so pleased when Alice shared this recent update. Food for my soul – I love it!

However, there does come a point when you can't continue to ask your fans, followers, friends and local organisations to give you support on the basis of a verbal pitch. They'll start asking for documents to support the pitch and, the more money you want, the more evidence they're likely to ask for. You'll need to set out a plan of how you're going to get your idea up and running.

Funders want to validate they're investing grant funding into ideas that deliver results. You're operating in a more competitive environment, where others will provide information and evidence you don't have. It raises standards and funder expectations.

Most funders refer to what they're funding as projects. This is because they want you to deliver and report on your idea within a 12-month period. Projects have defined start and end dates, like the funding period. Some funders will support, or the project will continue, beyond 12 months; however, the majority are only 12 months. Throughout this book, I use the term 'projects' to guide your thinking of a realistic and defined funding time period.

As an assessor, I can assure you it's clear when applicants have taken the time to plan their project. Well-planned projects shine through in the application – people can provide specific details when responding to the questions, and those details work together when you reflect on the project as a whole, across the application.

When people haven't spent the time planning the project, their answers aren't as detailed, and they generally don't include critical information, or the information they do provide is too general. All of these are signs to the assessors the project hasn't been planned out.

Looking at the different types of plans

In this section, I review the different types of project plans, their purpose and when it's generally useful to use them. These documents include information about research you've conducted (both desktop and physical market research), why the project is needed and who has been involved in designing the project.

As shown in the following figure, you'll generally choose one of the four main documents that can demonstrate the viability and loveability of your project:

1. Feasibility study
2. Business case
3. Logic Model
4. Project plan.

Project plans for outlining the viability and loveability of your project

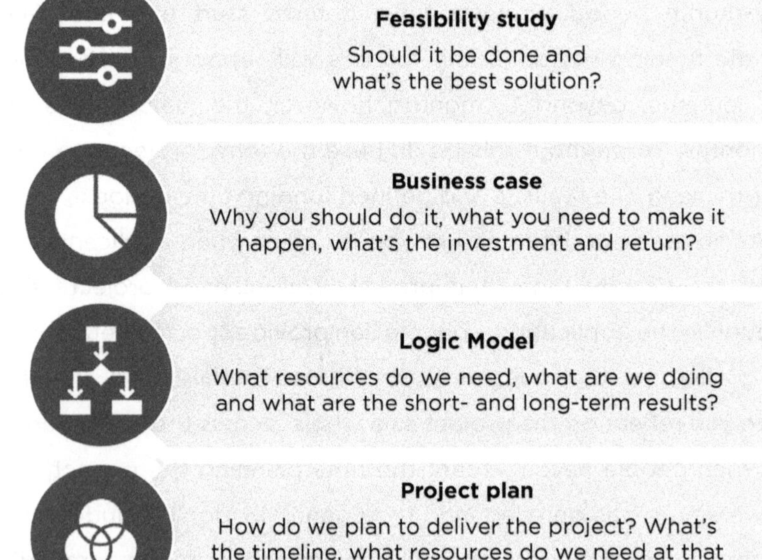

Feasibility study

Feasibility studies convince a funder that your idea is the best option. Feasibility studies are generally undertaken when hundreds of thousands, or millions of dollars in funding are needed and you're seeking state and/or federal government support. For this level of ask, funders want sound, well thought out planning, showing applicants have considered all the avenues to address the need.

For example, if you believe you need to build a new sporting facility, the feasibility study would analyse different options available. The plan would outline how you've critically assessed the feasibility (financial and otherwise) of those options to address your need.

The feasibility study broadly looks at how you'll govern and manage the project. For example, if it's a new tourism tour product, how will you staff it? What are your costs? What will the tour include? Sometimes feasibility studies include more detailed information, especially if the study is serving a dual purpose of identifying the most viable option and then building a business case for change.

The purpose of the feasibility study, however, is not to go into too much detail about each of the ideas and the operation of them. It's there to decide which option is the most feasible to explore further. For example, we're growing and need to expand our space to meet demand. Will we build, lease or buy? What options are there in the short and long term?

The feasibility study will explore the viability of the idea and how much it's really needed or wanted by your target group. This is the 'loveability' aspect. You don't build something hoping 'they will come'. You have to know that the target market will love it and use it.

You may have seen local councils awarded funding to produce a feasibility study because they are a higher cost with a larger depth of research and analysis required than for any of the following plans.

Business case

A business case differs from a feasibility study because it explores one solution only. For example, say you undertook a feasibility study that recommended building a new space as the best option. Your business case then dives deeper into the project and explores the value of the project, the costs and benefits.

A business case is good for larger financial investment projects that have positive economic returns, such as a job creation, new product or service, new markets, infrastructure or a new business. It will incorporate financial viability, project pay-back periods and financial modelling such as internal rate of return and economic impact. A business case assists when trying to convince investors – be it your manager, board or funder.

Developing a business case for these larger projects will support you to write a strong application, because it answers a lot of questions. Some funders also require a copy of the business case.

A lot of business case templates are available, and most follow a similar structure. Whatever department you're likely to seek funding from, check their resources and download any business case templates you find. Government departments often use the term 'case for change' when talking about business cases, because you're developing a business case to convince someone the change is worth investing in. Using 'case for change' is a good way to describe a business case to others who may not understand what a business case is.

A business case typically includes the following elements:

1. background
2. rationale, including alignment to strategies (yours or the identified funder)
3. expected outcomes (qualitative and quantitative)
4. scope of works

5. environmental analysis
6. stakeholder analysis, including input and feedback on their need and demand (this I where the 'loveability' aspect comes in!)
7. quality areas, including legislation and regulation compliance
8. details on implementation, including timeline, risks and project team
9. detail on ongoing management and operations
10. financials, including costs, ongoing costs and cost-benefit analysis, and proposed funding.

Logic Model

You need a Logic Model if you want to demonstrate how your resources and activities directly deliver the outcomes of your project. This model is particularly useful for showing how 'soft' outcomes deliver 'hard' benefits – for example, developing financial knowledge results in financially sound organisations, or developing grant writing skills with this book, assists you in writing strong applications, which increases your chance of winning grants.

As mentioned in step 1a, a Theory of Change framework outlines your high-level strategy. Your Logic Model (or Program Logic) is more operational. It might look similar because it uses the same framework; however, it is activity focused and works through the elements of the project. It outlines, 'With these resources and activities, this is how we make a difference'. In other words, your Logic Model makes it clear why a funder is being asked to pay for certain activities because it demonstrates how those resources and activities result in outcomes.

Using the Logic Model, funders can then identify how the project aligns to their objectives. Everyone should clearly understand what's important, and what activities don't add value to the outcomes. This is useful because we never have as much money as we'd like, so you can prioritise activities that contribute the most to achieve those outcomes. You can cut out the elements that are less useful as the budget gets tighter.

For example, iClick2Learn's Theory of Change framework shows capacity building as a strategy to build inclusive, healthy and adaptive communities. So, if this book were a project, its Logic Model would demonstrate how this book contributes to capacity building, to achieve the impact. The model would map how winning grants leads to increased knowledge and grants received, to deliver projects that contribute to iClick2Learn's impact. We would use evidence of past performance to project expected outcomes and impacts. A Logic Model offers so many opportunities for you to better understand your project. This information is invaluable when writing a strong grant application.

A Logic Model is my go-to planning tool after exploring the idea with the NDOIS tool. I've used Logic Models to understand projects as varied as a carbon sequestration project, an online system tool and a youth development workshop. For most projects I complete a summary Logic Model before I write up the rest of the project plan.

I cover Logic Models in much more detail in the next step of The Grant Writing System.

Project plan

Project plans are useful for any type of project. You can use them for ongoing programs, workshops, research projects and minor infrastructure, such as play equipment. Depending on your project, you may need to include other specifics. For example, if you are running an event, you might need to add in event specifics such as information on the venue, including a site plan, event production, security, traffic management, waste, cleaning and emergency procedures.

The following list outlines the kind of information to include in your project plan. For smaller projects, you may only need the one-page summary in points 1 to 7 initially. The one-page summary is a good overview to provide to stakeholders and potential funders. Whatever your project, I do recommend completing the whole plan, though, because you will need this to provide more information in your grant application. The depth of information you include in your plan will depend on how complex your idea is.

Here's what to include in your project plan:

1. need statement (incorporates need, demand and target group/s; 100 to 150 words)
2. solution
   - project title (10 words or less)
   - project summary (40 words or less)
3. outcome goals
4. budget summary
5. capacity to deliver (your organisational and project team experience, skills, knowledge, systems, processes and resources)
6. strategies, policies, standards and frameworks
7. implementation plan
8. mini Logic Model (anticipated benefits/outcomes)
9. stakeholder analysis (other organisations and people impacted by the project)
10. risk management (including risk mitigation strategies, key assumptions, barriers and weaknesses, and potential unintended consequences)
11. milestones and activity timelines
12. detailed budget.

A project plan is the most common document the majority of funders either ask for or expect you to have, and developing a project plan has so many benefits. Everything in your grant application requires you to answer questions that this project plan addresses. For example, you'll find questions about need and evidence of demand, stakeholders, engagement, milestones and timelines. You'll be asked other questions about implementation, capacity and budget. If you've already prepared your project plan, you can easily provide answers to these questions.

Ideally, you should go through this process with the priority ideas identified in The Grant RICE Score, because funding doesn't get announced at the exact time you want it. Some projects take a while to find the right funder. You might find while you're focused on getting project A funded, an opportunity comes up for project B. Or you talk with a funder, and they say, 'It sounds great, but we're interested in this type of project.' You're able to say, 'Oh we do have another project that might suit. I can send you the project plan.' When you develop projects to this stage, you can then 'shelve' the project, and this creates a range of projects you can pull off the shelf when an opportunity comes up.

You can also get other supporters excited and share the project plan with them. You never know – there may be discretionary buckets of money that need to be spent, or political funding that's been allocated and not assigned. Many a project has been funded this way! Plenty of funders with a few thousand dollars are happy to support or fully fund a project that has a documented project plan to assure them you know what you're doing.

Regardless of which plan you choose; I recommend you complete a summary project plan. You'll need this guidance to develop a business case or feasibility study or to provide to those developing these plans for you.

Summary

In this step, you learnt how to take your ideas and critique them to identify the best idea to invest time, energy and resources on. You've been able to rank ideas and use The Grant RICE Score to lead discussion on how to strengthen other ideas. You've also explored the four key plans that are useful when further developing your idea for funding.

What can you do now?

Here are some actions from what we've covered here in step 1b:

- ☐ Be critical of your ideas to make sure you're working on the right idea - the one that actually makes a difference and addresses your challenges and opportunities.
- ☐ Use the Grant RICE Score to rank and prioritise ideas.
- ☐ Decide which plan is right for you to continue planning your idea.
- ☐ Take your team through the NDOIS tool to understand relevant aspects.
- ☐ If you are co-designing your project with other stakeholders, use the NDOIS tool to brainstorm.
- ☐ Develop a pitch (or four!) using The Grant NDOIS Pitch frameworks.
- ☐ For additional opportunities, pitch your idea a few months before the end of financial year. Some funders have discretionary amounts of money they need to spend quickly! Support your pitch with a one-page project overview you'll find in the next stage.

Step 1c

Get your project grant ready

Funders invest in projects with outcomes that align to their objectives. It's now time to take your idea from pitching to a plan. Your ideas need to be soundly supported and you need to demonstrate you've considered a lot of aspects in your application. You don't want this written on your application:

> Applications did not provide detailed information and evidence, or highlight the applicant has the required knowledge, skills and systems. They did not demonstrate sustainability. Budget and timeline were unrealistic. Limited evidence was provided on how the activity will continue to contribute to outcomes for stakeholders.
>
> Grant Assessor's Feedback

Note that I had to consolidate about seven pages of feedback notes into this one quote!

So many assessors pick up gaps in applications. Yes, this may be because the writer didn't feel it was necessary to include the information, but in my experience it's because the writer didn't have the information to include and ran out of time to find it. Without the required information, they often fill their answers with unnecessary information.

In this step, I cover the Logic Model and the project plan in much more detail, outlining how they are universally applied for the majority of funded projects. In fact, I've developed The Grant Project Plan to incorporate the Logic Model, and so I also run through this tool.

The Grant Writing System: 3. The Grant Project Plan

As the following figure shows, we're now at the stage of getting your project grant ready, using The Grant Project Plan template.

Stage 1: Plan - Step 1c. Get your project grant ready

1. Plan

Get grant ready!

Step 1c. Get your project grant ready

Tool

v. The Grant Project Plan™

The Grant Project Plan answers the why, who, what, where, when and how of your project. A good starting point is to bring relevant people together to brainstorm the answers to the following questions. (Some answers you may have already from developing your NDOIS in the last step.)

Answer the following:

- Why is this project needed in the community?
- Why is it important?
- Where's the evidence of need?
- When will the project start and finish?
- Why is your organisation the best to deliver the project?
- Who are the key stakeholders?
- Who will benefit from the project?
- What is the project about?
- What will the impact be on the key stakeholders?

- What will it cost?
- What resources do you already have, or have access to?
- What risks are there?
- Where will the project take place?
- How is the project going to be funded?
- How will the project be managed?

> *If you don't develop a plan, you won't have the information you need to address the questions in the grant application.*

You can use The Grant Project Plan template to record answers to these questions, or just work through the template from the start. (You can download the template in editable format from the online kit.)

In the following sections, I take you through each page and row in the template, with each number relating to the numbered area in the template. As you're working through and completing the template, remember it's about documenting the thinking and approach. Some things won't be perfect. Things will change as circumstances change.

Need, solution, outcomes and budget

The first page of The Grant Project Plan template takes you through from need statement to implementation plan, as shown in the following figure.

The first page of The Grant Project Plan template

One-page summary

<table>
<tr><th colspan="3">1. Need Statement</th><th colspan="3">2. Solution</th><th colspan="3">3. Outcome goals</th><th colspan="3">4. Budget summary</th></tr>
<tr><td colspan="3"></td><td colspan="3"></td><td colspan="3"></td><td colspan="3"></td></tr>
<tr><th colspan="4">5. Capability to deliver</th><th colspan="4">6. Strategies, policies, standards and frameworks</th><th colspan="4">7. Implementation plan</th></tr>
<tr><td colspan="4"></td><td colspan="4"></td><td colspan="4"></td></tr>
</table>

In this section, I cover the elements in the first row of the template, starting with the need statement.

1. Need statement

In the last step, I covered using NDOIS to develop a pitch framework. The need statement builds on this and focuses just on the project and what can be achieved within the funding period, e.g. 12 months. NDOIS was broader and included impact to motivate and influence your supporters. NDOIS also didn't critique your need to develop a stronger position, which is what we'll do here.

We use the word 'need' in a lot of different ways, and this can cause confusion for new grant writers. If you ask a new parent what they need, they might yawn and say, 'Strong coffee', but is this the real need? We naturally understand that an unspoken conversation is happening, and we fill in the blanks. Without realising it, we conduct an internal needs analysis process by asking and answering the question 'Why?' Why do they need coffee? Because they're tired. Why are they tired? Because their newborn keeps them awake at night. So, what is the real need? Sleep. Coffee isn't the need;

it's one solution. It's also a short-term solution, because, ultimately, they need more sleep.

This analysis process feels so obvious because much of our communication is unspoken. But you can't ask a grant assessor to assume and to fill in missing information you haven't provided. It's not their job to assume. Assessors must justify why they're saying yes to your application. Their decisions can be investigated – even formally in such bodies as senate enquiries – so it's important they do their job well. They'll only assess what you've said, so be specific and clear.

To give the assessors what they need, you must unpack the obvious. You know why you started developing the idea. You know the motivation for the project and the support you have. Remember, though, that assessors and funders don't know this. They haven't been on the journey with you.

When you start exploring the need for your project, be sure to reference the target group who benefits from the project. Being specific is important here. If the project has multiple target groups, describe them. Include numbers of each target group impacted and those you expect to service or involve.

Clearly identifying the target group will focus you on the actual need, rather than being distracted trying to fulfil everyone's need, and being everything to everyone. Funders genuinely do want to contribute to the difference you make. They want to fund projects and organisations that are clear about what they'll do, and having them understand what you won't do is also important. For example, stating a program is for '13- to 17-year-old people who are refugees' makes it clear who the program isn't for.

All right, here's where you bring your team around a whiteboard – it's time to workshop! It's time to use the 5 Whys process to get to the core need – that is, the real need your project will address.

Understanding the 5 Whys process and how you can use it

The first thing any funder wants to know is what your project need is. Project need and demand has to be clearly communicated. You need to demonstrate you can resource and deliver the outcomes and impact to address the stated need. For example, have you planned for enough volunteers, staff, skills and experience to deliver what you are promising?

This all has to fit with the funder's priorities and grant objectives. When these three things align, you've hit the Grant Funding Sweet Spot (refer to step 1a), which means your project has a greater chance of funding success. However, to clearly communicate these things, you need to understand them yourself.

When asked about the need in their grant application, applicants often state the solution their project is offering instead. Sadly, they lose points and the funder's interest by doing so. Also, the problem is when you don't do the work to deeply understand the need, all you're doing is offering a band-aid or temporary fix.

> *Applicants mistakenly state the solution, not the need.*

I understand why people jump to talking about the solution – because it's what they need funding for! But it's not the need for the project. To discover the need for the project, you need to dig deeper.

The 5 Whys, developed by Sakichi Toyoda, is a simple process with powerful results. It uses a foundational cause and effect problem-solving approach.

In this step, I guide you through this process using a simple example in linear format. I'll then show you another example using a visual mind map.

In this first example, John works at a local school and is seeking funding for shade sails. In this case, the answer John gives for the need is, 'To install shade sails'.

This is what I call a 'level 1' answer. You need to keep asking 'why' until you get to at least three levels. Sometimes, you have to keep digging to level 5, which is what we'll do in this example.

Level 1 answer to the need for a project

What's your need? | To install shade sails

So, say I ask John, 'Why do you need shade sails?' John then tells me it's because the school doesn't have enough trees around for shade. But a lack of shade still doesn't explain why the school needs shade sails.

Level 2 answer to the need for a project

My third 'why' focused question would then be, 'Why do you need more shade?' John now tells me, 'Student numbers have grown at the school, so there are more children who need shade.'

Level 3 answer to the need for a project

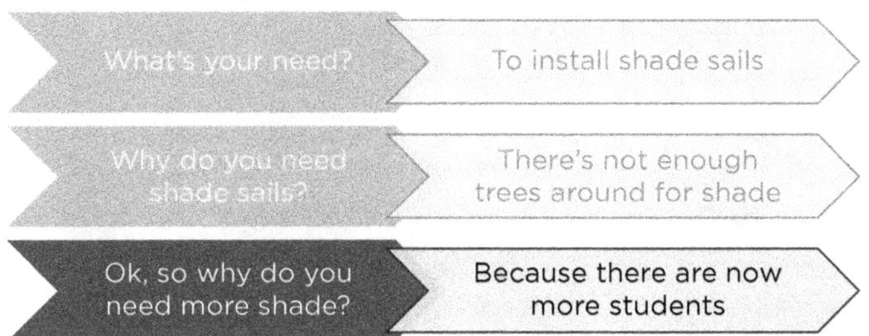

But the school growing in numbers still doesn't explain why they need shade sails. So, I ask John for more information, this time linking the explanation to the first statement John made. I ask him why the students need shade and the response is, 'They're outdoors a lot during the day for recess, lunch and sport, and it gets hot in the summer.'

Level 4 answer to the need for a project

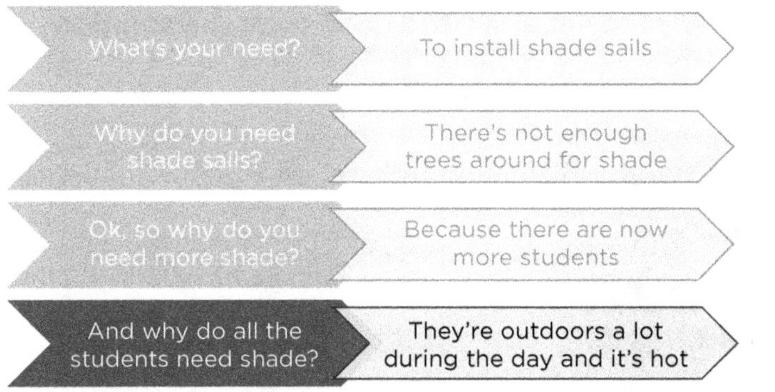

Now we're starting to get closer to the root cause. Next, I ask, 'Why is it important for students to be in the shade when they're outdoors in the heat?'

At this point, John states the project need: students need protection from the sun to prevent skin damage and cancer.

Level 5 answer to the need for a project

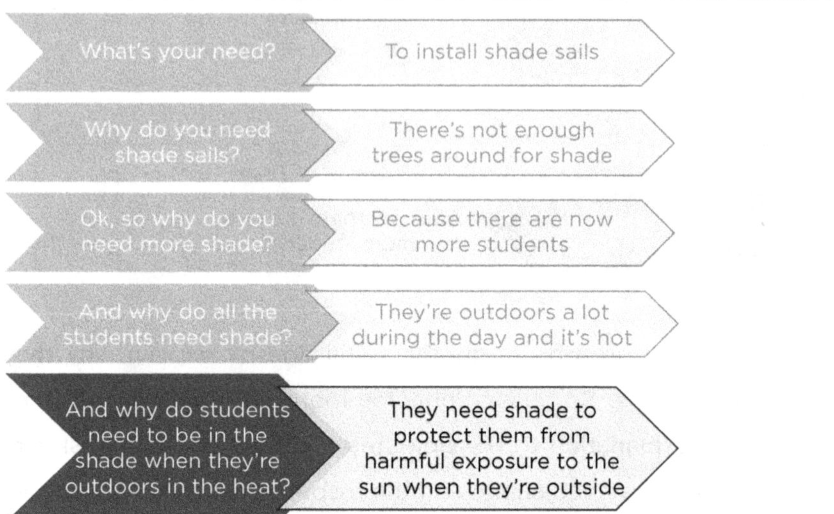

That's the need. Shade sails are a solution, while protecting students from skin cancer developing due to sun exposure is the need.

Using the 5 Whys to separate the need from the solution

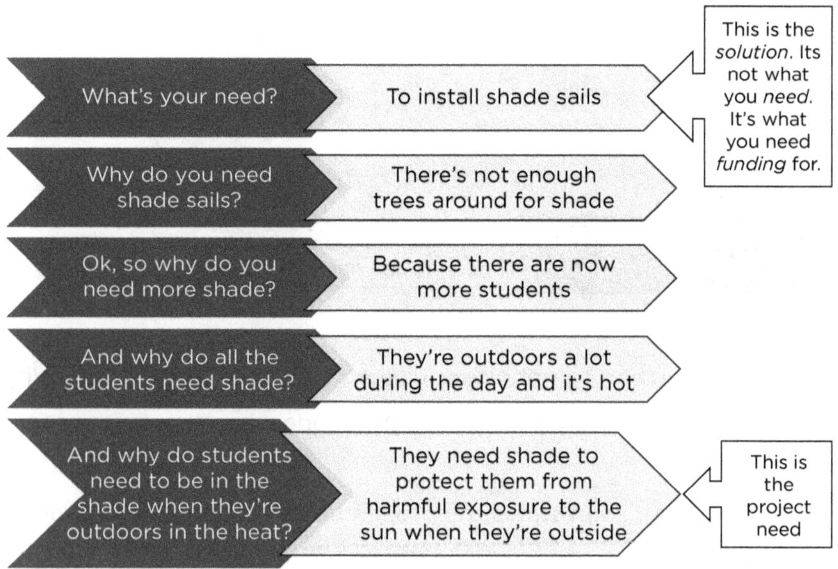

The need is also the impact, reversed - for example, the need is, 'Children need to be protected from harmful exposure to the sun when they're outside,' and for an impact statement this becomes, 'Children are protected from the sun, reducing their chance of skin cancer from childhood exposure, by 40%'.

These are more powerful statements to motivate people to invest, rather than simply buying a shade sail.

> *Stop talking about the solution and talk about the need and outcomes.*

You may be reading this thinking it is such a basic conversation, but it's essential. Every time I've done this with a group of people, they've had huge lightbulb moments when they realise they've been trying to sell the funder on the solution by talking about what they're going to do and their activities. They haven't been talking about the need. Funders want to hear about need and they want to know that you understand the need.

I've used the shade sail example to break the method down for you; however, I always use a mind map when doing this exercise because it's never that simple. What we do and the difference we make with our work has multiple benefits (outcomes) and those benefits have a ripple effect (impact).

Let's have a look at another example, showing it as a mind map. In this example, the local cycling business has decided to run a 'Hub and Spoke' festival. **Using the Why process, we have uncovered four key level 1 needs. These are:**

1. responding to market demand for the cycling festival
2. promoting a cycling safety message
3. increasing tourism and economic impact
4. increasing community inclusion, health and wellbeing.

You can use the why process to explore each of these four level 1 points in more depth, until you have listed as many outcomes your project delivers as possible. As the following figure shows, you can then present these as a mind map.

Mind map showing level 1 needs and possible outcomes for Hub and Spoke cycling festival

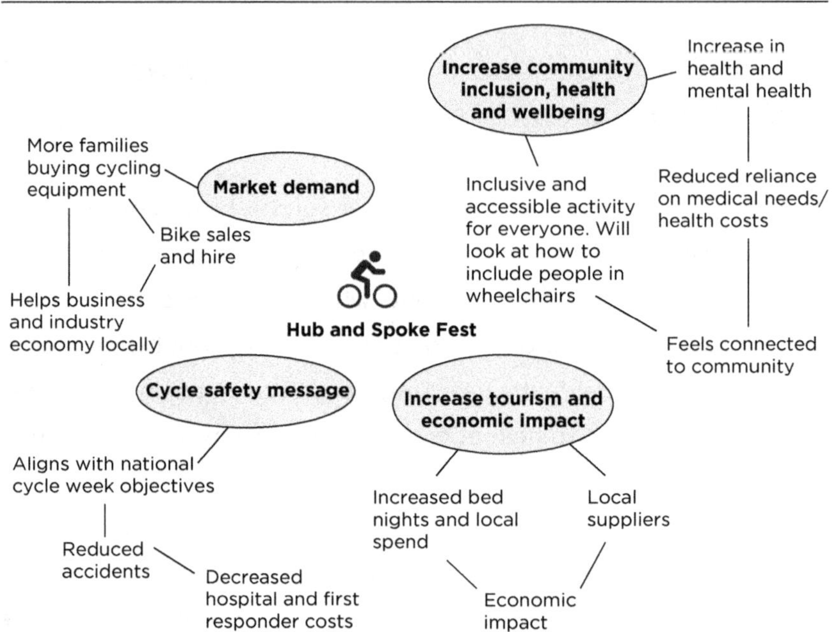

You can then use the visual aspect of the mind map to quickly identify the key themes your information is showing you. For example, business growth, tourism and health themes are coming through. This means when you start looking for the right grant, you would look for business, tourism and health-related grants.

Drawing a mind map of all the different answers to your 5 Why questions and digging down on each of these answers will assist you capture the core needs. If you need inspiration or want to see how this process works in other examples, go to this step in the online kit.

Using the 5 Whys process to identify further needs

In the previous section, the answer John gave would be enough to then write the first draft of the project need statement, which is: The school children need shade to protect them from harmful exposure to the sun when they're outside.

Your need statement will give you the non-negotiable heart of your project and provide a starting point for finding reliable evidence. As the first question generally asked, it's the first one assessors' score. To explore this further, you'd move onto the next stage and start talking about evidencing this need, and the demand (covered in the following sections).

But before you do ... have we forgotten anyone? That's right – the stakeholders.

John could include other teachers, parents and students in the conversation. This would provide John with additional information, and they may share stories to build the evidence base.

For example, students and teachers might share that because they're not in the shade at lunchtime in the hottest part of the day, they feel tired and weary, which means they aren't engaging in the afternoon lessons. John would add this to the mind map and project need statement. A parent might state they've recently had cancerous cells cut out, which their doctor linked back to childhood sun exposure. This could be used as a testimonial from a concerned parent. This is a good example of using a story to bring your statistics to life.

If you've asked people for feedback in a workshop, take photos. Funders want to know projects are designed 'with people' who are impacted, not 'for people'. These are your stakeholders and stakeholder feedback is evidence. If a grant application asks for evidence of stakeholder engagement, pull out the feedback from the people your project targets. You could even use these photos in a project plan and attach them to the application if you can.

Solution thinking

Up to now you've been exploring and breaking down the elements of need for your chosen solution. You've been approaching this with a solution-thinking mindset, not a need-focused mindset. It's important though for me to hit pause and reinforce to you that your solution may not be the best option to address your need. So, if you haven't already run through a list of ideas and discussed them, now is a good time to do it. Also, funders often see the same old, same old and this is your opportunity to really consider the best solution that meets the need and the solution that presents a stronger, competitive case for funding.

The Why process should have helped you think your need through. So, first get agreement on the need and be specific. Next, get your team together and put your solution on a whiteboard under the heading 'Ideas to meet our need'. Then brainstorm with the team. Ask what other ideas people have to address the need. For now, just write each of these up, you don't have to critique and discuss them, you're in brainstorming mode.

Now, use The Grant RICE Score from step 1b to rank your ideas. Then you can discuss and critique each idea based on these scored elements. This will help you develop a solution that is designed to meet the need. For example, you may find that permanent fixed shade is a better long-term solution than shade sails. This may mean an adjustment to your project plan and timeline. Sometimes though we can't have the gold-plated solution and you may decide for a few reasons to go back to the shade sails. That's okay. The main thing is that you went through the process of considering all options. The reason this is important is in many cases I find people accept the solution they think will be the best and they don't apply critical thinking to really assess if something else would actually be a better return on their time and investment. Often this critical thinking results in a far better solution and some creative approaches that make your project competitive.

Presenting need positively

Sometimes talking about need encourages a scarcity mindset because doing so puts your focus on what's wrong or what's missing.

However, need is also about opportunity, and thinking this way switches to having an abundance mindset. When you change something, you need to ask what additional opportunities are presented. Ask your stakeholders what other opportunities the project offers. The key is not to be constrained by your resources. Focus on what's possible.

Funders understand you want funding to address a need. Showing how you've thought about additional opportunities the project delivers demonstrates additional added value – providing, of course, this extra value is also something the funders care about. This also demonstrates the depth of stakeholder engagement in your project.

One of the ways you can discover other opportunities is by asking your stakeholders, 'If you had access to this or this was done, what difference would that make to you or how would that make a difference to you?'

As an example, we were applying for funding to reseal an airstrip in a regional community, which at the time had no passenger services. The position we put forward was that we needed the airstrip resealed so it could also cater for passenger services. Looking for need and demand within the community assisted; however, we also needed to understand unknown demand from others living outside the community, who still had an interest there.

The community we were working with has a strong 'return to the town' annual event and a few thousand people on their Facebook Group. So, we developed a survey and asked people in this group to tell us what difference passenger services to the town's airstrip would make to them. Here's one story we received via Facebook that we used to support a statement showing demand:

> I love the community, I would return there to live and work because a regular air service would mean I would be able to visit family in Sydney. Without air services, the time and distance is too hard to manage by myself.
>
> Respondent, air passenger services survey

We further demonstrated demand by estimating additional accommodation nights, based on the responses from the Facebook comments and survey. The sentence we included in the relevant section in the grant application stated:

> **Evidence from *[town we were working with]* community air services survey (Attachment B) projects demand of an additional 550 flights per annum (estimated 1,519 bed nights).**

This isn't the only reason the funding was received, of course - we submitted a strong application in a lot of other ways. However, anything you can do to strengthen your case around the demand builds that picture. You're telling the story of need and demand, and how the proposed solution addresses this.

Building demand into the need statement

Demand has two sides: people and the data. On the people side, it's not enough to say 15 people in your bicycle users group need a new track across the creek to link to a river walk. You must prove demand is bigger than those 15 people. How many other cyclists, runners and walkers would like a track linking to a river walk? How many would use it? And that's only from the community. What about tourists? Does it add tourism and economic value?

On the data side, you need to research and gather information to turn it into evidence. You need primary and secondary market research. For your primary research, ask stakeholders what they need and how this project would impact them, both positively and negatively. You need to consider any negative or unintended impacts so you can address them early and reduce or remove them. An example of a negative impact for the river walk might be people who use it early morning and early evening may be at greater personal risk because the plan doesn't include lighting.

Secondary research is researching via your computer, called desktop research (hello, Google!). You can access data such as community profiling data from the Australian Bureau of Statistics, community profiling data from your local council and industry data to support your project. (I've included further examples of data sources with up-to-date resources and links in the online kit.)

Importantly, you need to focus on gathering primary research first. If you're claiming demand exists for the need to be addressed, you need reliable and persuasive evidence to back up your claim. If you say 90% of the community will benefit from your project, you must be able to show evidence of how you know 90% will benefit. This is what grant assessors are looking for.

Your primary research will inform your secondary research. So, conversations with your stakeholders will give you information about different aspects of demand you wouldn't have otherwise known about, similar to the school shade sail example – where a key point gathered from primary research was that student engagement in afternoon lessons reduced after they were in the sun at lunchtime. You could then use this as a research focus to identify if industry research supports the anecdotal information.

Evidencing the four types of demand

You can evidence demand in four aspects: current known demand (also called 'unmet need'), projected demand, unknown demand and urgent demand.

Let's review an example. Say a community hall wants to refit their kitchen. The kitchen is 60 years old, and the cupboards and benchtops have been damaged over the years. The 10-amp single phase power needs to be upgraded to three phase throughout the hall, to run the lights and commercial-sized freezers and fridges. Hot water scalds and burns are also a considerable risk because the old hot water system pipes water into the kitchen at uneven temperatures, getting up to 60 degrees Celsius (which can scald people within five seconds).

For current known demand, you would include statistics of how many people use the hall and complain about the kitchen, or the number of reported incidents with the scalding hot water and what you've done about it. You would include information about where the people who use the hall come from – for example, if they're locals or if, say, out of region car clubs use the hall. Fixing the kitchen to address these needs would address the current known demand.

For projected demand, you would include statistics of people who have either withdrawn their booking after doing a site inspection and checking the kitchen, or those who don't book after they find out the kitchen facilities won't suit. You can use this to demonstrate that by delivering the project, you won't lose those bookings in the future; therefore, you project an increase in bookings. You could also use evidence of projected demand from responses via a survey (as in the airstrip example, earlier in this step), or based on target group population growth. For example, if 37% of demand currently comes from the target group and the target group is projected to grow by 10% year-on-year over the next three years, you could highlight how demand would increase as the population increases.

Projected demand tells funders what can happen based on known statistics. Unknown demand is about exploring the other opportunities. While you still need to have an evidence base, your focus is more about exploring additional opportunities. To explore unknown demand, for example, you can ask stakeholders what would change for them once the kitchen was upgraded. What additional opportunities are created as a result? What different uses could be explored? You could research who uses other venues. By upgrading the kitchen, you might find an out-of-state car club wants to book the hall for the weekend for their club gathering and show. (Yes, this is based on a real example, and this does now happen!) You can use these examples to show how you're aware that unmet demand exists and, based on this, you expect further bookings.

The final demand aspect you need to consider is the urgency of the issue. For example, say the hall's 100-year anniversary is coming up and a week of activities is planned that can't proceed with the kitchen in its current state. Or wedding season is coming up and, over the next four months, couples will be booking venues for their wedding. If the kitchen isn't upgraded, the hall won't be booked for these celebrations. This means you'll miss an estimated *x* number of bookings and *x* dollars of income – which could pay for other items in the kitchen. For other projects, the sense of urgency could be because the situation will worsen if not addressed within 12 months, based on the projections , or the safety risk it presents.

Keep a list of reference sources in The Grant Writing Kit (introduced in step 1a). This list identifies where you got the information from in case you need to reference it in your application.

Gathering evidence is something you definitely don't want to leave to your AI Assistant or trust the results it might give you if you try! Your AI Assistant is not a reputable source of relevant data. It can't critically assess the information it sources to define if it's an opinion or researched data. It also can't validate the reputation of the researchers, or if its relevant for your project and industry. So, use the links from the online kit to get you started on research.

If you're stuck for ideas on stories, it can offer some interesting suggestions on the types of target group or client stories you can share. It might send you down the wrong path though as it doesn't know the key message you are communicating in your answer. So again, AI Assistant for brainstorming and suggesting only, you'll have to apply strategic thinking.

Writing the need statement

The function of a need statement is to demonstrate the problem and engage the funder in wanting to fund your solution that addresses it. Your need statement should make the following clear:

Problem/Opportunity + Action = Solution

Here's how these three elements work together:

- **Problem/Opportunity:** This is the reason you need the project, and should be a result of the 5 Whys process. If you have uncovered multiple needs, for each funder you can target your need to align to the funding program. You should communicate the significance of the need and the cause of the problem. I know we're focusing on problems here; however, don't forget it's also an opportunity! We just mainly talk about it as a problem because we have to demonstrate need.
- **Action:** This is what your organisation proposes to address the problem. You should also include how this is achievable.
- **Solution:** This is the positive results of the action on the problem (without detailing the specifics of the solution itself!).

Drafting a simple evidence-based need statement is the starting point for all projects, and all grant applications. In fact, 90% of the time, the need question is the first question you're asked in an application. Keep it to 150 words or less. You could wait until you start writing your application to draft this; however, as you start communicating your project and persuading influencers the need statement will be invaluable.

A need statement comprises five points: the current situation, the ideal situation, the gap between the current and ideal, what will happen if the problem isn't addressed and how you plan to solve the problem (see the following figure).

The five points of a need statement

Currently	***This is the lived reality of the need***	Funders now understand the situation
Ideally	***Show what life would be like with it***	Demonstrates the change that can be made
To address this	***Explain how you'll get from current to ideal reality***	Shows them what will be done to bridge the gap
If we do nothing	***Highlight the consequences of not meeting need***	Creates urgency and exacerbates the reality
So, we will	***Your solution***	Reinforces the action and result

The best way to start writing a need statement is to write each element as bullet points, as follows:

1. **'Currently, ...':** Summarise the lived reality of the need. Make it a catchy, evidence-based claim. Ensure it's short and repeatable. Try to keep it between 15 and 20 words. You include known demand here (refer to last section).
2. **'Ideally, ...':** Highlight the need by showing what life would be like with it.
3. **'To address this, ...':** Explain how to get from the current reality to the ideal reality.

4. **'If we do nothing, ...':** Highlight the consequence of not meeting the need. Consider including relevant projected, unknown and urgent demand here.
5. **'So, we will ...':** Offer your solution.

Once you have your main points, weave a story in – generally, no later than the middle to re-engage assessors in the human side of what you're proposing.

For now, try to capture the main needs for the project. You will, of course, modify the emphasis in this need statement to align to the funder's priorities in your application. You also may not need to include the solution in the need statement as it's generally asked about in another question. It's good to be clear now though.

Going back to the example of the school shade sails from earlier in this step, John's first draft need statement is:

1. Currently, the school has 289 students with no adequate protection from the sun while outdoors.
2. Ideally, students would have access to shaded play areas to protect them from the sun.
3. To bridge the gap, the school needs 500 m^2 of shade.
4. If we do nothing, students will suffer harmful sun exposure and the increased risk of skin cancer. Teachers report children feeling hot and tired after eating lunch outdoors in the sun, so doing nothing also reduces students' ability to learn.
5. We will erect 10 shade sails on the school grounds to protect the children while they play outside.

Now it's time to ask questions and research the statistics and stories that support your statement. So, continuing this example, John would need to ask – and research the answers to – the following questions:

- What is the local legislation about school shade?
- What does a reputable source (for example, the Cancer Council) say about sun exposure?
- How many square metres are needed to meet industry standards or legal requirements?
- How many shade sails are needed to provide the required shade?
- What material will be used for the shade sails?
- Will the material meet the need?
- What's the lifespan of the shade sails?
- Who will be responsible for maintenance?
- Who will be responsible for replacement/disposal of the shade sails at the end of their lifespan?
- What is the long-term impact of providing shade to students?

Research like this often reveals hidden knowledge you might not think to ask about. For example, when I googled 'how much shade for 289 children', the very first result was a step-by-step guide for planning a shade project called *Guidelines to Shade* by Cancer Council NSW. The guide includes how to run a shade inventory and shade audit, and UV protection best practice for different contexts. I found some states do not permit shade sails in schools; instead, schools need to build shade structures with specific requirements about the materials used.

One thing to keep in mind as you develop your need statement is what you're comparing your need against. The data has to be local to you, and relatable to your project. Unless you are a state-based or national organisation, that level of data isn't 'local to you'. If you're going to use industry statistics or national statistics, you must compare.

For example, an application I assessed, stated, 'Soccer membership is increasing right across Australia.' Now, the applicant wasn't Soccer Australia; it was a local club. So, this statement provided little value in their need statement – in fact, it detracted from it. They hadn't included any statistics demonstrating their specific increase. They did not relate the national trend back to what it meant for them as a local club.

A better answer would have been, 'Our membership has grown 22% (62 children) annually on average in the last two years. The increase in membership is higher than the national average annual growth of 18%.' Or reduce your word count to, 'Annual membership growth in the last two years is 22% (62 children), higher than the national average (18%).'

After research and further consultation about the shade sail, John will need to amend the need statement to include more specific data. He might even get creative and find a new way to meet the need. The following example shows you what I mean; however, please remember this is only an example! Your local safety standards and legislation will be different!

Here's how John could start to develop his need statement:

1. Currently, the school has 289 students with approximately 110 m^2 of natural shade from evergreen trees and 85 m^2 of shade from a 10-year-old polyethylene shade cloth. The shade cloth has exceeded the lifespan of effective UV protection *[cite here the shade inventory and audit]*.
2. Ideally, students should have access to 1.48 m^2 of shade (minimum UPF of 40) per child to comply with state guidelines *[cite guidelines]*. For 289 students, this equals to approximately 428 m^2 of shade required rated UPF40+.
3. To bridge the gap, a minimum of 318 m^2 of compliant shade must be installed.
4. If we do nothing, students will suffer harmful exposure to UV radiation, which causes skin cancer. Research shows 60% of children in Australia will be diagnosed with skin cancer later in life *[cite reputable source]*. Teachers report children feeling hot and tired after eating lunch outdoors in the sun, so doing nothing also reduces students' ability to learn, impacting their future opportunities.

5. We will install a permanent shade structure to protect the children while they play outside. The structure will exceed UPF40 and cover the whole play area of 500 m^2 (photos attached).

Depending on how the need statement is worded, you may present the solution as the starting paragraph. This way you're telling funders what the solution is and then why you need it.

This framework guides you to write a need statement that flows and contains all these elements. When I write my need statement, I don't use the sentence starters I've used in the previous bullets in the final version. Here's how the shade sail example points could be written in a 150-word need statement answer limit:

> **60% of our 289 students risk harmful exposure to UV and increased childhood skin cancer *[source]*. The school has sun-safe policies. However, in summer, students access outdoor areas in 30+ degrees Celsius heat. The current shade sail has exceeded its recommended lifespan. Shade covers less than the area required for enrolled students (318 m^2 short).**
>
> **The inability for some children to access shade has also decreased their engagement and learning opportunities. 'Lack of available shade and children feeling tired in the afternoon in class and going home sunburnt is concerning. We've discussed this in P&C meetings. We've fundraised $35,000 and need another $48,000 to protect our children.' P&C President.**
>
> **We will install a permanent shade structure in the playground. The structure exceeds UPF40 and covers the playground area of 500 m^2. It will meet *[state]* guidelines and local government regulations for permanent structures.**

Here's another example for another project. This need statement doesn't include a quote or testimonial and is 100 words:

> **500+ children in Perth access community language learning through 18 not-for-profits. These organisations deliver community events including Perth Unity Festival, attracting 15,000 visitors. Grant funding is essential for cultural celebrations to take place. Demonstrating child safety practices is a requirement to obtain event funding.**
>
> **Without documented child safety processes, we can't access financial support. The community won't be able to unite and celebrate our rich diversity. An external resource audit found two childcare resources. These are not relatable and use complex language. We will deliver in-language translated resources and training, so the community can continue to strengthen and celebrate unity.**

Now, let's add in a quote/testimonial to this example, while still keeping it to 100 words:

> **500+ children in Perth access community language learning through 18 not-for-profits. Collectively, they deliver the Perth Unity Festival, attracting 15,000 visitors. Government support is essential for cultural celebrations to take place. Demonstrating child-safety practices is a requirement to obtain event funding.**
>
> **'Funders need documented child-safety processes to access financial support. Without this, we can't celebrate our diversity and unite our community.' Laleh Ahmadi, President Unity Festival**

An external resource audit found two childcare resources. These are not relatable and use complex language. We will deliver in-language translated resources and training, so the community can continue to strengthen and celebrate unity.

You may also notice some word changes and a 'sneaky' writing trick. I've joined the words 'child safety', so it's only counted as one word, not two. This wouldn't save much if you were writing to a strict character count, but for word counts it works. It also works because it's connecting these two words to represent a single descriptor, so it's excusable. As a general rule in assessment panels, as long as what you say makes sense and is clearly not a first draft, you won't be harshly judged on spelling and grammar. I've had applications with minor spelling mistakes that have won the grant!

Once you've finalised your need statement, use it as an anchor. During any negotiations about your project or concessions you need to make, keep anchored to the need statement. For example, when your need statement is 'protecting our school children from the sun with adequate shade', you know when someone suggests hats and sunscreen it's only a short-term solution and won't fully meet the need. It might be a good option for now, but you'll still have the same problem. Children can forget hats and sunscreen. What will you do? Using your need statement as an anchor assists you to avoid such short-term thinking. You may have to accept less funding than you need to get you started on stage 1 or a smaller part of the project, but at least now you won't accept a solution that's not addressing the need.

When you're completing research for your need statement, keep notes of where you find answers and gather evidence – for example, letters, emails, photographs, reputable websites, testimonials and minutes from meetings.

Earlier we discussed how your AI Assistant can be useful, and sometimes how they can send you off track. Here's our AI Assistant's response when we asked it to develop a need statement for the Perth Unity Festival example.

> **We need funding to establish child-safe policies to guarantee the safety of the 15,000 attendees at our lively multicultural festival. Over 500 children benefit from community language learning programs facilitated by 18 not-for-profit organizations, emphasizing the necessity of developing these policies in multiple languages.**
>
> **Laleh Ahmadi, the President of Unity Festival, shared a powerful story underscoring the significance of child-safe policies. Once, young Amir attended the festival with his family. Amir's parents, predominantly Farsi speakers, encountered difficulties in expressing their concerns about his safety due to language barriers. Tragically, this hindered their ability to seek assistance from festival organizers, exposing Amir to potential risks.**
>
> **Your generous support will enable us to formulate child-safe policies in multiple languages, bridging communication gaps. This will ensure a secure environment for all children, irrespective of their language backgrounds. Stand alongside Laleh Ahmadi and the Unity Festival in championing child safety by funding these crucial policies, protecting the 15,000 festival-goers, including the 500+ children benefiting from community language learning programs provided by 18 not-for-profit organizations.**

Now compare it to my written example. As a brainstorming tool, the sample story has an interesting angle with a higher emotive pull than my written example. So, I would consider what testimonial or story Laleh can offer that might put more emotion in the story. However, it doesn't speak to the multiple needs and challenges, such as the gap in the market because existing resources aren't suitable. If you didn't include this in your answer, then the assessor may know of some resources and feel that these are appropriate. Highlighting they aren't shows the gap and reinforces the need for funding. It also doesn't link how the 500+ children in 18 not-for-profits relate to the festival. I've used this example to start demonstrating the pros and cons of our AI Assistant.

Now let's move onto the next part of the template - your solution.

2. Solution

The solution section of The Grant Project Plan template is where you provide an overview of the project, providing the project title and summary.

a. Project title

Give your project a title in 10 words or fewer. You'll use this title to communicate your project to stakeholders. You might also use it in your grant application (which is why keeping it to 10 words or fewer is important), with a few tweaks to align to what the funder cares about. This title can be a simple description, such as 'Innovating the tile industry with an online home design system' or 'The Victoria Park inclusive play equipment project', or it might have something snappy, such as 'Your home, your tile design' or 'Project Sandbox'.

When you've found a grant, you'll find a purpose statement or statement outlining objectives for the grant. This statement will sound something like, 'To strengthen community connectedness and increase positive play experiences for children living with disabilities in regional areas'. Use as much of the grant's purpose statement in your project title as you can. So, 'Project Sandbox' could be renamed to 'Positive play for children with disabilities in regional Tasmania' (or

'Project Positive Play'). Use the full title at the start of the document and use 'Project Positive Play' in the rest of your application. I talk more about this in stage 3.

A project title should be interesting enough to capture attention, but not so ambiguous funders don't know what the project is.

b. Project summary

Your project summary is also called a 'scope statement'. It's focused on 'what' you're doing. Try to keep your summary to 40 words or less because that's often the word limit in applications. Include the location/s the project will be delivered in.

You can use your need statement to create your summary, focusing on the final part. For example, using the information in the first and final paragraph in the shade sail need statement your summary is:

> **We will install a permanent shade structure in the playground *[include details of location]*, shading 289 school children per day. It will be 500 m² and exceed UPF40. It will meet *[state]* guidelines and local government regulations for permanent structures.**

3. Outcome goals

In this section, list the key priority outcomes you plan to achieve by delivering the project. Outcomes are the benefits your project delivers, and can be tangible, such as developing a product, or intangible, such as offering training that leads to increased knowledge and improved job opportunities.

Your stated outcomes must be achievable during the funding period (generally 12 months). However, be sure to factor in aspects such as seasonal holidays. Sometimes such holidays mean the project outcomes must be achieved within nine months. Your stated outcomes should address the challenges and opportunities you've identified in your need statement.

You'll commit to delivering outcomes in your grant application and you'll need to report on these at the end of the project when you submit your final report (called an acquittal - see steps 7a and 7b).

Some project outcomes lead to change beyond the funding period, and these are called impacts. For example, say a therapist is delivering a wellbeing project to isolated elderly people living alone. This increases their social interaction and confidence in meeting new people (outcomes), resulting in 75% of participants joining new social groups, which reduces their social isolation (impacts).

You're only providing a summary of outcomes here. If you want to expand on this summary, or your stakeholders or funders want more information, you can provide a copy of your Logic Model - see '8. Logic Model', later in this step, for more.

4. Budget summary

In this section, you state the project total first and summarise your project income and expenses, either as a total or with some broad descriptive groups.

For income, include the money your organisation will contribute and the things you will pay for, the money you're seeking to be funded (listing all types of support, including grants and sponsorship), and the total of all in-kind contributions. (In-kind amounts are things that cost someone else.)

For expenses, summarise these in natural groups. For example, say you're applying for a grant to develop a website, email promotions and site hosting, and have included costs for graphic design, brochure design and printing 100 brochures. One budget summary group would be website costs, and this group would include a portion of the graphic design costs, development of the site costs and the hosting fees.

For more on budgeting and what items to include where, see '12. Detailed budget', later in this step.

Capability, Strategies and Implementation

Let's now move on to the elements in the second row of the template, as shown in the following figure.

The first page of The Grant Project Plan template, second row

5. Capability to deliver	6. Strategies, policies, standards and frameworks	7. Implementation plan

5. Capability to deliver

Many grant applications will include a question covering capacity – such as, 'What is your capacity to deliver?' Depending on the structure of the question, you'll also need to prove 'capability' to deliver this project. Capability is as much about your organisation as it is about the individuals within your organisation. So, when 'capacity' is included in the question, stop and consider if you should include 'capability' in your answer or if another question asks about experience.

Capability is really about proving these two things: capacity and ability.

Capacity

Capacity is about your resources to deliver the project. Include human, physical or financial resources. Some examples at an organisational level would be the number of staff and volunteers or the physical and virtual resources. Some of these may also be through partners such as offices in other communities.

To increase capacity, consider who the natural partners and supporters are for your project and have a conversation about how they might be involved. If you're not sure who you should consider here, your stakeholder analysis (covered in detail in '10. Stakeholder analysis', later in this step) is a good starting point.

For community projects in particular, funders want to maximise their investment and there's often an expectation that you'll partner with other relevant organisations. This means they may question why *xyz* group isn't involved. For example, if your organisation were seeking funding for your staff to run a youth program in schools, they may question why only one school is currently involved in the program. If it's a broad community youth project, funders may question whether a good mix of other youth organisations are involved – including local council, youth councils and organisations that support youth.

When considering capacity, you should operate on a basis of, 'I don't know 100% what a person's background, experience or skill level is'. This is the ability part of capability.

Ability

Ability is about the skills, knowledge and experience of the people who are working in or supporting your project. The number of times I've come across projects with an apparent gap and supported the team discover an internal strength is amazing. People don't often stop to explore the value people have. Our brains tend to pigeonhole people based on what they could do when you first got to know them or what they now do – which might be only a small part of their ability.

I've even had this situation occur with a couple! A childcare centre committee needed $750,000 for a fit-out. We had to address a question about capacity to deliver the project, and the president, Mark, couldn't think of anyone who had the skills to manage a commercial building project. Mark then said Aleesha, his wife, could probably manage the project because Aleesha 'has managed our house build'. But, I was looking for something stronger to demonstrate the person had the capacity to oversee a commercial project of this nature. When we called Aleesha, we ended up having the opposite problem - Aleesha's previous job had been managing multimillion-dollar commercial building projects, so we had to ask for examples of managing builds under one million! That question was an easy one to answer, after all.

Include your board, staff or volunteer biographies or CVs (which should be all easily accessible in your Grant Ready Kit). Consider the partners and contractors you're involving and their experience and knowledge. Link their experience to the project activities and outcomes.

6. Strategies, policies, standards and frameworks

Aspects such as strategies, policies, standards and frameworks are external to your project, but your project is subject to them.

These include things such as relevant industry and government strategies and policies, legislation and industry standards and industry frameworks.

Once you find a funder, you can also add in here anything important to them, as it applies to your project. Demonstrate how you'll assist potential funders achieve their goals through these areas. For example, the Foundation for Rural & Regional Renewal (FRRR) manages funding programs, funded by other organisations - such as the ANZ Seeds of Renewal program. So, if you were applying for a FRRR funding program, you might go through the guidelines and also research ANZ to identify if there's anything else you could include in this section, or link to in your project, such as their financial training programs.

If you're applying to your local council for funding, you would research their overall plans and strategies. For example, if you're running a business tourism event and applying to your council, you would review its community strategic plan and related plans such as the tourism and economic plans. If one of your project's outcomes is about inclusion, then the council's inclusion plan would also be useful. I'm going to pause here to reinforce that inclusion is not just useful, it's vital. Imagine if you couldn't participate in a great work or school event because your inclusion needs weren't considered. Let's build inclusion into everything we do.

So, you then need to research the external standards that apply to your project and make some notes about how you'll meet them. Conversations with your stakeholders and project leadership team, and a Google search, will help you track down any external standards your project needs to meet.

Now this isn't only about alignment and compliance. This is also about finding the influencing factors to convince decision-makers (and delivering best practice). When I say grants are 80% strategy, this is part of it. If you can show how you align and support the funder's work, it demonstrates value for money and a return on investment.

Doing this alignment will assist you to address questions in your grant application around capacity, compliance and governance. The funding guidelines will provide additional information about other organisations involved in or influencing the funding program.

Best practice frameworks also guide a funder's strategies, policies and standards. These could include aspects such as how your project aligns to the Web Content Accessibility Guidelines for developing a website, or to frameworks for delivering human services, such as the Queensland Out-of-Home Care Outcomes Framework. These kinds of outcomes frameworks help funders justify their investments (and also why I recommend you write a mini Logic Model so you can demonstrate how your outcomes align to their framework).

7. Implementation plan

Your implementation plan should summarise how you'll deliver the project. A list works well here, and you can base list items on timelines - for example, 'Month 1/Week 1' and so on - or achievement milestones - for example, 'Trainer and workshop venue booked'.

Think about the key things you want your stakeholders and funders to know in this implementation list. For example, showing a mid-project evaluation in your list gives funders confidence you're planning on monitoring what's working and adjusting as needed to achieve stated outcomes.

For some organisations, this is where you would reference or show your service model. This is a list of the steps and stages in your delivery process. A diagram is a useful visual for supporting information. For service-based organisations, a service model is a basic requirement to demonstrate how you implement what you do.

Project details

Now, let's look at the second page of the plan, which covers your Logic Model (see following figure).

The second page of The Grant Project Plan template: The Logic Model

Project details

8. Logic Model							
a. Resources	**b. Key activities**	**c. Short-term outputs** (immediate result from activities)		**d. Medium-term outcomes** (within a funding period generally 12 months)		**e. Long-term impact** (over 12 months)	
What resources you need.	What you need to do. Also consider key activities that help the project sustain itself after funding.	What do the activities deliver? What are the outputs?	How will you measure for the funder?	What outcomes are achieved from those outputs?	How will you measure for future projects?	Impacts resulting from outcomes.	How will you meausre for future projects?

8. Logic Model

A Logic Model is my go-to for designing projects. I use this thinking when I'm working through ideas. Often, I'll develop this before the project plan, because much of the information in the model informs the project plan.

Why use the Logic Model?

It was around 2009 when I first started noticing a trend in evidence-based impact assessment approaches coming into Australia. I was mentioning Logic Models in grant writing workshops just prior to the release in 2010 of Western Australia's 'My-Peer Toolkit', which was one of the first impact-evaluation resources developed in Australia. (This toolkit was developed by the Western Australian Centre for Health Promotion Research at Curtin University in Perth – see mypeer.org.au for more information).

I then started seeing draft models on the education minister's advisory board in New South Wales and the South Australia health advisory board. I was telling everyone it would only be a few years and we'd see widespread use of impact models to direct funding.

Developing a Logic Model used to be an advanced grant writing tool, I've been using it since 2009 as a basic must-have for any project delivering intangible benefits – and particularly projects involving state or federal government funding. Governments use this methodology to develop their outcomes frameworks, and philanthropists use it to design and evaluate programs they support. Logic Models justify investments. Many organisations seeking funding have to develop Logic Models for everything they do – it's their status quo. They can't access funding without it.

Understanding Logic Model basics

The key headings in the template are as follows:

a. resources
b. key activities
c. short-term outputs - the immediate results from activities
d. medium-term outcomes - achieved within a funding period (generally 12 months)
e. long-term impact - a result of the outcomes and achieved beyond the funding period.

The following figure shows how these sections of the model work together.

The basic elements in a Logic Model

Resources	***What resources do you need?*** *E.g., people, systems, assets, equipment.*
Activities	***What will you do?*** *List key activities that will be delivered by you, your organisation and others.*
Outputs	***What do those activities deliver?*** *List results from each activity. Include results for different target groups.*
Outcomes	***What are the benefits from these results?*** *What changes do we expect to see in the funding period?*
Impacts	***What is the ultimate goal?*** *What is the big difference this project contributes to in the long-term?*

A simple example of a Logic Model is as follows:

- Your *resource* is a person to answer the community health advice phone line.

- The *key activities* are to answer phone calls, web enquiries and emails to provide information on available options, including how and where people access health services.
- The *short-term output* of this is the number of (actual or projected) calls, emails and web enquiries answered.
- The *medium-term outcome* is you've supported (actual or projected number of) individuals, families and organisations access information about local health services and programs. These people have increased their confidence in seeking further health information. This has resulted in them being able to access the right services faster than they otherwise would have done. This has reduced the callers' stress, and the time and funds they would have otherwise spent seeking this information.
- The *long-term impact* is the people you have supported have improved health and wellbeing by (actual or projected) percentage faster than they may have done otherwise. The reality is you won't measure long-term impact during the funding period, but highlighting this impact shows the funder what can be achieved. This long-term impact should link to what you're measuring in your strategic plan or Theory of Change (refer to step 1a). So it demonstrates that alignment to your team and your funder.

Getting the elements to work together

Let's start with a simplified example of a program we're currently delivering at iClick2Learn, shown in the following table.

Simple Logic Model for an example program

Resources	Key activities	Short-term outputs (immediate results from activities)		Medium-term outcomes (within a funding period generally 12 months)		Long-term impact (over 12 months)	
Input	Activity	Output	Measured by	Outcome	Measured by	Impact	Measured by
Grant writing training and mentoring program	• 3 in-person training workshops • 3 online workshops • 15 organisations receive mentoring • Attendees able to access monthly online grant Q&As during and beyond funding	• 90 people attend in-person workshops; 213 attend online • 15 organisations mentored • 293 workbooks distributed	Bookings	• 47% increased knowledge, skills and confidence • 74% increased grant readiness • 62% improved application quality • 43% increase in funding received • 85% increase in value of grants applied for • 67% increase in value of grants received	Survey	• Capacity across organisations increased by an average of 75% • More funds secured for businesses, enterprises and community organisations, building inclusive, healthy and adaptive communities	Mentoring case studies

For simplicity, I've grouped resources and activities in the table. This is good as a one-page overview. However, for larger projects, splitting these up into each defined resource is worthwhile. So, in the prior example, the in-person training would be separate from the online workshops. Separating projects out in this way means you can track the results of specific elements – for example, the difference it makes having the right trainer. However you do this, the basic point to remember is that your resources deliver your activities.

You may be tempted to then ask yourself what is the result of this activity – for example, 'If I get a trainer, what is the result?' – and simply use the result as your output or outcome measure. Instead, I like to use the 'So, what?' method. It's more critical – and it's far better for you to critique your project than an assessor.

Using this method, you continue to ask, 'So, what? What difference does that resource make?' If the result or short-term output of the resource is something like a workbook, you continue to say, 'So, what? What difference does that workbook make?' In this example, this output can deliver increased retention of knowledge from the workshop. Now you ask about the outcomes: 'So, What? How does the outcome deliver a long-term impact?' You keep going until you've explored all the benefits of your project.

This process maps the resources and activities you're asking funders to invest in to the outcomes and impacts the resources achieve. This helps the funder understand justification of your budget items – for example, why you need to spend $30 per person on the workbook. The outcomes are also clear – in this example, how the program builds capacity in knowledge, skills and confidence, improves the quality of grant applications and increases number of grants, and value of funding received. And the long-term impacts are included – the projects in this example support community building, through delivering inclusive, healthy and adaptive communities. This also links to the Theory of Change for iClick2Learn.

The Logic Model also makes your timelines clear. The timelines I've provided in the outputs, outcomes and impacts columns in the preceding example are because we're focused on the common 12-month funding period. Some Logic Models define two-year outcomes as medium term. Whatever time period you use, check it's clear to funders what's going to be achieved in the funding period, and what these outcomes lead to after the funding.

As mentioned, this is a more basic walk-through. To access different examples, including a sports mental health project, and video demonstrations, just go to the online kit.

Some Logic Models include the proposed outputs, outcomes and impacts without any projected measures. You should, where possible, strive to include measures. If you've already delivered something similar, you should be able to use those to estimate improvements. When thinking about projected measures, you need to consider how you're going to evaluate these and report on them. This is important because it will affect your budget and timeline.

Note that some Logic Model templates include sections for assumptions and influential factors, which are important. If you were only developing a Logic Model, you would need to include these. However, when using The Grant Project Plan, these aspects are included in the risk and stakeholder analysis sections. Before we explore each element of the Logic Model let's refresh on the importance of setting goals.

Setting goals

Industrial engineer Allen Morgenstern coined the phrase 'Work smarter, not harder'. It's a good one to remember when setting goals. As shown in the following figure, goals should be SMARTER.

SMARTER goals

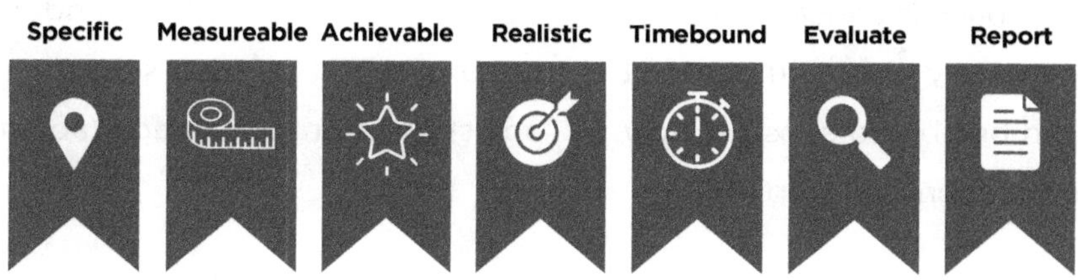

SMARTER is an extension of the **SMART** goal principle. **SMART** is an acronym used to remind us to set goals that are:

- **S**pecific
- **M**easurable
- **A**chievable
- **R**ealistic
- **T**imebound.

The **ER** in the **SMARTER** method adds two elements. It reminds you to set goals that you're able to both:

- **E**valuate, and
- **R**eport on.

The **SMART** principles, developed by George Doran, Arthur Miller and James Cunningham, are useful, but for me lack the robustness you need for programs and grant applications – this is where the 'ER' comes in. Far too often in applications, people talk about what they're doing and measuring, but don't outline the resources that will need to be spent on evaluating and reporting. These aspects are important to funders – and they use resources you need to plan and budget for. When I do community development work for funders, the time spent evaluating and reporting is one of the things they ask me to include – that is, how I'm implementing and providing feedback. I'm working on one project across four communities at the moment, and feeding back insights to the funder about their nominated approach is critical to inform the next stage of their project. Funders genuinely want you to monitor, track and report on what's working, and be able to consider how you adjust what isn't. (For more about evaluation, see step 6b.)

Developing your Logic Model

Now you understand the principles of Logic Models and setting goals, let's develop one. To develop your Logic Model, in this section I review each of the five key headings from left to right, in a logical order. I also outline how I reverse the order to assess your model with a critical lens.

The five key headings of the Logic Model are:

a. resources
b. key activities
c. short-term outputs – the immediate results from activities
d. medium-term outcomes – achieved within a funding period (generally 12 months)
e. long-term impact – a result of the outcomes and achieved beyond the funding period.

Set up a table or grab a piece of paper and draw up a five-column table. Pretend you're part of an organisation delivering a diabetes management program. This organisation could be a diabetes management business, or community organisation. You can also use this example to follow along as you develop a Logic Model for your project.

The proposed diabetes management program includes one group fitness workshop per month for five consecutive months, a diabetes management diary and two follow-up emails to participants in months 6 and 12. The expected impact over 12 months is 20% improvement to fitness and diabetes management. The follow-up emails will ask questions about the participant's blood sugar levels and daily step count. The answers would provide the measurements to demonstrate the success and impact of the project.

a. Resources

Resources are anything needed in the project. In this example, a fitness trainer, project coordinator, scheduled emails and a survey system would be needed.

Also consider aspects such as human resources, financial systems and physical assets.

b. Key activities

For key activities ask, 'If we have those resources, so what? What will they deliver?'

List all activities the resource delivers – for example, the fitness workshop and the follow-up emails. If you decided one of the fitness workshops is a meal-planning workshop, you would write this up as a separate activity because it will deliver different outcomes.

c. Short-term outputs

Outputs are the direct and immediate results achieved as a result of those activities. So, you ask, 'If we do this activity, so what? What does it result in?'

Consider tangible results, such as the diabetes management diary participants are provided with, and intangible results, such as an increased feeling of being supported.

You can use these outputs to monitor and assess your achievements in a mid-term stakeholder or funding report. This gives you early signs if things aren't working, and you can make adjustments. You don't want to get to the end of the project and say, 'Oh well, that didn't work.' You – and the funder – want a successful project. Successful projects increase your future chances of funding.

d. Medium-term outcomes

Outcomes are the results from the outputs. From a grant application perspective, essentially, you're giving yourself and the funder a benchmark to measure the success of your project and the return on investment against.

The question here is (you guessed it), 'If that's the output, so what? What outcome does it produce?' You would also ask, 'What do we and our stakeholders expect the outcome to be?' When you've found a funder, you would come back and revisit this to check alignment to their outcome expectations. Again, document both tangible and intangible outcomes.

Continuing the example, you could include that having a diabetes management diary is expected to result in a 37% improvement in diabetes management and a 65% increase in movement and fitness.

e. Long-term impacts

When you get to this column, I want you to ask the 'So, what?' question and also ask what might prevent the long-term impact from succeeding. Consider what activities you can build into the project to increase the likelihood of achieving the impact.

Okay, so you ask, 'If we achieve those outcomes, so what? What do they lead to?'

The impact from increased movement and fitness might be a 50% increased feeling of physical fitness, sustained or increased weight loss, and a reduction in amount of medication needed and associated costs.

Also ask what risks exist that prevent or reduce your achievement of the planned long-term impact. Asking this enables you to consider the risks and mitigation strategies you might include to remove or reduce the impact.

Congratulations! You've just built your first Logic Model.

Critiquing your Logic Model

When critiquing your Logic Model, keep in mind the following:

> *Funders invest in outcomes not ideas.*

I outline the two key ways to critique your model in the following sections.

Work backwards from impacts or outcomes to resources

When working backwards, I like to start with outcomes because the connection between outcomes and resources is what you need to be clear on in your funding application.

To achieve this, reverse the 'So, what?' question and ask, 'Is this the best way to achieve this?' Asking this, you may realise when the project (and funding period) is finished, you won't have anyone from your organisation continuing to drive the project outcomes with participants. So, this means if you want to give your participants the best chance of achieving the long-term impacts, you need to find a cost-free option. In the example of the diabetes management program, if participants have been active in the program, it doesn't mean they'll continue beyond the program without accountability. So, how do you build this in?

You could set up an online peer group so all participants can connect during the program and beyond. You could offer options or upskill participants so they can take turns 'leading' the group. If you're applying for a commercialisation grant, you would of course project future paid services such as one-to-one or group coaching. If it's a community-focused project, though, it's worth noting that many funders' policies prevent them giving an organisation a competitive advantage, which means including this could make you ineligible for funding.

Ask what other benefits you're missing. Let's review the group fitness workshops being offered as part of the diabetes management program. More is going on here. What happens when a group of people come together over a common interest? They start discussing this and their experiences. In this example, if I've recently been diagnosed with diabetes and in the group are other people with the same diagnosis, I want to learn from them about the experiences and how they manage their diabetes. So, another outcome of this is people are being exposed to different management strategies to support them in different situations.

Apply this critical lens to your organisation and your actual or proposed activities right from the start of your planning. Don't wait until the funder is assessing the submission and noticing the gaps or misalignment between your outcomes and your proposed activities.

Get stakeholder input and target market feedback

Discuss your plan with key stakeholders. They'll think differently to you; they have different lived experiences and the people they're working to support may have different needs or expectations.

For example, say you consulted with your trainer and people who have diabetes about your diabetes management program. They will have given you ideas about other impacts they would expect. You could then decide if these were achievable and potentially add those to your impacts. An example impact you may have missed is a projected 80% increase in confidence to self-manage diabetes and a 100% increased knowledge of referral pathways to access support.

I cover engaging stakeholders in more detail in '10. Stakeholder analysis', later in this step.

'I'm a small group, why should I do a Logic Model?'

Have you ever asked, 'Why do all these other organisations get more money than we do?' Most of it is down to the time they invest. For example, they plan, they produce Logic Models, and they understand how to show the funder they're a good investment.

Even if you're a small organisation, a Logic Model will add value to your project and assist you to submit a stronger application.

Let's use an example of a local soccer club – YourTown Soccer Club in Western Australia – to explore why you would use the Logic Model for any type of organisation.

Say a volunteer asks, 'Why do we need to think about this, when we're a group of volunteer parents and just want our kids to play sport?' So, how does this work for a local sporting club?

Now, as you no doubt know, playing sport is more than the physical act of the game itself. Being involved in your local sports club has so many other benefits, I'd need another few pages to cover them all. For brevity, I'll use how the Department of Local Government, Sport and Cultural Industries (DLGSCI) in Western Australia summarises these benefits. They state, 'It's our belief that sport and recreation can be a vehicle for positive social change', and list a range of impacts (which they call 'benefits to sport') on their website. (See www.dlgsc.wa.gov.au/department/publications/benefits-of-sport-and-recreation for more information.)

These benefits include:

- stronger and more connected communities
- inclusion of minority social groups
- diversion and education of at-risk youth
- healthy child development and contact with nature
- economic outcomes
- education outcomes
- tourism outcomes
- environmental outcomes.

Since YourTown Soccer Club is in Western Australia and is applying to the DLGSCI, they could use this list as a starting point to demonstrate how their program achieves some of these outcomes. DLGSCI needs this to do their work – they need to report on the achievement of outcomes to the national committee that develops and has input into the national sporting strategy (see www.sportaus.gov.au).

YourTown Soccer Club knows larger, more resourced organisations will apply for funding, so they need to be more strategic to be competitive at the decision table. To demonstrate alignment to the outcomes DLGSCI fund, they develop a Logic Model. They incorporate the state-based outcomes expected, and relevant national outcomes mentioned in the national strategy. This makes them more competitive when their application is compared to other organisations that have failed to do this.

This is exactly what I did for two local sporting organisations who partnered to jointly apply for state funding. I not only considered these outcomes, but also aligned and brought in regional health strategies in the application answers, because the grant program was designed to achieve outcomes in mental health and wellbeing, and was funded by the state Ministry of Health. Giving the funders a one-page Logic Model showing outcomes across the three target groups of junior players, adult players and coaches significantly increased the project's competitiveness and contributed to the organisations receiving the full funding ask. Historically, the recipients of funding at that level were state-based organisations.

Avoiding starting from scratch

Why waste time developing something when others have done it for you? You can access and review a lot of relevant outcome frameworks, industry and funding frameworks to identify the benefits of your work. This is also a good check-in if you're wondering what you may have missed in your Logic Model. A good tip is to go to Google Images and use search terms related to your project – for example, 'aged care' – with the words 'logic model' or 'program logic' after them. You'll find documents and visual examples that will guide you as you work through your project or introduce concepts and outcomes.

You may also turn to your AI Assistant and ask it to develop a logic model for a diabetes management program to help you consider other outcomes and impacts. I did and there are some good general points to reflect on if you've never delivered a program like this before. They are points that someone experienced would have identified. It didn't include the specific approach, insights, strategy, statistics, or stories. For example, it didn't raise something as simple as the peer-to-peer network and the shared experience aspect that adds strength to the program design, outcomes and impacts.

These examples are, however, just to guide you and get you started. Make sure you do put the time in to developing a Logic Model that's correct for your project.

Taking advantage of the other benefits of the Logic Model

Completing your Logic Model ahead of time, including working out how you'll define and measure success, and how you'll avoid unintended negative outcomes, will help you significantly with mid-project and final reports to your funders. Project evaluation and receiving timely acquittals from those who have received funding is one of many funders' big pain points.

The other thing I like about the Logic Model is that you can apply a critical lens when you analyse the model backwards - from the difference the project makes through to the resources needed to deliver it. A lot of projects have desired resources or activities, but they don't directly influence the likelihood of achieving the desired outcome. So, assessing this by working backwards will filter the necessary from the desired. Remember - you'll never get enough money to do everything you want, and you'll need to cut less important resources and activities. The Logic Model assists you to decide what to cut.

Timelines, stakeholder analysis and risk management

Let's move onto pages three and four of The Grant Project Plan, where you find the project timeline, stakeholder analysis and risk management. I look at each of these separately in the following sections.

9. Project timeline – milestones and activity timelines

Your project timeline (see the following figure) is your planned sequence of events from the moment you receive the grant money to delivering your acquittal report.

The project timeline section of The Grant Project Plan template

9. Project timeline					
Milestones	**Activity**	**When**	**Who**	**Resources needed**	**Estimated cost**

No rules exist about how your timeline should be presented in The Grant Project Plan. For your plan, I do recommend you use weeks, months or quarters rather than dates that will change. Later in your grant application, you'll have a template to follow and you can give indicative dates.

For a summary project plan, the first page of this document, estimates of the work being done will suffice; however, for this part of The Grant Project Plan you should be able to be more specific in the resources needed column. You need to include all costs including labour – for example, 5 hours weeding + 2 hours admin @ $50 per hour = $350. This will assists you in avoiding common mistakes, where organisations don't adequately include the time or resource costs in the project budget. It may seem like doubling up, but doing this step will make sure you don't miss documenting the resources and costs.

Go back to your Logic Model. Check the resources and key activities column. Make sure you include these factors in the resources needed or estimated cost.

If your project requires approvals, such as an approved Development Application (DA), you will need to factor in achieving this prior to applying for funding. For funders that fund building works, 99% require an approved DA.

If you're able to provide supporting evidence as an attachment in your application, you could provide a timeline showing what you've done to get the project grant ready. Funders won't fund things you need to do to get your project grant ready, such as research or approvals. This is called 'retrospective' funding. An example would be if you've already started promoting your proposed workshops, the funder may not fund them.

However, mentioning this preparation in the application briefly in a relevant question, and then showing the detail in an attachment can give strength to your application. It demonstrates your ongoing commitment to the funder.

Keep in mind you wouldn't detail this in your application timeline or budget, because it then appears like you've started the project and they won't fund the work.

10. Stakeholder analysis

This area of The Grant Project Plan documents who your stakeholders are and evidences your relationship over the project, including their expectations of outcomes and any concerns (see the following figure).

The stakeholder analysis section of The Grant Project Plan template

10. Stakeholder analysis					
Who	**Their interest/ what they need from us**	**What we need from them/how they help**	**Outcomes they want/ expect**	**Concerns to resolve/ negotiate**	**Communication/ advocacy plan**

In my workshops, I often talk about identifying your influencers so you can persuade them – and that's what this section of The Grant Project Plan is all about. My colleague Megan uses a similar approach for her projects and called this section an 'influencer map' when she saw it, and that's a great way to look at it. The more people who know about your project, the more people they share it with. You may be cautious about sharing ideas because you fear that another group will 'steal it'. Put it this way – people are going to talk anyway. Making your idea public actually brands it as yours, and it's a lot easier to claim ideas when they're public. Plus, you never know who will hear about your project and think, *Great, that's something I want to support.*

Use The Grant NDOIS Pitch from step 1b or the need statement formula earlier in this step to develop a few pitch frameworks and start sharing what you're doing.

I've included a column in the template to make notes on any communication you need to undertake with your stakeholders, including any advocacy plans you might want to make. For example, say the relevant minister knows who you are, but you need to demonstrate how critical the project is. An advocacy plan might then include inviting the minister to your community to meet your clients. You could ask your client to write letters to the minister, expressing their need and urgency for support. You can also share client stories through media channels and get your fans to raise awareness of the need and urgency for funding.

While you want to identify influencers who can progress your goal to get this project funded, you also want to identify who is impacted by the project. It's important to identify all stakeholders to understand how deep their involvement is in your project and what you need from them or need to know from them.

Identifying stakeholders

For most grants, you must show you've consulted with the right people – that is, the stakeholders. Broadly speaking, a stakeholder is anyone who will have influence on or is impacted by your project. To work out who these stakeholders are you need to do a stakeholder analysis and decide who will be involved and the depth of their involvement.

Some organisations will have undertaken a stakeholder analysis as part of their strategic planning or marketing and communication plan. If you already have one, you can use this list as a starting point. This analysis needs to be project-specific, though, so while some of the stakeholders on your existing list might be included, you'll also likely need to consider other organisations and stakeholders for your project.

Brainstorm which people or organisations to include on your list. Then take this list and decide where each fits on the following impact and influence stakeholder matrix. You can draw the matrix on a whiteboard or download the template in the online kit.

Impact and influence stakeholder matrix

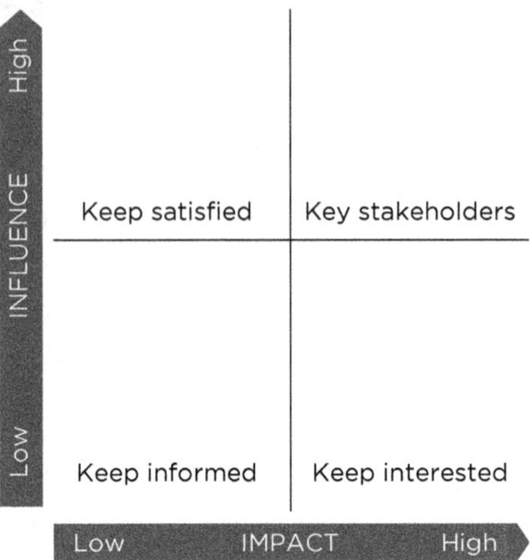

Continuing the diabetes management program from earlier, key stakeholders for this project are people who have been diagnosed with diabetes and need support managing it. The following figure shows where they would be placed in the stakeholder matrix.

Stakeholder matrix for diabetes management program

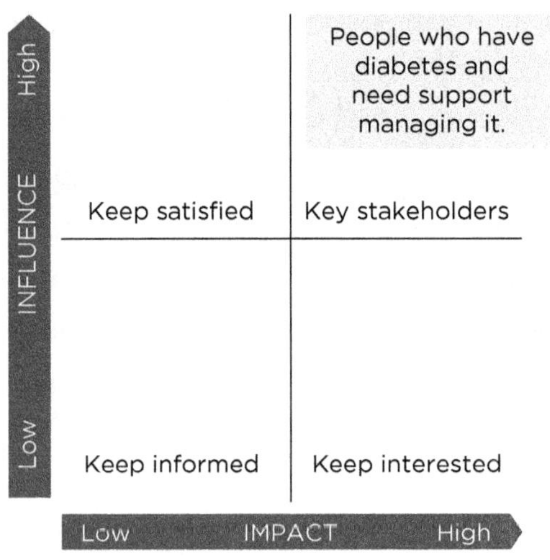

When you think of who your stakeholders might be, also consider stakeholders beyond the immediate direct stakeholders - that is, those who can be impacted if the project is set up. For example, say your project has the potential to change the space, or change the usage of an area, and, in particular, change an area with existing use, such as a community green space. You need to think about consulting with those current and future site users, both people and groups, as key stakeholders.

I know of a project that proposed to build sporting facilities on community land that was open green space surrounded by a walking and cycling track. The project succeeded in securing funding to the tune of $1 million; however, based on the community commentary and evidence that emerged afterwards, the adequate community consultation hadn't been undertaken.

Community members protested this proposed usage change. Some didn't want the facilities built there because of the inappropriateness of the location due to flood risk. Others argued having a clubhouse and stadium on the site would reduce their personal enjoyment of the quiet space. Some highlighted environmental, flora and fauna reasons for their objections. The combined community outcry stalled and eventually stopped the project. The project was also then the subject of parliamentary questions, and a freedom of information application. Based on the funding period and acquittal, as of time of writing, the project group have three months to produce a building on land they don't have.

Now, here's the real kicker. Someone who was connected with the project's sporting organisation posted a request for support of the project in a community Facebook group and asked for feedback. Of total responses to this request, 95% were negative, citing the reasons already outlined. This simple request for feedback should have been made much earlier in the planning stage, or seeing this reaction they should have considered consequences of moving forward. The responses should have been treated as a risk, demonstrating to the organisation they needed to do more work getting community support for the project, before they submitted the grant.

For the club, this has had a huge impact on their dreams and future goals. It's a strong club and the project is needed to offer facilities to a growing community. Achieving the project will be good for the community. At this stage, however, we're all expecting them to have to give the funding back. From the funder's perspective, they've had to answer questions in parliament about the decision. So, while I'm sure they believe it's a great project as well, the reality is for the same organisation to be successful the next time they apply, the funder will be very focused on making sure their decision can't be challenged like it was this time. You don't want this to happen to your project.

This is an example of stakeholders who may not have been considered key stakeholders, but who became the driving force to halting a project – in some part, at least, because they weren't consulted. No-one can say if the project would have continued even with consultation; however, the organisation would have saved themselves and the community a lot of stress, money and time by doing the work earlier to identify stakeholders and consult with them. Based on this, it wouldn't surprise me if, in the next round of this grant program, we see a question related to evidence of community consultation about any changed land use.

Engaging with stakeholders

After identifying all potential stakeholders, the next step is determining the depth of engagement with these stakeholders. Stakeholders who are identified as high impact and high influence should be engaged with deeply and asked to give feedback on the design of the project. This engagement could be showing them what the project does and how it will be implemented (perhaps using your Logic Model) and asking what their interest is. In the diabetes management program example from earlier, the local community health officer may want to come and speak to those interested in the program. The organisers could involve them as co-designers of the program, so they know what approaches and methods work for them.

Ideally, the people involved in the delivery and target participants (or those who represent them as a sample size) should be involved in the design. In this example, this would mean asking the trainer how to design the workshop and asking participants what else they feel is needed in the project. This is a process called 'co-design'. For most projects, increased levels of ownership and engagement are ideal. Ask yourself, can your project be designed by the target group with your support? Just because you have an idea of what should happen, that doesn't mean it's what the target group want or really need.

The following figure shows how you can use the impact and influence stakeholder matrix to determine level of stakeholder involvement.

INFLUENCE	Low IMPACT	High IMPACT
High	***Feedback/input*** Keep satisfied	***Co-design/ engagement*** Key stakeholders
Low	***Marketing*** Keep informed	***Communication/ advocacy*** Keep interested

Understanding why key stakeholders should be engaged

Some funded projects did nothing but increase tensions and problems. Services and housing have been funded that didn't work for the relevant communities. Why? Because the people who they were being built for weren't involved in the design. They weren't asked if they wanted the project or weren't included in the project design. They were instead given the solution by well-meaning people who had no lived experience in the reality of their lives and what they really needed.

One of the biggest issues within the world of community development is volunteers and staff being forced into a scarcity mindset – the mindset that says 'There isn't enough to do what we want'; the mindset that knows we must beg, borrow or secure partial grant funds to achieve the impact we want. We all want to live in a world where our communities are inclusive, healthy and adaptive. To achieve this, we need sustainable community organisations.

The funding world today expects more of you, and demands more of you, and I understand why this is. No-one wants to get involved in a project that fails. No-one wants to put their efforts into a project where the people it's designed to support aren't involved.

Authenticity in stakeholder involvement is crucial

It doesn't matter who you're engaging, authenticity gives your project the resounding ring of truth. So, while I might discuss a certain approach to stakeholder involvement (and provide a template in the online guide), ask yourself if this is the best approach to engage the people you want to involve.

A lot of communities are fatigued by a constant flow of 'heroes' trying to save them, and feel 'over-consulted' with not much action or money on the ground. They have no time for new people to town, or those who have flown in just to talk to them, or ask them to talk. So, how do you engage a community like this? You build relationships and involve them in the development of your approach. You deliver by offering support and showing them you're authentic.

One project I worked on for a funder was across five communities of varying culture and connectedness to each other, and we needed a model that could be adopted by all. We needed to show we were authentic, so we offered a contribution to the relationship upfront. We also made sure our communication was authentic.

I designed a large visual roadmap, coloured to represent a river. This reflected the traditional owners' special connection to the river in the communities we engaged with. They sat outside on Country and completed a five-year plan for their community, adding words and drawings to the visual. This process further demonstrated we were authentic and genuine in our desire to improve community. The result was high-quality engagement, and the community consultation was supported by all groups – from children and youth through to Elders in the community. In other communities, we had youth involved in the development process. This same process was used with other community members who saw it as a roadmap or a journey from where they were currently to where they wanted to be.

You're likely going to be brainstorming and talking with all different types of people, with different lived experience, literacy levels, physical and mental abilities, cultures and languages. So, you need to think about the best method to use to engage them and develop customised or multi-purpose engagement tools.

Building project ownership with key stakeholders

Key stakeholders should be engaged to the degree they feel some ownership in the project. An unintended negative consequence of pushing through a grant submission when, as the writer, you don't get support or the level of information you need, is it feels you are the only one 100% committed to the application.

Another consequence is you don't feel the project is ready. I was working with a regional organisation and a local council to develop an application to improve a World Heritage-listed site. This was one of those, 'Yes, I'll assist you because I like you and the project outcomes.' But I had nothing. It was a new grant project, and my client couldn't give me a lot of information beyond what they thought they would do. The regional organisation had the idea and a partnership with the council that was managing the site in trust. The relevant council staff member, Belinda, who is also my friend, was about to go on leave but was able to provide some information. And, despite being on leave, Belinda then followed up and answered some questions for me. However, while being aware of the site in question, Belinda hadn't been involved in the project discussions, so it made it difficult for her to provide the details I needed about the site.

So here I was, on the final few days of submission and still no substantial evidence from the client. Fortunately, I have good working knowledge of labour programs, culture and heritage requirements and, with a bit of research to fill some gaps, I was able to write a sound submission and Win the Grant. However, the project wasn't 'owned' by the client or the council. My friend later confided it was a messy project and she had to be more involved as a partner than originally expected. Do I believe the project was successful? Yes, it did deliver benefits to the site. However, it didn't necessarily strengthen relationships between my client and the council, so the outcomes weren't as successful as they could have been.

Ownership is a measure I now use to determine if a project is worth proceeding with, or not.

In summary, if you can't get buy-in and ownership for a project early in the process, it's likely not going to happen later down the track. So, you need to work out if that's an acceptable consequence, or if you can improve or change something before proceeding.

Useful questions when asking for feedback

Here are five questions you can ask to guide your stakeholders to provide useful feedback:

1. **What do you like about the project?** Try to understand the parts of the project they believe are valuable to them, their clients or their community.
2. **What can we improve about the project?** Even good projects have elements to improve. It could be how the project is delivered or who's involved. They may have ideas you can't include but you still should listen to understand their motivations, interests and objections.
3. **Why do you support this project?** This helps you understand why the project is valuable for them. For example, they're not supporting the project because you're a good organisation, but because they know there's a need and they have some knowledge and experience of it.
4. **What difference will this project make to you and your community?** You'll understand the outcomes and impacts the project will deliver to them. Be mindful of your need statement (refer to earlier in this step). If stakeholder responses to this question don't include all the items in the need statement, this will cause doubt in the funder's mind.
5. **What do you want to achieve from this project?** This final question might feel like a repeat of the last one. However, its focus is to develop key success measures. It's important to understand exactly what they need from the project. Be clear on determining

if it's something they need, or something they want. Find out what their 'non-negotiables' are. In other words, 'If you can't deliver *x*, then we're not involved.' I would classify these as project success measures. Discuss scenarios with them to gauge how they might react as the project moves.

Stakeholder input will give you evidence to show real demand exists for your project. Often, in discussion, you'll find other needs the project could address or other sources of demand.

For example, say you're an obstetrician who is planning a new community health building. You'd like to section off part of your space to provide a permanent area for people to hire for parents' and carers' groups. You talk to the local council community officer, and they tell you the local Arabic Women's Group (AWG) are searching for a space to run a new mothers' health class. You contact the AWG and discuss what outcomes they want, and realise with a minor change your project can meet their needs. You can add their outcomes to yours, creating one space used by two groups. To a funder, this will show value for money. It may also expand the range of grants you'll be eligible for.

Challenge your project idea to improve it. If any groups of people don't love it, ask them why. Ask them what they'd change. If you want to make a difference, encourage input from others to design the best project you can deliver - one you'll all be proud of. Too many projects have failed or not even been started because people got caught up in their own ideas and didn't seek fair criticism.

11. Key risks

Some projects may require a detailed, comprehensive risk management plan. For the project plan we focus on key risks (see the following figure), which is on page four of the template.

The risk management section of The Grant Project Plan template

11. Key risks					
What are the risks?	**What could happen?**	**What are we doing to mitigate the risk?**	**What resources do we need**	**What will it happen**	**Who will do it**
Use STEEPLE to consider risks. Also consider any assumptions you're making and any potential unintended consequences.					

Now you've gone through each of the previous elements in the template, you should have a solid foundation for the types of risks you need to consider for your project. And if you already have a risk management plan for your organisation, you can refer to that to avoid doubling up. While you don't have to include everything, a trend I've noticed is funders are starting to ask for a minimum number of risks in grant applications – for example, they're asking for a minimum of five risks.

I'm not going to go into the detail of risk management templates here. You can find best practice templates on the websites of state regulators that deal with workplace health and safety. They're a good resource to think through the types of hazards and risks that may occur, and provide a wealth of information about how to undertake risk management and mitigation. I also provide information on this area in the online learning library at iClick2Learn.com.au.

For grant project planning purposes, risks can be divided into three categories: strategic, operational and project.

The way to think about risks is shown in the following figure – with a hierarchy of risks (dark grey boxes in figure) and categories (light grey boxes).

Hierarchies and categories of risk

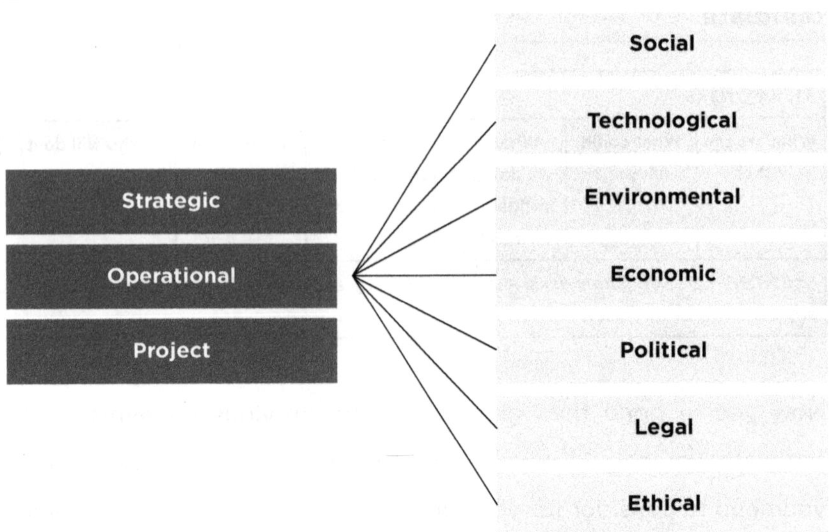

As shown in the figure, the hierarchy of risks you should consider including are strategic, operational and project risks. Applicants generally focus on project risks but miss the others.

Examples of strategic, operational and project risks include:

- Strategic risks are those where the risk is so great your organisational viability is at risk. Examples include insolvency, reputational risk, loss of key major funder, loss of accreditation and governance risks. These are also risks that impact or change the direction of your organisation or your project - for example, changes to the environment such as through flooding, bushfires, internet access problems and weather. Strategic risk can also come from changes to legislation, a major partner withdrawing, or even a global pandemic!
- Operational risks are factors that cause disruption or limit the achievement of your goals, outcomes and impacts. This is from an organisational perspective, and includes aspects such as staffing

or contractor issues, equipment breaking down, and health and safety risks. Other risks can include a landlord not renewing your office lease, minor sponsorship loss or not meeting service standards.

- Project risks are where your project is at risk of completion or achieving its goals. Such risks can include loss of key project team members, loss of project partner or other resources. It could also include loss of a project funder, partner or trainer, or lack of participant engagement.

Using STEEPLE to think through risks

As mentioned, state health and safety regulator websites provide a lot of useful risk management tools. In addition to the best practice risk management templates they share, and example risks and hazards, I refer to the organisation's risk management plan. I then use the STEEPLE method to think through risks. You may have heard of the PEST analysis tool, which looks at political, environmental, social and technical factors when in the planning stage for a project. **STEEPLE extends this analysis, and stands for:**

- **S**ocial: What social trends might impact on your project? For example, I was recently talking with a cultural group, and they mentioned that their members won't use Facebook because of a range of privacy and scamming concerns. There may also be stakeholder risks here.
- **T**echnological: Consider here cybersecurity, such as privacy information. What about risks of people not being able to use the bookkeeping software system the grant is paying for?
- **E**nvironmental: Environmental can mean environmental risks such as lack of waste facilities at an event, but also other things such as the system environment, including networks and partnerships or referral pathways.

- **E**conomic: This category generally relates to financial risks. Strategic financial risk might be insolvency; project risk might be increased supplier costs.
- **P**olitical: This may or may not apply depending on your organisation, industry and project. Political doesn't necessarily mean political parties in power. It could also mean the politics within your community – for example, between traditional custodian language groups and families, political actions or policies that can divide communities.
- **L**egal: This is more straightforward and incorporates things such as legislative, regulatory and accreditation compliance.
- **E**thical: Aspects such as alignment to values, standards, codes of conduct and industry codes may apply here.

Remember risks aren't only the hazards you can identify; you need to also forecast and project *possible* risks. Consider potential unintended consequences. Going back to the diabetes management program example from earlier, let's say you're intending to provide an online group for the project participants. An unintended consequence might be created because people who don't want to, or who don't have the technology or budget for data access can be disadvantaged.

Anticipating what can go wrong is an under-appreciated skill. As human beings, we tend to favour problem-solvers over problem-finders. Most people in the community development sector are full of hope and motivation for a positive future, so some of us aren't necessarily good at identifying the potential negatives in projects.

Someone who can identify gaps or point out things that are wrong is ideal at this point. These people are gold when you're developing a risk management plan. If someone like this is part of your organisation, share the project and what you want to achieve with them and ask them what could go wrong. Check each step you've outlined in your Logic Model.

Also, involve stakeholders in your risk brainstorming process, and check if suppliers and contractors have a risk management plan you can use to identify key risk. You can also turn to your AI Assistant for some ideas.

Once you've identified risks and worked through what could happen and what your response would be, you can start to work out the resources you'll need for risk management. This will assist in the next step - your project budget.

Financials

Last, but definitely not least, we're talking financials. While you can start the template in any order you like, it's important to always do a final check on the budget.

12. Detailed budget

A project budget (see the following figure) is your plan of what you're doing and how much it's going to cost. It shows the funder how you plan to spend the money they give you and demonstrates the support of others.

The budget section of The Grant Project Plan template

12. Detailed budget		
Milestone, activity or item description	**What will it cost** *Note if actual or estimate*	**Income/funding options**

Note that if you only want to include a summary, the budget points you've stated on the first page of the template might be enough. This table is intended to support you to develop a simple budget.

Some projects, though, benefit from more detail and, to be honest, a spreadsheet with formulas would be better to develop your budget. You'll find a bonus spreadsheet template in the online kit.

If your organisation ran a similar project in the past, search for a copy of the original budget and a breakdown of the actual final costs. This will help you anticipate any unexpected expenses. Keep in mind that prices change over time, so you'll need to get updated information and double-check any new requirements to your project that were missing in the previous project. Your AI Assistant can also share ideas.

Developing a simple project budget gives you a template to tweak to fit different grant guidelines. Not all grants allow the same expenses, and different grants will have different expectations about division of costs.

Funders want to fund projects designed to meet the specified needs by delivering outcomes and impacts. These outcomes and impacts come from the people you're trying to support. So, you're designing something that, in essence, meets their needs. Funding limits will constrain what you can ask the funder to contribute. This either means you need to get others to fill the gap, or you reduce your costs. For example, say you wanted to fully fund 30 people in a workshop. Due to the funding constraints, though, you either can only fund 20 participants or need to seek more funds to meet your goal of 30.

Your budget should include income, expenses and in-kind donations – regardless of who pays for it, and even if it's donated, it's still a cost to factor in your budget.

Description

List your expenses by milestone, activity or individual item. Ideally, you should use descriptive language here so anyone else who's reading the budget knows what the cost item is.

Some things will be easier than others to explain. For example, if your project is delivering workshops in regional communities, 'travel' is likely one of your budgeted items. 'Travel to workshops' is a perfectly simple and acceptable justification. What gives that statement more strength though would be to state 'Travel to workshops × kms return @ × $ per km' = the amount needed to pay for this'.

Some entries can be a bit more ambiguous, and so need more detail. As an example of why this is important, I was asked to review a failed application. I noticed a curious entry in the budget: $250 for a stapler. I went back over the project and couldn't understand how $250 for a stapler was justified. I wondered if it was a typing mistake – was it meant to be $2.50? When I asked the applicant, I was told the cost was for an industrial stapler for heavy-duty work – which, given their project, would have been a justifiable cost price to pay. What was obvious to them, however, was not initially obvious to me and neither would it have been obvious to the funder. It wasn't mentioned in the application; it was only priced in the budget. One mistake like this is sometimes all it takes for a no decision. I've been in those decision rooms and have had to make the call on similar mistakes. We can't assume it's a mistake. We have to accept what you've said and judge that.

So, make sure to add relevant clarifying comments and descriptions to all costs.

Cost

This is the dollar amount cost of the item, regardless of who pays for it. You need to assign a cost to every item. Even donated time and objects need to be listed as a cost. Perhaps putting a dollar amount on people's generosity feels wrong to you. If so, you're not alone – it's a common reaction. But I want you to try a new perspective. Try thinking of this process as recognising and acknowledging the generosity of your supporters in a concrete way. It demonstrates genuine demand and stakeholder support for your project.

You need a researched cost forecast. It's time to ring around for price lists and quotes! If you're using a budget from a previous project, you'll need to check the price is up to date and includes consumer price index (CPI) increases.

CPI is measure of inflation and is factored into companies' new sales prices, generally in July or January. This can be a big surprise and change your budget if you don't know about it. If you're applying for a grant in one year but your project is planned for the following year, your costs could be higher.

For now, estimates from suppliers who are giving you an idea of costs are generally acceptable. Getting specific quotes from suppliers can be difficult and many suppliers won't give written quotes for a grant project. I understand – if they've quoted 12 months before you wrote the grant application and it took another six months before you were ready for them to do the job, how can they be held to the same price?

When you put in your grant application, however, you may require written quotes and you'll have to follow the instructions in the guidelines and application. For rural and remote locations, these quotes may be exceptionally hard to obtain. If this is the case for you, contact the funder, explain the difficulties of distance and ask if an alternative is possible.

When you're ready to get a formal quote from a supplier, ask them to forecast the price to the time you'll be ready to do the work. For example, if you're applying in October and won't be ready for work until March, ask them to forecast the cost factoring in annual CPI and other industry increases. Also, make sure they provide specific information in their quote that matches the project activity and the funder's requirements. For example, if the quote seems to include items the funder won't pay for, this may eliminate you during the assessment process.

One cost you'll have is unpaid labour - be this your labour as the business owner, or that of volunteers. Costing this does depend on a few factors, primarily what the funder will accept. So, for now, note the hours in your budget. (I discuss how to cost it in step 4c.)

A common mistake here is applicants take out costs for things someone else pays for or provides. For example, if your local council offers to do all the printing for your project's mail-out, you'll pay $0. However, a cost to the council still exists. Items like this are called 'in-kind' payments in the grant writing world. The simplest way to estimate the cost is to check the market rate. In the scenario just mentioned, if the council is printing 500 copies of your newsletter, you need to find out how much it would it cost for the same 500 copies if you went to the print shop. Most printing shops have prices online you can use to estimate the cost. If your project involves catering and a local café wants to support your project with a 50% discount, the 50% is being donated and counts as an in-kind contribution.

If a graphic design business offers to design your flyers for free, you might be inclined to remove graphic design costs from your budget. Please don't. You miss out on sharing the true value your supporters are offering and this shows stakeholders how much support you do have. Be aware of the risks. If you receive funding as per the budget, for example, but the graphic designer has now moved away or doesn't offer these services anymore, you'll be short of resources! How can you afford the graphic designer now? So consider if you should put the total amount for the graphic designer in the expense column and ask the funder to pay for it (if they will), or decide how you might fund this if not.

Adding a contingency

A question I'm often asked about costs is, 'How much can I add as a contingency or miscellaneous cost?' My answer is to ask the funder. Some funders may allow it for justifiable reasons, such as transport costs to a remote community. Otherwise, you'll likely find the answer is $0. You can't include costs without justification.

Instead, you need to minimise unbudgeted costs. Invest in planning and getting detailed quotes, including CPI or annual price rises. Review previous projects and their unexpected costs. Did they have to pay surcharges for remote delivery? Did they forget GST?

Be descriptive in your budget. If you're budgeting above market rate, explain why. For example, if you're ordering $1,000 in building supplies and delivering these to a regional location will cost an extra $400, you can't simply add $1,400 as the cost. The funder will need to know why you're paying $400 over market rate. The assessor probably knows regional projects cost more for delivery, but you can't rely on assessors joining the dots for you. Simply adding 'includes $400 regional delivery surcharge' to the description and the quote could save your application.

Summary

In this step, you learnt how to develop your idea into a grant ready project plan. This will give you a lot of information to start writing your grant application. You now know a lot about your project and this will assist you find funding in the next stage of The Grant Writing System.

What can you do now?

Here are some actions from step 1c:

- ☐ If you don't feel you understand your project need, take your team through the 5 Whys process.
- ☐ Develop your need statement and make sure you have evidence to support the need and demand. Add this evidence to The Grant Ready Kit.
- ☐ Complete a mini Logic Model (at minimum) or complete The Grant Project Plan in full.
- ☐ Start sharing your one-page project overview with influencers and stakeholders you've identified who can support you.
- ☐ Ask your stakeholders for feedback to improve your project design and Logic Model.
- ☐ Research strategies, plans or frameworks relevant to the area the project delivers outcomes in. You might find your project aligns to one and you can start talking to people in the department or the influencer to share how you can assist them achieving their goal.
- ☐ Create a page on your website called 'Projects'. Do a case study on all the projects you've completed and what's coming up. (Take this information from your plans.) Describe the background, show images and even get people to record testimonials saying why they need (or needed) this project. For past projects ask them to share the positive outcomes they experienced. You can post those videos on social media. Showcase existing partnerships and projects on your website.

Summary of Stage 1: Plan

The steps in this stage give you a lot to take in – they make up almost a third of the book! This highlights the importance of planning, and how important all the funders believe it is.

You should now have a project plan for your grant application. Of course, the reality is adjustments to this plan will be needed. However, going through this step-by-step process means your efforts from here on will save you time and stress. You'll also be in a strong position when you're persuading the funder. They'll be able to clearly identify this project has been designed to meet a need. They will feel confident you've thought the project through and you're not simply trying to do a 'money grab'. The funding request is genuine, and it already has a good chance of succeeding.

Let's take a moment here to celebrate!! Congratulations. You've completed the main step for your project to succeed.

What can you do now?

Added together, the steps in this stage assisted you to get grant ready. There really aren't any shortcuts in this process – although I will say, it's better to start small if it feels overwhelming.

To start putting the tools and tips from this part into practice, you can:

- [ ] Start adding to The Grant Ready Kit (refer to step 1a) whenever you renew your insurances or someone updates information listed in The Grant Ready Checklist (also step 1a). Just keep adding to and updating your kit and, in no time, you'll have your organisation grant ready!

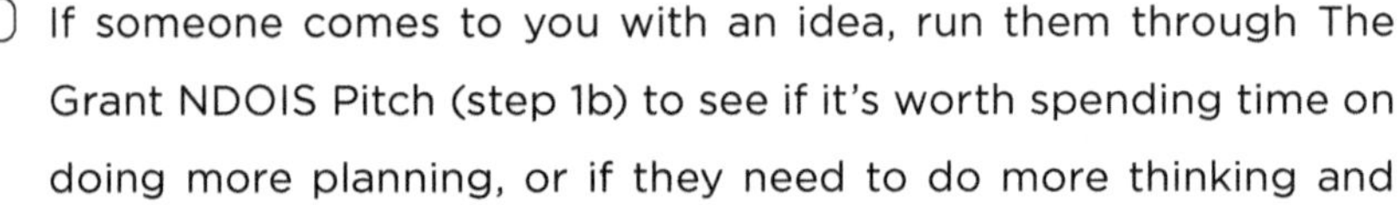

- [ ] If someone comes to you with an idea, run them through The Grant NDOIS Pitch (step 1b) to see if it's worth spending time on doing more planning, or if they need to do more thinking and research. If they have a few ideas then take them through The Grant RICE Score to identify the strongest idea.

- [ ] If an idea is worth spending time on, either get out The Grant Project Plan (outlined in step 1c) and start completing it, or at minimum run through the first page overview or Logic Model (also step 1c) to better understand the project strengths and weaknesses.

You've just learnt how to:

- ✓ support your organisation to get grant ready
- ✓ develop an idea to get it grant ready
- ✓ design the project with stakeholders
- ✓ develop a project plan.

Now it's time to have some fun and find the right grant with the right funder. Woohoo! Who doesn't like finding money?

Stage 2: Find

The Grant Writing System™

© Natalie Bramble

1. Plan **2. Find** 3. Align 4. Write 5. Submit 6. Manage 7. Report

Finding the right grant with the right funder

We're now starting the second stage in The Grant Writing System - Find, as shown in the following figure.

Find: Stage 2 in The Grant Writing System

Find grants and choose the right one.

2. Find

Find grants and choose the right one.

Steps in this stage

a. Search, pitch and attract funds.

b. Decide if it's the right grant to apply for.

Tools to guide you

vi. The Grant Calendar™

vii. The Grant Go/No-Go Decision Checklist™

If you've worked your way through the first stage in The Grant Writing System, your organisation, idea and project plan is grant ready. Now it's time to find grants to apply for. The steps in this stage explore the four main types of grants: government, philanthropic, corporate and individual. I cover different approaches to find grants, including how to search and pitch for grants and other ways to attract funds.

And I cover how to develop The Grant Calendar so you can follow funders that fund your type of organisations and projects to identify upcoming grants.

I also guide you through how to understand guidelines and assessment criteria. You'll learn how to decide if you should apply for a particular grant or keep searching for a better fit for your organisation and project, using The Grant Go/No-Go Decision Checklist.

Completing this step is important - you don't want your grant assessors to write the following feedback on your application:

> While it seems to be a worthwhile project, the applicant is not eligible. The applicant has requested for the grant program to fund expenses we don't fund, as we've clearly stated in the guidelines.
>
> Grant Assessor's Feedback

Step 2a

Search, pitch and attract funds

Before you get to pitching for and attracting funds, you need to find the right grant to apply for. And tracking down the right grant from the right funder starts with searching in the right direction - using either a proactive or responsive approach. I cover these aspects in this step. However, before we get to that, let's take a moment to really understand what funders want from you.

Understanding what funders want

There are four key types of funders. Each funder has a different reason for awarding grants. Understanding their motivation can assist you to narrow your search for a funder who fits your project.

The four types of funders are:

1. government
2. corporate
3. philanthropic
4. individuals.

I separate them into these four groups because who they are drives the kind of funding they provide, and their risk appetite for adaptability and change. You need to understand why funders are motivated to give money. Fundamentally, once you decide they might be worth pursuing, you should research the funder enough to understand the motivation behind their funding.

For example, I've identified that individuals are generally more driven by personal motivation to support a project or cause, than by a strategic goal they have. However, every rule always has an exception. While the grant guidelines will provide information on motivations, it's useful understanding this holistically as well.

The following figure shows where the four funding groups generally sit in terms of their motivations and appetite for risk and change.

Motivations and risk appetites of four main funding groups

Let's review the four funding groups in a bit more detail.

Government

This includes Commonwealth/federal, state and local government funding. All levels of government have policies and plans, some of which have to align with international targets.

The driver for government funding is for the government body to achieve its goals. They're looking for applicants and projects to deliver outcomes that align and help them with their work. They can be demand-driven goals set by environmental conditions (refer to the introduction), or strategic goals they set in their policies and strategic plans.

These goals can be influenced by the advocacy industry associations offer. One example would be the Country Women's Association of Australia's advocacy for funding to increase telecommunications to rural, regional and remote communities. They show government bodies (at federal, state and local level) how they have a groundswell of support, which raises the importance of support and funding. Other approaches can help these bodies meet goals they've agreed to, such as the United Nations Sustainable Development Goals (UN SDGs), which even local councils align to.

Government funders will have different departments that focus on different aspects of society. For example, most local councils have a sport and recreation department, or a sport and recreation officer in smaller councils. They have processes to follow and can't 'give away' funding.

Other plans originate from the overall strategic plan, such as local council's community and strategic plans and youth plans and cultural plans. In these plans, the council might also list or acknowledge how they support state goals, industry goals or international goals such as the UN SDGs.

Philanthropists

This includes organisations, foundations and individual philanthropic-minded donors. This can also include PAFs - private ancillary funds or PuAFs - public ancillary funds - with the basic difference between the two being where they receive funding from, as identified in their name (private or public).

Philanthropic donors and organisations are interested in causes, and value and impact alignment are important to them. Their interests may change or be consistent. For example, the Vincent Fairfax

Family Foundation changes its funding strategy as they decide, and from time to time, however the NSW government Elsa Dixon Aboriginal Employment grant supports organisations with targeted employment, and while they've changed eligibility over the years, as at the time of writing it's never changed that employment focus.

Philanthropic organisations' purpose is funding positive change in social, environmental, cultural and community contexts. Different organisations will have their own priorities - some fund sector-specific projects; others prioritise certain regions.

One of the valuable things about philanthropists is they can choose a flexible approach to funding. They're in a better position to provide responsive action to assist communities address challenges. You only have to look at the critical areas of society and communities who are in crisis to know it's philanthropists who are often the most responsive to financial support. They don't often have multiple layers of decision-making to get through. I was working on a project when a crisis hit, and three philanthropic organisations combined within weeks to extend funding across six communities they were supporting. They funded responsive services, such as hamper drops to isolated and vulnerable community members.

The biggest challenge with a philanthropic funder is that 97% of the time you need deductible gift recipient (DGR) status to be eligible to apply for their funding. **I say 97% because options are available that allow you to still get funded if you don't have DGR. These options are:**

- ✓ Work with an organisation that has DGR status. This arrangement is called 'auspicing'. Check the philanthropic organisation you're considering accepts auspice arrangements because some don't.
- ✓ Apply to join a foundation. For example, you could start a fund-raising account with the Foundation for Rural & Regional Renewal (FRRR), which can accept donated funds from philanthropic

organisations and then provide these funds to you. Or you can join another organisation such as the Australian Sports Foundation where, with their permission, you could use their DGR status for your sporting project.

✓ Become a partner in a project that a philanthropic organisation is supporting. If it's a good fit for what you and the funded organisation are doing, it will increase reach and outcomes and you can access funding for the work you do.

✓ Reach out to the funder and tell them what you're doing. Ask them if they're aware of any groups or organisations that are doing similar things and you should talk to. Some funders act a little like brokers. They may guide a couple of organisations to talk together about what they're doing, and support them to apply for the right grant to access funds.

✓ Convince the funder to work with you. Perhaps the funder loves you regardless and will find another way, perhaps through another organisation, to get you the support you need. I've seen it - it's not common practice, but it can happen!

Corporations

Company giving is decision-maker driven - for example, decided by the business owner - or through policies such as Environment, Social, Governance (ESG) or Corporate Social Responsibility (CSR). While they support others, the grant will align to the funder's strategy and support brand awareness. For example, the Innovate with nbn Grants Program is linked to NBN Co's goal to increase digital capability of regional Australia.

Many corporations adopt a policy of Corporate Social Responsibility. Their CSR should promote and protect human rights, address the social and environmental impact of their business, and give back to their stakeholders. Small to medium businesses might have a local giving program. Sometimes in these programs the community chooses who receives funding by voting, and sometimes the organisation's staff choose. Giving back can be funded through grants, sponsorship and partnering.

The key here is to understand the decision-makers and what makes them give. What type of organisations and projects have they supported in the past? How can you build a relationship to understand who the decision-makers are and what drives them?

Individuals

Individuals will support you if they believe in the project. Some individuals give through crowdfunding platforms, donation campaigns or investor pitch nights. Fundraising from individuals is one way you can diversify income shown on your application budget. It also demonstrates community support. You should support your grant application with funds you've raised elsewhere, so implementing a fundraising plan to attract funds will support your application. Individuals give to individuals, so have the right person pitching and the right personal stories to tell.

I cover pitching in more detail in step 2a.

Working out how to search for, pitch and attract funds

As the following figure shows, we're now up to the first element in the finding step – searching for, pitching and attracting fund.

Stage 2: Find - Step 2a. Search, pitch and attract funds

2. Find

Find grants and choose the right one.

Step 2a. Search, pitch and attract funds

Tool

vi. The Grant Calendar™

As you research grants in this step, you'll find funders and closed grants that may seem to fit with your project and organisation's purpose. You may even find other opportunities such a sponsorship program. You can use The Grant Calendar to document these opportunities.

The Grant Writing System: vi. The Grant Calendar

The Grant Calendar assists you to track opportunities and applications. It's also useful because it gives you a record of past grants you've applied for, the result and acquittals of successful projects. Some organisations have tried to apply for grants in the past without knowing that the organisation was successful with a funder and hadn't finished the acquittal for that funding. This means the funder won't consider a new application until you acquit the last one. So, if you're unsure it's worth checking with the funder.

The Grant Calendar is a spreadsheet you can download from the online kit. The following figure shows the first four columns in the spreadsheet. You record the months or dates you're expecting the grant to be available. If you're using it as a record of grants applied for and received, you can use different colours in the cell. So those that are coming up I would colour a bright yellow, for example. If you use a date format, you can then also sort that column by date. This assists you to check in every month as you add new opportunities.

The first four columns in The Grant Calendar

Date/month expected/due date/acquitted date	Status	Organisation name	Have you applied to this funder before and have you acquitted this past grant?

The value of having it as a calendar system is you can start to get your idea and project plan grant ready well in advance. Someone was telling me the other day that the way they use their Grant Calendar is to track a regular funder they know who always opens their funding around May and closes on 30 June. So, in February or March they start discussing what project they'll start developing in order to be ready for the grant round.

The next six columns in The Grant Calendar documents information, if known, about the grant program (see the following figure).

The next six columns in The Grant Calendar

Grant program name	Max $	Min $	Funding purpose	Our project alignment	Asking for

Make this calendar a shared document so your team can access it, keep it updated and bring it up at every meeting to start planning to get grant ready.

Finding grants

You'll increase your chances of success in this process by heading in two directions: proactive and responsive. Neither direction is better than the other and you'll achieve most by following both; however, they require different skill sets. The proactive direction is focused on getting out and talking about your project, so you need someone who is confident and can persuade people. The responsive direction is focused on desktop research, newsletters and searching online to find grants.

The proactive direction

To understand this direction, let's review the Hub and Spoke Fest I introduced in step 1c. Remember this 5 Whys mind-map?

Mind map showing level 1 needs and possible outcomes for Hub and Spoke Cycling Festival

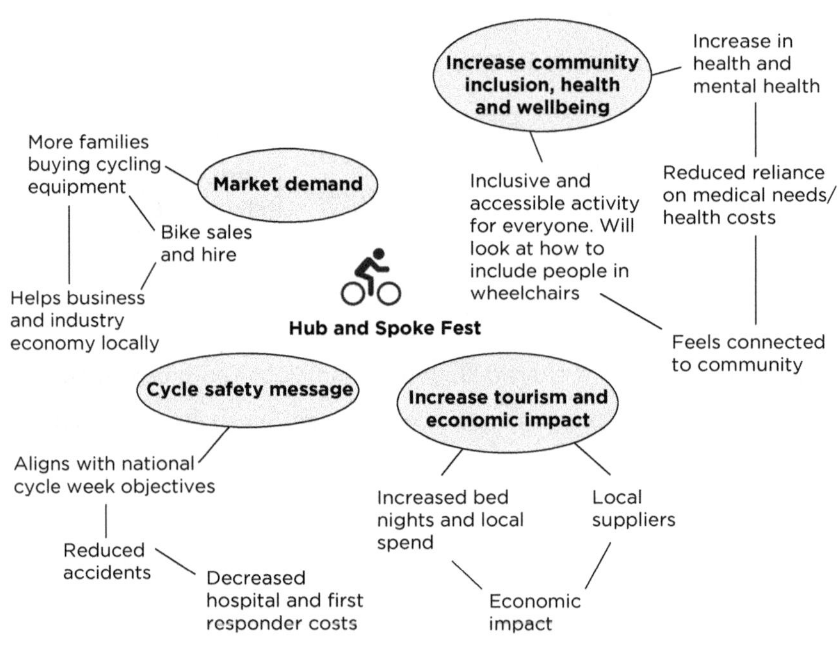

Through using the 5 Whys process, we discovered four level 1 impacts. These were:

1. responding to market demand for the cycling festival
2. promoting a cycling safety message
3. increasing tourism
4. increasing community inclusion, health and wellbeing.

So, without digging any deeper into the impacts, we know, at minimum, we can use these four avenues to find funding. Looking at the themes, we can also consider other funding options.

Okay, let's delve into the themes:

1. **Responding to market demand for the cycling festival:** This angle would work for business growth grants or new product development, especially if they could link hosting the festival with bike hire and sales.
2. **Promoting a cycling safety message:** The cycling safety message would be a good project to seek funding for from local or state government, especially if the festival could be held during Road Safety Week. The relevant state government may also hold 'Bike Week' events. If you can't find a grant from these bodies, remember discretionary funds might be available and pitch a sponsorship opportunity. Events are great for brand awareness for sponsors.
3. **Increasing tourism:** For this angle you could look for tourism and event funding. Destination management organisations, and local and regional tourism associations would also know about other opportunities.
4. **Increasing community inclusion, health and wellbeing:** Sports, mental and physical health funding are potential options that align to this impact.

Now you've identified some options, let's get into grant searching, pitching and attracting. Searching includes using search engines and newsletters, as well as a strategic search method I call a 'reverse search'. Pitching can create opportunities to access discretionary funding and bypass the grant application process for smaller projects. Attraction marketing harnesses the power of community and media to broadcast your message to funders.

Searching

You can search for grants in four ways:

1. **Find grant websites and register your email to receive updates:** Doing so you're likely to receive updates and funding possibilities well in advance of some of them being announced via 'projected notices'. This means you'll have a bit of head start - sometimes up to two months - to prepare a potential project (or two) before funding is officially announced. Because websites change, I provide an up-to-date list for you in the online kit. Subscription grant finder services are also available, some free and some paid. Subscribe to as many as you want (or can afford!) and use their filter to keep the notifications relevant to your project.
2. **Consider who your ideal funders might be:** For example, if you deliver youth services, then council, state-based youth organisations and government youth departments could be possible funders. Departments of sport and recreation and philanthropic organisations are also potentials. Research them. Check if your organisation or project aligns to their objectives. Find them and sign up to their newsletters.
3. **Use automation:** If you know the name or funder of a grant that's going to be announced, or there's a grant you'd like to apply for but the current funding round is closed, set up a Google alert for keywords. For example, I would use the funder's name and grant or, if known, the grant program name. When information

is published on the funder's website, you'll receive an email from Google notifying you within 48 hours.

This is how many organisations build their grant newsletters that you then pay for. Why wait for their newsletter? Set up automation and save time. Even finding out two days before you receive the paid grant newsletter or local members' free newsletter can be a big help.

Google alerts are particularly useful when funders open multiple rounds, either during the year or over a number of years.

4. **Use what I call the 'reverse Google search':** This is my last tip, and my favourite go-to search method. Most people search Google the normal way, using search terms such as 'wellbeing grant for youth'. The reverse search is designed to identify a funder who has already funded a program. Search as if you are writing a social media post thanking the funder. Use terms like 'wellbeing project funded by'.

   To delve deeper, go back to your Logic Model (refer to step 1c) and check the key outcomes you're planning to achieve. So, for example, if you're planning a coaching program for young sporting achievers and the potential outcomes are leadership skills, confidence, behaviour management, improved communication and personal development, you might find that the largest outcome area aligns to youth leadership. So, you could replace wellbeing with 'youth leadership skills', and search again. Examples might be 'youth leadership workshop funded by' or 'grant awarded for youth leadership'.

   Using this kind of reverse search, you can find articles and newsletters about projects like yours. You can then find the name of the funders and research them. Those funders might have an ongoing interest in your area of impact (for example, youth) and have more funding rounds coming up. So now you can sign up to their newsletters or set up a Google alert.

Pitching

Some grant programs have a pitching element. For example, individuals are asked to contribute at investor pitch events to support a business or community organisation. When you're ready to pitch or approach potential funders, it's time to pitch your heart out! Pitch Your Heart Out is my four-step method to pitching like a pro, even if the idea of pitching makes you want to run and hide under the nearest spreadsheet! You don't need to be an outgoing, rapid speaker. You need the confidence to make the calls, get the appointments and talk with people. If it's not you, maybe another staff member or volunteer would be best.

I outline the four ways to Pitch Your Heart Out in the following sections.

Plan your pitch

Identify organisations who are influencers. (Check your organisations or project stakeholder analysis from step 1c.) Also look for other similar organisations you can work with to collectively seek funding and increase your impact, or businesses that deliver services and may be able to support your next project, program or service. Start to build relationships with these organisations and let them know what's coming up for you. Identify the influencers you should put on a regular communication schedule - for example, connect with your local member of parliament, and keep them updated on what you're doing.

Check in with those locals who know what's going on in the community world - this includes economic development organisations, or local council economic development officers, community services officers or grants officers. Maybe they've heard about opportunities you can take advantage of. Check with your staff or board members and find out about any prior relationships your organisation had with funders. Can you rekindle any relationships? And tell as many people as possible that you've got an opportunity for the right sponsor!

You can then research your potential funders. Ask yourself what the funder wants. What are their goals and purpose? Frame your project as a way of supporting them to achieve their goals. A common mistake is to try to convince a funder to meet your project's objectives - don't do that! Go back to your project plan and Logic Model. Map your outcomes to the funder's objectives to show them how your project outcomes align to their goals.

Develop a winning one-pager

A one-pager is a one-page digital document containing a brief overview of your project. Your one-pager should spark curiosity and interest from potential funders. You could use the one-page project plan as a starting point but make it more presentable.

Keep this document simple and brief and use visuals instead of dense text. Visuals can be photographs of the people who will benefit from your project, graphs to show statistics, and any mock-ups or diagrams so the funder can understand your project quickly.

Include a short impact statement explaining what your project will achieve over the long term. You can use The Grant NDOIS Pitch frameworks from step 1b, or the need statement framework discussed in step 1c, using the 5 Whys process to dig down into the full impact. Just make sure you also put a human face on all the information and use storytelling and testimonials to highlight the lived reality of the people your project supports. If possible, include links to videos funders can watch.

Keep a section you can modify for each funder. While you're pitching the same project, different funders are interested in different outcomes, so focus this section on sharing key outcomes each funder cares about. If you aren't sure what might interest them, research them or use your need statement.

Include your contact and website details in this one-pager. Double-check the document for typos (they happen to the best of us) and you're good to go! Publish the one-pager to your website. Send it to your local council, your state MP, and your federal MP. Keep a list of the potential funders you've sent your one-pager to and follow up with phone calls. Don't forget to email or mail out the one-pager to your stakeholders and other community groups - you never know what opportunities will come.

Pitch your heart out in person

You might be face to face or video conferencing - either way, this is your chance to present your project. Keep telling everyone what your plans are and what you're trying to do. You never know who will be interested. One project received $200,000 from a resident who was only aware of it because the project organisers had been talking about the project in the community. An aged care service received $1.5 million, and they had been talking about their project for three years. Some things take time so keep talking!

When pitching in person, be presentable - consider it a bit like a job interview. Take a hard copy of your one-pager (plus a couple of spares in case more people are at the meeting). If you're pitching via video conference, still present yourself well and have a slideshow or screen share you can show them.

Emotive storytelling supported by statistics and evidence is useful here. Also be sure to have the right person pitching, sharing the right stories. As an example of this, I was mentoring a founder and CEO of a social enterprise who was pitching. Joh, the CEO, had founded the social enterprise to give opportunities for at-risk young people from life skills to employment.

The majority of Joh's beneficiaries identify as Aboriginal. In the past, Joh would do the pitching herself, but Joh has had pushback from some stakeholders questioning her authenticity because she doesn't identify as Aboriginal. Her story comes from the heart, and the programs she's created have made a huge difference to the lives of young people in the programs.

I recommended to Joh that she have her team, who reflect the youth she works with, both Aboriginal and non-Aboriginal, pitch their story of change – if they were comfortable. Some were also previous participants in her program and then employed as youth workers in the program. A couple of them embraced this opportunity and have learnt skills that have taken them onto other roles in the organisation and other jobs elsewhere.

This removed objections and barriers, but also connected with funders on a more personal level. The story wasn't being told second-hand. Funders were hearing directly from the people who had been positively impacted through the work Joh started. This motivated funders to support their goals.

If you're sharing a story, note that a line exists between appreciation and appropriation. It's not using another person's story to 'sell'. You have to share your journey authentically and have to be relatable to the beneficiaries. Stories of change are better told by those who have been personally impacted. If you're sharing evidence of the impact to others, tell your personal story about the difference it makes being part of that magic.

Start a conversation

The last way you can pitch your heart out isn't for every influencer or funder you've identified. Sometimes, however, simply starting a conversation is useful. Instead of asking for money, you ask for feedback on your project, particularly if they've funded or been involved in projects like yours before. You never know where these conversations might lead.

A note here on government organisations: simply starting a conversation is less likely to work because they can't be as flexible as philanthropic or corporate funders. You could, however, ask someone who's not in the same department for feedback or insights on your project. You just never know who they might talk to.

Attraction marketing

The third proactive direction for you to take is attraction marketing. Pitching took your message directly to funders, and now you'll get it to them indirectly. This part of finding funders is often missed, but it's important because you never know who's searching to fund you. Foundations employ people to search for worthy projects that align with their objectives. And sharing your message with your community will give them what they need to spread your message even further.

So, do you need a degree in marketing to start? Absolutely not! But in today's media-rich environment, it might be worth collaborating with people who will complement your skillset to get your message everywhere.

Social media is a great way to connect with some of your stakeholders and share your message with the world. Most social media platforms have set-up tutorials - or you could enlist a tech-savvy person, who will probably get it done in seconds! Link your website on your social pages.

Fill your online presence with real and engaging content, such as short video interviews with stakeholders and organisation representatives. Your local MP might even agree to be interviewed (especially if they've awarded your project some funds). Make your content shareable and interesting. Ask existing funders and sponsors if they would share their experience supporting you. If they're open to it, film an interview and post it on your website and socials.

Websites are a wise investment to showcase what you're doing. If you're a part of an organisation with a website, ask if you can have a page dedicated to your project. If you're flying solo, you can purchase a domain with your project's name and create a website. Have a dedicated page for each project and include the project title and need statement, a project summary, your one-pager, videos, testimonials, survey results, stories, interviews and any other content to build the legitimacy of your project.

Does it work? You bet. One organisation I worked with received $750,000 over five years to support their project. The funder said they had been searching to fund an organisation with a genuine focus on a particular area of health. Where did they find them? A Google search led them to the organisation's website. One call and a business case later (lucky I had done that work already!) and they got funded!

Another example is a church who received funding of $20,000. The individual wanted to fund a faith-based organisation to run a community event. Again, the website did the work in connecting the funder with the service.

Let's not forget the power of traditional media. Newspaper articles, radio and letterbox drops are still effective for some types of funders. Think of the three things you want everyone to remember about your project and focus your marketing messages on these.

The responsive direction

Being responsive means finding and applying for the grants announced by funders. Most of the people I work with find this direction the most stressful – typically, they find out about a grant a week before the deadline and madly dash around trying to develop an application. They're being reactive, however, instead of responsive.

The best way to get ready is to plan and research the funder to understand the information you may need when the grant program documents become available.

Of course, I live in the real world and know funding announcements do sometimes surprise us and we think, *Oh, what project can I develop so I can apply for the money?* If this happens to you, it's important to work through The Grant Go/No-Go Decision Checklist, covered in the next step. Don't consider the funder's document with your project in mind; instead, do it with a 'What projects are they wanting to fund?' lens.

For example, I recently worked with a grant writer in a local creative group. Kellie came to me with a potential project for a grant program. As I had just delivered training on the grant program in question through our regular Q&A sessions, I knew the project Kellie was proposing wouldn't work. I reinforced the funder's objectives and outcomes with her and talked about the types of things they'd be searching for. Kellie went away, worked on a different project and applied. Her organisation now has access to a piece of equipment they wouldn't have been able to afford otherwise.

Once you understand the funder a little, you're more likely to work out what type of project you should quickly pull together so you can apply for funding.

Will I still need to fundraise?

I know you probably want me to tell you that grants are the solution to everything and you won't have to do any further fundraising, but sadly I can't. Funders like to see that you aren't just waiting around with your hand out saying, 'I can't do this until we get a grant.'

They want to support motivated people and organisations that, pardon the language, get off their backside and do something.

The reality is you're not going to win every grant you apply for, so there will be shortfalls. You also may not be able to find the funds to do everything you want - not many organisations do - but you can start. Often starting your project shows it's worth funding, because you've proven demand or proven you can make it work.

I had a community centre in regional Queensland say to me, 'We want to run yoga classes but can't because we need to pay the yoga teacher. We need a grant to pay the teacher.' They didn't want a project grant; they wanted an ongoing grant for what funders deem to be operational. I talked to those involved at the centre about why they needed to think about this as a project and how they could build a project. One idea I shared was to bring people together as a group via a free downloadable app that allowed participants to watch an online yoga class and do it together. Starting the project in this way assisted them to demonstrate the need, demand and outcomes for their project. The following year their grant application to council for an in-person community yoga masterclass was successful. Their next step will be to use the information they've gathered on the outcomes and consider different grants, sponsorship or for people to pay for classes, because the local council won't re-fund this indefinitely. Funders want to know that their initial investment supports a project that has potential to become self-sustaining.

The other reason you won't be able to simply stop fundraising is because your grant application needs to show that you are bringing a contribution to the project - and this includes a financial contribution. Fundraising and sponsorship committed to a project also shows the funders that you have supporters, which is positive.

The good news is, while you're searching for grants you just may find potential sponsors or other funding opportunities.

Sometimes grants aren't the right option

The other thing that's important to recognise is grants aren't suitable for all projects. For example, only very specific targeted grants will fund business-as-usual operations or assets. I was having a coffee meeting with a business who wanted more information on grants. They offer a certification program and need to upgrade their equipment and wanted a grant to pay for this expense. This is not a grant opportunity. This is a business-as-usual cost. What I mean by that is it's actually the business's responsibility to make sure they understand their costing model and to put money aside for asset renewal and replacement.

Another example is a writer who wanted to publish a book on all the bushwalks in the region to make them more visible and accessible to people who didn't know they existed. This would be seen as a tourism project and publishing a book alone is not a strong proposition. However, combining it with a destination campaign with collateral could also get the book published. This also opens sponsorship opportunities.

I had a similar conversation with a not-for-profit rescue service. In that case they wanted a piece of equipment that would save them a lot of money. They thought that they had a strong business case for a funder to pay for the equipment if they demonstrated cost savings and those savings would be put back into operations and rescues. If they were funded by an organisation for operations, then yes, that organisation would be smart to fund the equipment. However, this was not the case. They were seeking a grant, any grant, to fund this. So from a funder's perspective this again is a business-as-usual cost. In fact, they could get a loan, use the savings to pay off the loan and when it's paid back then reinvest those savings where they need the funds. It's a hard call, I know. It is a life-saving rescue organisation. However, you also have to be realistic. If this ultimately means more lives saved and more money for the organisation, then a loan or high-value sponsorship might be the quickest return on investment.

Summary

In this step, you learnt how to find a funder using different approaches.

What can you do now?

Here are some actions to implement the learning from this step:

- ☐ Check the type of funders you usually seek grants from. Are you missing any types of funder? Would it be worthwhile investigating these funders to see if they would be a suitable fit?
- ☐ If you've identified an influencer, take along a one-page pitch document that follows the NDOIS formula (showing Need, Demand, Outcome, Impact and Solution) I talk about in step 1b. You can also find more information about pitching in step 2a.
- ☐ Go to the online kit and download The Grant Calendar and find the funding website list.
- ☐ Sign up to all the free funding newsletters.
- ☐ Start completing your Grant Calendar.
- ☐ When funders offer workshops or grant program information sessions, be sure to sign up for these and turn up - or if you can't, email your apology. Funders make a note of attendees and no-shows. This is a good opportunity to connect and become known to the funder, particularly if you're engaging in the workshop.
- ☐ Research funders who generally fund the work you do, or the industry you're in. Work out how you can get an introductory conversation with them to explore aligned goals.
- ☐ If you haven't already done this in previous steps, make sure that you have a project page on your website sharing information about what you're seeking funding for, and ways that people can support the project.

Now let's move onto the next step to work out if the grant programs you've found are right for you.

Step 2b

Decide if it's the right grant to apply for

Once you've identified some potential grants or funders (refer to the previous chapter), you need to get some documents together and then use The Grant Go/No-Go Decision Checklist to determine if it's the right grant for you. This is the second element in the Find step of The Grant Writing Cycle, as shown in the following figure.

Stage 2: Find – Step 2b. Decide if it's the right grant to apply for

2. Find

Find grants and choose the right one.

Step 2b. Decide if it's the right grant to apply for

Tool

vii. The Grant Go/No-Go Decision Checklist™

This checklist assists you to critically review whether you should apply for a grant using three lenses: grant eligibility, the funder's requirements and your organisation's position. I run you through this checklist in this step. First, though, you need to gather some basic documents.

Gathering documents to start making decisions

When considering whether a grant might be right for you, first get together the following:

- **Project plan and outcomes:** Because funders invest in projects with outcomes that align to theirs, you'll need your project plan and outcomes as a reference when you review The Grant Go/ No-Go Decision Checklist. You may amend these aspects to better demonstrate alignment to the funding program.
- **Application pack:** Find and download all the documents the funder provides for the grant program. This is your application pack, and these documents contain critical information you'll need to refer to. **The pack may include:**
  - the grant guidelines, also called program guidelines
  - the application form and any templates. If the form is online only, go through the online application as a test, and copy all the questions so you know what you need to address
  - sample contract, possibly also called draft contract
  - any additional documents, such as frequently asked questions or addendums.
  - any strategies or policies mentioned in the guidelines.

The following figure outlines what you might include in your application pack.

Grant application pack

Guidelines	Application form and templates	Sample contract	Other docs e.g., policies mentioned in guidelines	Funder strategies	FAQs or addendums

The Grant Writing System: vii. The Grant Go/No-Go Decision Checklist

A recent Grants in Australia report found 54% of grant seekers had failed to lodge an application they had commenced. The reasons for non-lodgement included running out of time (38%), discovering they didn't meet the criteria (16%) and or deciding the grant 'wasn't right for us' (27%).

The number of people who start and then abandon an application they've spent time on is sobering. So many applicants start working on an application, only to realise halfway through it's not right for their organisation or project! That's so much wasted time for people like us who have a lot going on already! So, how do you avoid being one of these statistics? You use The Grant Go/No-Go Decision Checklist.

Refer to the documents you've just gathered in the last section as you work through The Grant Go/No-Go Decision Checklist to decide if you should continue. Adding this stage will save you time, stress and money down the track. The checklist can be used either for a quick check or for a more detailed reflection before you start writing your application.

The Grant Go/No-Go Decision Checklist guides you through the application pack from three lenses, covered in the following sections. If you can't answer yes to each of these angles, you need to pause and reconsider how you can align to the requirement or if you can't, consider stopping because it's likely the funding isn't right for you.

If you know you can meet each of these aspects, it's a go-forward decision. For smaller amounts of funding, this may be all you need before starting the application. For more complex applications, I recommend you then do an additional step - a critical assessment using The Grant Application Tool (see step 3c).

One important point, regardless of the size of your project, is you need to make notes as you work through this checklist. You can either take your own notes or use The Grant Application Tool to break down the grant requirements and pull out the information you need from the documents.

Should you apply? The eligibility lens

Smarty Grants, a grants management system I worked with to train funders on grants management, manages thousands of grant applications every year.

Their data shows 30% of all applications received are ineligible - 30%! That's one in three applications! So, save yourself time and disappointment by first considering if this is the right grant and the right funder for your project. If not, maybe another project would suit this funder?

> *Remember - 30% of all applications submitted are ineligible.*

Eligibility has a hidden complexity. It's not only about your organisation being eligible to apply. It could also be the project you're applying for. You might have asked the funder to fund a project they've said they won't, and because of this the application is ineligible.

Eligibility differs between grants, even from the same funder or the same grant in different rounds. So, if you've identified a grant program that's not open yet based on past guidelines, when the guidelines are released for the new round, you may actually find you're ineligible. Even though nothing has changed about your project, the funder may have changed one sentence or one word in the guidelines or the application form and now you're ineligible. But it may not mean you walk away.

Eligibility falls into two main categories: the yes/no and the maybes. The yes/no questions can easily be answered with a simple yes or no – for example, 'Are you incorporated?' The maybes are a bit trickier; these answers require careful attention to detail and possible amendments to your project plan. One of my favourite sayings is guidelines are goldmines – everything you need to answer both kinds of question should be in the guidelines and other documents you've gathered.

Yes/no eligibility is fairly straightforward when you understand what the question is. If the guidelines say something like, 'This funding is open to incorporated bodies with Deductible Gift Recipient (DGR) status', this creates two yes/no questions. Are you incorporated? Do you hold DGR tax status?

Maybes have a little more wiggle room. You might be able to amend your project to better fit the funder's requirements, or work with a partner who fits the geographical area or target market better. Unlike the yes/no questions, you have some flexibility with your answers.

The hidden complexity here means checking your eligibility with four steps, shown in the following figure and then discussed in the following sections.

The four-step eligibility process

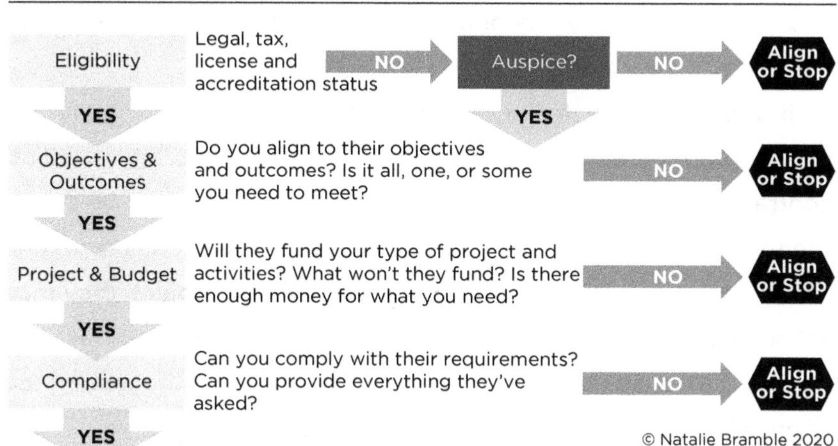

Are you eligible?

Check requirements for legal status, tax status, geographical location, types of organisations and any licensing or accreditation. If you're already accessing a grant from that funder in another program, you might not be eligible for another one. It's sometimes seen as 'double dipping'. If you don't meet these, options might be available to still apply. Fortunately, being ineligible might not be the end of the story. As mentioned in step 2a, many grants allow for something called an 'auspice' or a partnership arrangement.

Essentially, auspicing combines the partner's eligibility with your project. The partner will be the applicant responsible for managing and acquitting if you do Win the Grant.

An example of an auspicing arrangement might be where only a legally constituted not-for-profit association is eligible for an event grant from a local bank. The local library is council owned and operated so they can't apply for a grant for the book fair they want to hold. However, they can work with Friends of the Library, which is a legally incorporated not-for-profit association. So, in this case,

Friends of the Library apply as the grant applicant as the auspicor, and the local library becomes the auspicee (organisation being auspiced).

If you want to enter an auspice relationship, keep in mind the other organisation is the applicant, and it signs the legal funding contract. They receive all the funding and must do work to acquit the funds and report to the funder at the end of the funding period. This means even if they don't do any work on the project, they may ask for some of the funding to cover their operational expenses. This generally means they'll include an operational or a management fee of anywhere between 10% and 20% of the project.

When you're searching for potential auspice partners, review their objectives as stated in their constitution. The best way for this kind of partnership to work is if all sides meet their objectives, so partner with an organisation that has a similar purpose to you. If the auspicor has DGR status, it's critical for them to ensure your project aligns to their constitutional objectives and the purpose of the DGR given to them. If it doesn't, they could risk losing it and they won't take that chance.

Before you look into an auspice arrangement, check the grant guidelines allow auspice arrangements - most grants accept them, but not all. Finally, when you decide to enter into an agreement, get a written agreement signed. You may also need to provide this to the funder.

Objectives and outcomes

The objectives assist you to understand the purpose of the grant and the funder's motivation - why they're providing the funding and what they want to achieve. Funders will use different words to outline this, so scan the information provided for these kinds of headings: Background, Introduction, Purpose of program, Objectives and aims.

Do you and the funder align? What are the funder's objectives and how well does your project meet them?

Also review the stated outcomes and critically assess if your outcomes align to the funder's. You need to understand what they want to achieve and their measure of success. Check eligibility around outcomes. You may be required to meet one, more than one, or all of the objectives or program outcomes.

This is an example of the 'maybe' in eligibility criteria. You could maybe change your project to align to the required outcomes. Once you understand what the funder wants to achieve, check your Logic Model. Can you change anything that adds value to your project, and means you better align to the outcomes? If the project change is too much of a stretch, stop and ask if it's worth it. Assessors and funders can sniff out weak changes and add-ons.

Generally, the application form will have a corresponding question, and you'll need to specifically address how you meet those objectives and outcomes you've selected (if you had a choice). Addressing this correctly is important. You don't want to be the rejected applicant because you only aligned to one outcome, when eligibility required you to align to all.

If you're not required to align to all outcomes, a competitive position would be to see if you align to half of those listed. Don't try to meet all funder outcomes. This may come across as trying to be everything to everyone. The funder wants to know you're going to be focused. Trying to meet all outcomes has also just made your writing job that much harder as you try to fit everything into the word count. Most projects have multiple outcomes, so focus on those strong outcomes you're achieving that match the funders.

The funder may have some specific requirements, such as indications of the target people, including demographics and geographics.

Often, questions in applications ask you to specifically address how your project meets the objectives.

One last point here is to research any industry or funder outcome frameworks. The same approach applies to any frameworks funders use, such as outcomes frameworks (refer to step 1c). Knowing these frameworks and any outcome indicators at a strategic level can inform more complex, strategic grants. Even stating that you are aware of or align to the outcomes framework can be useful. For example, if you were applying for a community grant in the Northern Territory, you would mention how you align to the Social Outcomes Framework, and in the evaluation question in the application you can reference how you have adopted all, or components of, the Northern Territory Government's Program Evaluation Framework. Of course, it's not enough to say it - this actually has to be true.

Project and budget

Now you've aligned to outcomes, you need to establish if they'll fund what you need.

Review the guidelines to identify what the funders will and won't fund. They'll either use words such as 'eligible grant expenditure', 'eligible grant activities', 'eligible projects', or 'what the money can't be used for'.

Check your project is eligible for the specified funding. If it includes some activities they won't fund, make a note of this. Sometimes they'll fund your type of project, but they won't fund specific expense items within these types of projects.

Confirm you understand the financial contribution expected of you. Some funders ask for 50% of the project either in cash or a mix of cash and in-kind. Some require you to carry some expenses until the project is finalised. Here's an example clause from Community Sporting and Recreation Facilities Fund guidelines:

> Applicants are now able to claim 25% of their grant upon the signing of a major works contract. 50% of the grant may be claimed once expenditure has reached 50%. The final 25% of the grant is to be claimed upon the completion of the project. It is important to note the CSRFF program still primarily operates on a reimbursement basis. Grantees are required to demonstrate the expenditure of funds has occurred prior to submitting a claim for payment.*

This clause means if you wanted to apply for this grant, you need to be sure you can carry the debt until expenditure can be claimed. This can be done, of course, with your funds, loans or contractor negotiations; however, it's important to know up-front so you can consider how this will work for you.

The last thing to consider is a reality check. A lot of applicants get excited at the total pool of funding and the maximum amounts of funding available. They don't consider other aspects - which means they end up asking for too much money. This can sometimes be what culls you in the assessment, regardless of how strong you think your application is.

Check the budget they have for the whole grant program. See if they've stated an expected budget range for applications, the geographical area or number of applications expected. This gives you an understanding of what the funder determines a reasonable funding ask to be.

For example, the national Building Resilient Regional Leaders Initiative (Pilot) had up to $5 million in funding available over two years. They encouraged applications between $250,000 and $5 million. So,

---

* Community Sporting and Recreation Facilities Fund guidelines, 2022-2023 funding round

while it sounds fabulous, something like this is likely to get people over-excited and wanting the whole bucket of money. For pilot programs, consider who the ideal applicant might be. Given it was a pilot Commonwealth government grant, I felt confident they'd want to give it to a reputable organisation already delivering regional leadership programs. They would also have to spread funding around Australia – otherwise, they'd get backlash for only supporting a state or two. This is the type of program that lends itself to a few state-based organisations collaborating on a program to pitch for the whole amount.

A lot of smaller locally led community organisations were excited about this level of available funding, and I heard from quite a few across a few different states. Our social enterprise collaborated with a foundation on possible applications for three communities. We all discussed the potential drawbacks and decided we would apply anyway, because it was a program these communities wanted and, if unsuccessful, we could use the work to seek funding for the program elsewhere. For me, it was a volunteer love job, and just over a week's work volunteering.

After reviewing the grant guidelines, I recommended we produce one application across the three communities to strengthen the application. Despite this, the foundation decided to put in three separate applications, each for over $250,000.

This is an example of taking a risk and working out if the work involved is worthwhile regardless. Since this was something that lined up to the foundation's goals for these communities, we went ahead, knowing full well the decision was going to be based on the government's risk appetite. In other words, if it was a pilot program in the truest sense, they would want to fund a few different approaches to test what works, not rely on an existing tried approach. But if they were using the pilot to then roll out the program, not test a range of alternative approaches, they'd award funding to a brand name leadership organisation.

This grant was ultimately won by a consortium of leadership organisations, led by the Australian Rural Leadership Program. Based on the number of applications and total amounts of funding asked for, the chance of a win was 0.3%. I win over 80% of grants applied for, so of course there are some losses. But we went in with our eyes open, knowing that the work wouldn't be wasted if it was a no. We had a realistic view of the likely outcome. These communities will continue to seek support for a leadership program. I'm pleased to say that one community has secured other funds and has recently launched their program.

Some other things to check include:

- Are the funders asking for a financial audit? If so, will they pay or contribute?
- If your project involves staff, have they capped the hourly rate or on-costs?
- Is the funding including or excluding GST? This catches out even the most experienced applicants.
- Have they capped expenses – up to $2,000, for example?
- Have they given other instructions on maximum expenditure amounts on specific amounts, such as office expenses, total volunteer contributions or hourly in-kind labour?
- Will they fund evaluation, reporting and acquittal costs?

Guaranteed, the guidelines will include something they won't fund in your project, so you'll need to consider if you could make other arrangements or seek other support to fill those gaps. If you're going to make a large concession – for example, they won't fund 50% of the project or greater – filling the gap will be challenging. Check if you can modify your activities without a big reduction on quality and outcomes. If not, then perhaps this funding isn't right for you.

Compliance

Can you comply with their requirements? Check the guidelines for what you need to provide, or what goes on your 'to-do list'. Review the sample contract. Check for policies, and comments referring to legislation, reporting requirements and acquittals.

Sometimes you can make changes to align to requirements. For example, you may need $20 million in public liability insurance, but you only have $10 million currently. You can increase that insurance in order to apply, or you could ask if the funder accepts your application, on the condition you'll increase your insurance if you're awarded the grant. Keep in mind you won't be able to factor in the additional cost of this increase in your budget - funders won't pay if it's a minimum compliance requirement.

The guidelines also include general items that 99% of funders ask you to confirm compliance to. These will generally be listed on the last page of your application, and common examples include conflict of interest, child safety, workplace health and safety and modern slavery.

As you check the guidelines, make notes on these areas of compliance and check how your organisation complies with them. This is your opportunity to address any non-compliance before you submit the application. Some funders may ask for evidence, such as an example policy in the application; others may request it during or post-decision.

If you can't comply to a requirement and the funder won't accept anything less, this is considered by them to be a non-compliant application. You won't get through the first assessment stage. So, if you can't comply, the funding isn't for you.

Should you apply? The funder's lens

This lens helps you uncover what the funder needs from you. This includes aspects they've instructed you to cover in the application, and what's important to them.

Again, you have four areas to consider, as shown in the following figure and discussed in the following sections.

Four areas to consider from the funder's perspective

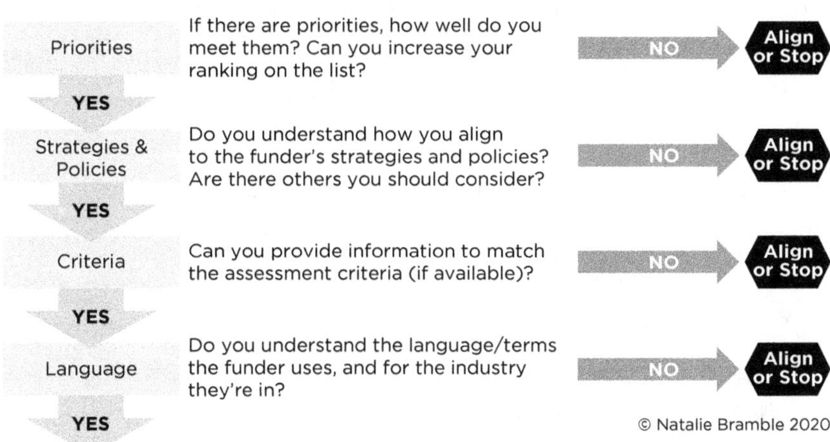

Priorities

While the grant objectives give you an understanding of the focus for the funding (refer to the section 'Objectives and outcomes', earlier in this step), priorities tell you not only if you'll be deemed eligible but also what order applications will be prioritised in.

You may find these priorities listed in the guidelines – sometimes they're not stated in the guidelines but instead become part of the assessment process, and you won't know what these are unless they tell you. For example, I was co-facilitating a funding workshop with a funder. It was mentioned by their staff in discussion that First Nations communities were a priority; however, this was not stated anywhere in the guidelines.

Examples of targeted priorities for business grants could be self-driving transport; for crisis funding priorities could be flood relief or social issues such as elderly homelessness for women.

Some funders may require you to meet their priority area to be eligible. If so, they will include in their guidelines. This means if you don't meet it, don't apply. I was speaking to a funder the other day who said their community and business grant program priority was to flood-affected communities. They had made this priority clear in the guidelines; however, sadly, the majority of applications were from organisations that were not in those flood-affected geographical areas. I say sadly because the time people had spent was wasted. They ended up in the rejection pile primarily because of one factor. I'm sure they're great projects, but the priority was made clear up-front.

Some funders select short-listed applications in order of the importance. For example, if they have a list of four priorities, they may select those that meet priority one first, then they'll look at short-listed applications that meet priority two. Others will work through the short-list in order of ranking then consider the priorities. These approaches are similar also to methods funders use who need to be seen sharing the funds around. For example, if they want a geographical or industry spread.

Strategies and policies

Take note of any plans, policies or strategies referenced in the guidelines. An example could be something like 'alignment to Brisbane City Council Sustainability Strategy'. What that's telling you is this grant is assisting the funder achieve these strategic goals. In fact, the funding has been approved because it will help them achieve these goals. So, it's important you find a copy of the referenced strategy. Consider this strategy and note down the strategies you align to and how. A specific question on this might be included in the application, or you may need to weave this alignment into your answer to a relevant question, with a short statement about how you help them meet their goals.

Even if the strategy or policy isn't mentioned, you should still research to see if there is one because it does help you. I was recently running a workshop and Larrash, from an aged care service, mentioned a grant for a workforce retention program that is being funded by Department of Health. So, I turned to Google and used the following search terms 'aged care workforce retention strategy department health'. I found the national Aged Care Workforce Action Plan and opened the document. We explored the document to discover that Larrash could refer to a lot of elements in the plan when answering questions in the application about workforce strategies, demonstrating how they are aware of the plan and align to the plan. In addition to that, Larrash now has a better understanding of the language the department uses when discussing the aged care workforce.

I've taken this to the next level in business cases and infrastructure project grants where I've had to bring some extra strength into the application to persuade government funders. I researched every local, regional, state and federal policy the project impacted. I mapped all the relevant policies and provided this in a table, addressing the relevant strategy and how we assisted funders to achieve this. Certainly, this wasn't the only reason funding was secured; however, it was part of building a strong, competitive case for funding, particularly when the 'value for money' assessment is applied (see step 3a).

You can use this information to then include relevant key words in your marketing collateral and in any pitch documentation you provide to funders in conversations.

Criteria

Like any competitive process, grant assessments use a considered, logical framework to, as best as possible, ensure best practice is implemented and the best project and organisation is funded.

Every grant process has a list of criteria your application will be judged against. Sometimes you're told what this is, sometimes you aren't. If the guidelines do include the assessment criteria (also called 'evaluation criteria'), review it and ask yourself, 'Can I demonstrate this in my application?'

I go into criteria and how this is used in the assessment process in more detail in step 3a. For now, consider these criteria more generally. What areas are you strong on and where might the weak points be? For example, the guidelines might be asking for participant co-design and you haven't done that previously. If you can fix that in time before the application is due, then move ahead. If not, it's likely not the right grant for you and you should not devote any more time to it.

Language

One of the common complaints of applicants is they don't understand the terminology funders use. Different words mean different things to different people. Unfortunately, if you use the wrong context of a word, you'll confuse those in the assessment process and send a message you don't understand the funder and their needs.

I do two things to understand terminology and context:

1. identify the main words
2. understand their context.

Identify the words

One simple way to discover what the main terms are is to copy and paste the guideline document into a word cloud generator. Word cloud generators use an algorithm where the word that's repeated the most is the biggest word. I use TagCrowd and love it. I copied 28 pages of one funder's guidelines to create the following visual.

The dominant words used in the sample guidelines

Note: don't copy and paste sections that cover costs they won't fund or ineligible projects. You don't want those words in your word cloud confusing the message.

Next, remove generic words such as 'department', 'grant' or 'page' until you get to terminology. The following figure shows the words I removed.

Remove generic words from your word cloud

Activity Australian Communities Grants Guidelines Program Resilient SARC Strong agreement and application assessment commonwealth criteria date decision department entity families funding government grant grantconnect guidelines including information opportunity organisation page processes state

You then get a final image and can select the option to show frequency. The following figure shows my final result.

Frequency of main relevant terminology used in the example guidelines

Understand the context

Once you've found the relevant terminology in the guidelines, you now need to confirm you understand what these words mean, and how they relate to your application. From the above figure, I chose the word 'inclusive' to focus on. A quick search of the guidelines showed me some important terminology was needed here to ensure context was translated to my application, should I proceed.

The word 'inclusive' essentially means you're including everyone, and not excluding anyone. So, you could think your project needs to support everyone. However, searching the guidelines and reading the sentences surrounding the word 'inclusive' shows me this grant is particularly focused on geographical areas of high socioeconomic disadvantage. So, if the project was supporting everyone in a suburb not considered to be disadvantaged, this grant isn't right for the project. The same paragraph provides more useful information that can be used in answers – such as the words 'vulnerable', 'disadvantaged', 'self-reliance', 'empowerment' and 'community-driven'.

The words funders use in guidelines are important. Words like these, and those listed in the objectives and outcomes, are important to understand because you'll need to show this alignment in your answers. You shouldn't be repeating word for word what they say, but you do need to show how you understand what inclusive means to the funder, as it relates to the grant program.

I do want to give you another example of a common one in community grant applications: the word 'community'.

The word 'community' is commonly misunderstood in grants. What a funder means by community is likely to be different from your version of community and the community your project serves.

You need to be very clear about who you call your community. Is it your members or is it your whole local government area? You also need to be clear about who your funder is talking about when they say community. Sometimes they'll use a different definition to yours.

As an example, a rowing club needed to upgrade their club toilets, which were only accessed by club members. They wanted to apply for a grant that was focused on support for the broader community; however, their project only benefited the club community. Despite my advice when I explained they wouldn't be deemed eligible because of this, they spent the time applying for the grant. Unfortunately, their time was wasted. When they asked why they were rejected, they were informed their project didn't meet the requirement of providing benefits to the community.

Words, and context, matter.

Should you apply? Your organisation's lens

This lens gets you to consider your organisation and your project. These are areas you may have to – and can – strengthen to be more competitive.

The four areas to consider here are shown in the following figure and discussed in the following sections.

Four areas to consider from your organisation's perspective

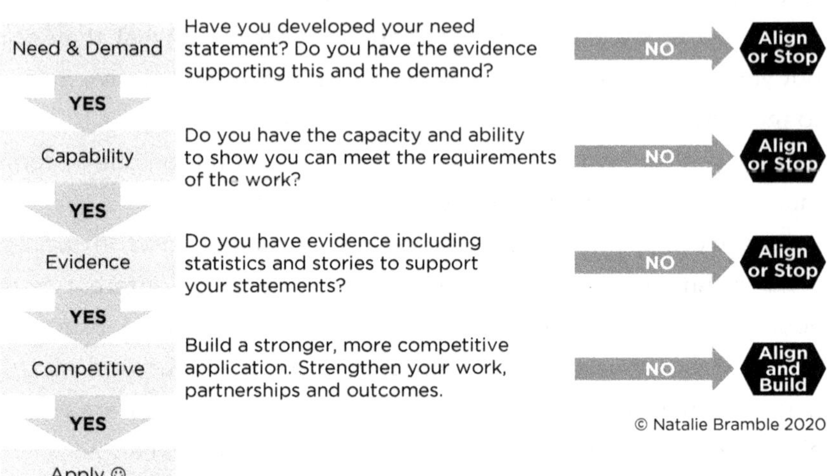

Need and demand

I discuss need and demand in step 1c as part of completing The Grant Project Plan. Once you get to this point, you should have crafted your need statement for your project. (If you've jumped to this part of the book, I recommend you go back and review the need statement in step 1c.)

Now to get a better understanding of the funder and the grant program, ask yourself what needs to be changed. Do you need to place emphasis on certain elements that align to the funder's objectives and outcomes, for example?

Capability

Do you have the capacity (resources, assets and people) and the ability (skills, experience and knowledge) to deliver? When you reflect on your project plan, the project and the funding program, do you think you'll need to change the scope of your project? For example, some of the Australia Post Community Grant rounds have focused on supporting community mental health and wellbeing. They stated in the guidelines they had partnered with a mental health organisation. This not only tells me they believe it's important to partner with a reputable organisation delivering in this area, but also gives me an insight that either health professionals, or even people from their partner organisation, may be on the assessment panel. I also found in the guidelines a requirement for organisations to demonstrate the effectiveness of their approach and a capacity to deliver.

So, with this information, I knew anyone applying for this grant would need to demonstrate to the funder their organisation had the capacity and ability to deliver a program addressing community mental health and wellbeing. They would also need a relevant health professional supporting them. This could mean this professional is involved in the co-design of the program, is an advisor, or is involved in the delivery of the program; or this professional had undertaken a professional review and could provide a letter of support telling the funder the organisation is on the right track.

It's important to consider your gaps after you've gone through the guidelines and considered funder expectations. One of the ways I tell people to think about this is imagine you had to contract someone to deliver your project. What would your expectations be?

Evidence

You should now be able to make some judgements about any other evidence you'll need to gather to share in your application. For example, if the funder is asking for evidence of a community-led or co-designed project, and you're able to provide attachments, you could include photos of a planning session you held with youth, showing how the session actively involved them and how they were running the session.

Check the guidelines and application form to identify other evidence funders want, or evidence that will strengthen your statements. You may find your existing research is too general, so you need more specific or recent research. Finding this out now, at the beginning of the application process, gives you more time to do the research.

I was supporting a local council to demonstrate evidence of need. We had to convince the federal government to extend an existing cycleway by funding a new bike path over a river. An existing old railway line couldn't be used, because it had been held for potential access for a rare earth mine.

Anecdotally, demand existed for this path, but the local council didn't have the hard evidence. I organised the local Bicycle Users Committee and wrote up rosters for volunteers to stand on the existing cycleway and ask users questions. These volunteers went out and gathered evidence over a two-week period, on different days and different times. I was able to use this data to demonstrate a strong need and demand for the project.

Imagine if I hadn't considered this earlier, and instead maybe only thought of it a day or two before the application closed. Collecting this data wouldn't have been possible, and we would have submitted a weak application – probably missing out on funding, wasting everyone's time. Above all, this result would have de-motivated a great group of volunteers and council staff.

Competitive

By now, you have a good understanding of the funder, the funding environment this grant program sits in, your project and what you may need to do to submit a strong application.

But you need to be realistic. Is this grant worth spending time on? Is there a chance of success? I remember talking to a client, Jeff, about a business advisory program he wanted to apply for. He was considering three regions. I went through the same process I've taken you through and told him that in the first region he was currently servicing, he had a strong competitive chance. I initially said he had about a 75% chance of success in this region. He was weaker in the second region, with around a 35% chance of success, and so I didn't recommend proceeding. However, I said if he collaborated with another business in the region, he could increase the chance dramatically.

The third region I said don't even bother. Jeff pushed for me to do the work but I'm realistic and won't do work on projects just to tick a box. It's a waste of time and energy and does no-one any good.

I could only make this kind of judgement, though, because I had developed a considered and critical view based on everything I discovered as I went through this process. Jeff ended up agreeing with me not to proceed on region three. Unfortunately, he didn't collaborate with another business on the second region and, as predicted, didn't win. We did, however, secure business advisory services for the first region.

Another example can be drawn from our earlier discussion of the word 'inclusive' (refer to 'Understand the context'). I mentioned the guidelines focused on geographical areas of high socioeconomic disadvantage. This gives me a hint to find the list of disadvantaged communities and identify where the community my project is focused on is ranked. This is an Australia-wide program, and they don't have endless buckets of funding, so if my community is less than 50% on the social disadvantaged list, we won't be as competitive.

The other thing to again reflect on is any priorities listed in the guidelines which we covered earlier. As an example, some grant programs, such as the Gambling Community Benefit Fund (GCBF) in Queensland, list a series of priorities in order of their importance. **In their previous round they prioritised:**

1. items destroyed by a natural disaster
2. equipment
3. vehicles
4. education, events and marketing
5. organisations that had received funding in this grant program within two years.

So, if the project you're applying for is a community event - number four on this list of priorities - how competitive do you feel your application is? Particularly when you know, based on conversations over the years, a lot of community groups across Queensland apply for this grant.

Ideally, you'd rethink your project and check if you have other projects that fit better with priority number two or three. I'm not saying you wouldn't go ahead; I'm saying be realistic with your chance of success.

Is it a go or no-go decision?

It's a big question I know. To answer it, we're going to switch hats. Stop thinking as the applicant, and instead think like the funder.

Stop, pause and reflect on everything you've learnt about the funder. If you started today as the person managing the grant program, who is your ideal organisation and what's your ideal project? This is one of the questions I always ask. This helps me to critically reflect on what we're offering versus what the funder wants. From this, I can estimate the chance of funding success.

I was supporting a business service that had a connection with an expert in the waste field. They wanted to apply for innovative waste practices, via a state government grant. After reviewing the guidelines, I told the CEO the best fit for this grant was with local councils. Waste in communities is a remit of local councils; therefore, a project like this would either be delivered by or in partnership with councils. There wasn't anything in the guidelines that suggested they were going to fund any innovative approaches and non-traditional service providers. So, I recommended the organisation approach councils for a partnership arrangement. The CEO chose not to and went ahead with the application. When the funding was announced, every single successful applicant was a council. So not having the partnership clearly weakened their application - and is a lesson for them to take away next time, when they're considering who the ideal applicant is that the funder's seeking.

Funders often have a list of previously funded projects. This is useful to review the types of projects they're likely to fund, but only if the guidelines and the application form haven't changed from the last round. Otherwise, it's interesting information, but may not give you a clear view of what they fund in the future.

Summary

By completing this step, you should now have a sound understanding of eligibility, the funder's objectives and desired outcomes, and how strong your organisation's application is likely to be. Importantly, going through The Grant Go/No-Go Decision Checklist should have helped you identify areas that you need to strengthen before you start writing your application.

What can you do now?

Here are some actions to implement the learning from this step:

- [ ] If you don't have a current grant you're applying for, review a past grant with guidelines and the application. Go through the checklist. What areas would you change or improve on? What have you learnt from this?
- [ ] Anytime a grant is announced that you feel is worth investigating, use this checklist first to determine if you should invest any more time.

Summary of Stage 2: Find

Congratulations for going through the second stage of finding the right grant with the right funder. I'm sure you learnt a lot of valuable information about the funder, the grant program and your project.

You'll now be in a position to make an informed decision about what you need to do to apply, or if the grant is right for you. Importantly, The Grant Go/No-Go Decision Checklist would have highlighted any weaknesses you may have and you've now got the time to strengthen these areas.

I generally move ahead to the next part of the process if I feel the application has an over 65% chance of success. This is because I know some programs don't receive a lot of applications, and I know I can find ways to strengthen my application. I've got confidence in how I address questions and I know even if other impressive projects are submitted, a lot of applications are going to make mistakes I won't make, which means they'll lose more points than I do.

So, I continue doing more work to better understand how to avoid mistakes in this application and to identify the valuable information I need to build in my answer.

In the next part, I outline how grants are assessed, and I introduce you to a tool I use to guide you through the guidelines and find those nuggets of gold. Because ... say it with me ...

Guidelines are goldmines.

What can you do now?

Your actions from this part are going to be driven by the need to find grants and assess the grants you find. While you're waiting on the grant announcements, you can still develop your networks and relationships with existing funders. Also consider other avenues to funding, including sponsorship and fundraising.

Stage 3: Align

The Grant Writing System™

© Natalie Bramble

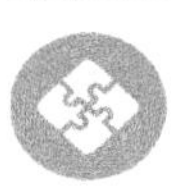

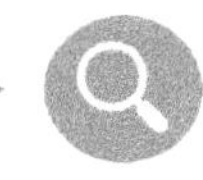

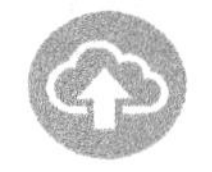

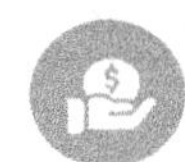

1. Plan
2. Find
3. Align
4. Write
5. Submit
6. Manage
7. Report

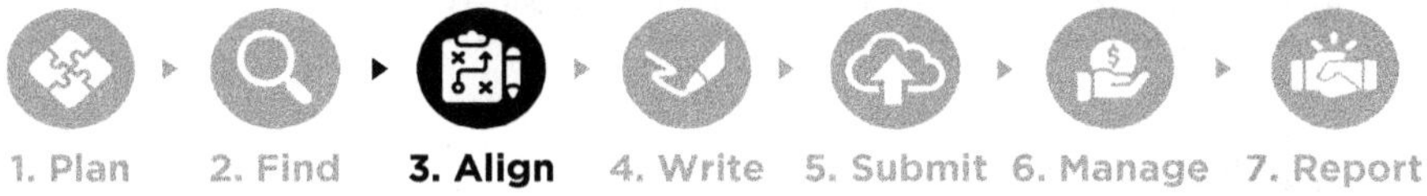

Align to the funder

We're now up to the steps in the third stage in The Grant Writing System - Align, as shown in the following figure.

Align: Stage 3 in The Grant Writing System

Align to the funder's goals

3. Align

It's all about the funder's goals

Steps in this stage

a. Understand the funder.
b. Think like an assessor.
c. Analyse the application documents.

Tools to guide you

viii. The Grant Application Tool™

This stage is all about strategy. You are grant ready and you've found the right grant to apply for. Now, you need to convince the funder your project is an ideal fit for their grant program. Other applicants are competing for the same grant and not everyone can win - the bucket only has a limited amount of money.

So, this part will guide you through what funders are seeking, how grants are assessed, how to align to the funder and how to think like an assessor. I take you through researching the funder and studying the documents in the application pack to understand them, and then finding those nuggets of gold you can use strategically to strengthen your answers.

I also outline how to use The Grant Application Tool for more complex grants. The strength of understanding is in the details, and this tool will help you avoid simple mistakes that, if missed, could mean you're rejected immediately.

Step 3a

Understand the funder

Before you start to explore the grant guidelines and the application form, it's useful to first understand how grants are assessed. As shown in the following figure, you now need to understand the funder.

Stage 3: Align – Step 3a. Understand the funder

3. Align
It's all about the funder's goals.

Step 3a. Understand the funder

We know how to persuade people we're close to because we know how they think, what objections they have, what's important to them and the decision-making process they use. But how do we influence a grant process? We need to know the same things. Each document in your application pack (refer to the previous step) relates to and impacts others. A lot of applicants, for example, jump right into the application form and start answering questions; some might scan the guidelines but few review them strategically. Doing so, however, makes a huge difference to strengthening your competitive position at the decision table.

You don't want this on the assessor's feedback notes:

> The application doesn't align to the guidelines. The relevance and alignment from the funding objectives to their project isn't clear. It seems rushed through, just to access funds.
>
> Grant Assessor's Feedback

It's easy to identify when an applicant has done their homework. For example, the application will reflect key messages from the guidelines. Guidelines include deliberate messages you need to understand. These assist you when you're writing your answers in the application form. Understanding how the application is assessed is also important, because this can influence what information you include - particularly if none of the questions directly addresses the assessment criteria.

Understanding how funders assess applications helps you understand funders. Now, we aren't mind-readers, and we don't have access to internal information about the funders. We can only use information they've made available to us, and grant practices we know about.

The two areas you should research are: who is assessing the grants, and what's the process?

Who assesses grants?

Check the guidelines to see if they give you an understanding of the assessment. Who assesses your submission depends on the organisation.

Internal staff only may be used, or a combination of internal staff, external experts or target group representatives. At a minimum, a program manager who knows the program and, in many cases, was the person who co-designed the current round, will be part of the assessment team. This individual is responsible for the process, probity and confidentiality, and any contracting arrangements.

Subject matter experts, if appointed to the panel, either would have been involved in developing the grant requirements or have a sound understanding of what's needed. Subject matter experts assess your application from a technical, practical or lived experience perspective. They'll have different experiences of projects they have led or been involved in. They'll be able to spot weaknesses - for example, in timelines or budgets. People with lived experience who reflect target groups will also likely be included.

What's the grant assessment process?

This assessment process can be application-based or include a personal approach, where you have an opportunity to pitch your project directly to an assessment panel. Or the assessment process is a mix of these. If a pitching component is included, go back and review the information I cover in step 1b on The Grant NDOIS Pitch and step 2a on pitching your heart out.

In the following sections, I outline a common process for grant programs I've been assessor on, managed or advised funders on. There are some differences within each of these levels, but these three levels are common across all programs I've been involved in, or discussed with funders and other assessors.

As shown in the following figure, the three assessment levels are:

1. due diligence assessment
2. application and project assessment
3. strategic assessment.

The three assessment stages

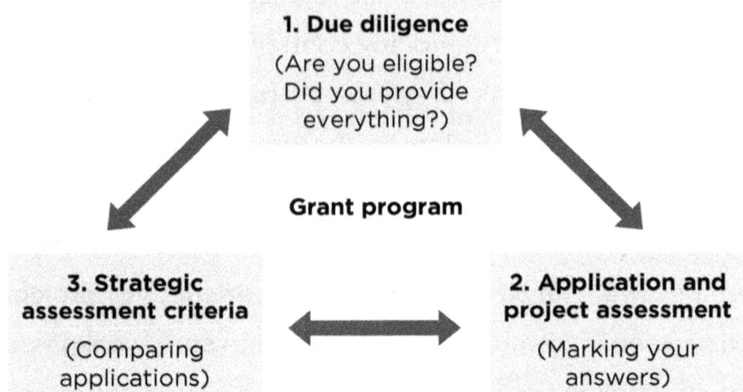

Due diligence

The first level is due diligence. This is where eligibility, compliance and other minimum requirements are validated.

This due diligence assessment may be undertaken by administration staff, assessors or program managers simply using a checklist. This includes checking you're eligible to apply, you aren't asking the funder for projects or budget items they have said they won't fund. Staff will also check compliance matters and probity, covering the specific questions in your application, such as declaring conflicts of interest. (You'll generally find probity questions on the last page of your application.)

Depending on the grant assessment process, in this step they may check your answers to questions and directly relate these back to the objectives. For example, if it's not clear in your written answer how your project addresses the funding objectives, your application may be rejected on those grounds.

Many online applications are developed to address some of these items on the checklist and if you can't provide a satisfactory answer, they won't allow you to progress through the application. Some guidelines include a submission checklist. If you're submitting an online application form, go through each question they ask, particularly if they have a final submission checklist.

Here's a simple example submission checklist:

✓ meets eligibility criteria

✓ outcomes and activities align to the grant program

✓ required information provided

✓ all questions have answers

✓ project starts within the funding period

✓ project ends, and will be acquitted within the funding period

✓ budget is within funding guidelines

✓ budget doesn't include expenses the funder won't pay for

✓ insurances are current and have required levels of cover

✓ no conflicts of interest declared, and conflicts declared are managed

✓ all requested documents are uploaded

✓ accreditation and certificates are valid.

Application and project assessment

The second level scores your answers in your application. You'll have a range of questions in the application to answer, and assessors use a scoring table to rank these answers. Assessors will go through each answer and give it a mark. Your total marks will rank you on a list of applications and, generally, only the top 10 to 20% of applications go through to the next level.

This application assessment step is where your questions are assessed. The funder appoints and trains their group of assessors and this is where a mix of people will be involved, such as internal staff, external consultants, community members and people with areas of expertise and lived experience. For example, if you've applied for an arts grant, a person who is a sculpture artist may sit on a panel to assess those applications for sculpture works, a writer may assess applications for written works.

The funder may give you some insights into who will be on the assessment panel, and this can certainly help. If you know something about the assessors, you can use language they'll understand. For example, if you're an educator writing an application for a school grant that's not education-specific you know you have to use language anyone outside of the education industry would understand.

Also keep in mind your application may be split between different people who review different questions. For example, your financial documents may be analysed by someone from the finance team, and for specific targeted grants - for example, for LGBTQIA+, a person with relevant lived experience may review your answer.

So, when answering questions, check you've provided adequate information in the relevant section. Don't rely on people having assessed the full answer to previous questions. Each answer should stand on its own.

Sometimes your application will go through different rounds of assessment at this level - for example, perhaps a first assessment round by internal staff at the head office, with applications then split up into the different regions and assessed by staff in those regional offices.

Assessors are given a scoring matrix to mark your answers against. A simple example of this is the following five-score matrix, with five being the highest you can achieve in each question. Assessors mark the answer on what you provided and how well they understood your answers.

Your goal is to get as many marks as possible. You can influence what that score is likely to be by understanding the question and giving the assessor the information they need. (I guide you through analysing the guidelines and grant application in step 3c.)

Not all scoring tables are the same, but the following example reflects a review of 152 program application forms offered across all states and territories in a two year time frame.

Example assessment application scoring table

5	Excellent	Answer is detailed and comprehensive and demonstrates how the requirements will be fully met.
4	Good	Answer provides enough detail to demonstrate a good understanding of requirements and how they'll be met.
3	Acceptable	Answer broadly demonstrates understanding; however, some answers lack detail on how the requirements will be met.
2	Poor	Answer provides partial information. Answer is insufficient or provides limited details to demonstrate understanding and ability to meet requirements. Answer requires further clarification.
1	Unacceptable	Does not demonstrate minimum requirements or fails to comply. Failed to address criteria.

One final thing that assessors will also reflect on and score in this level is your project. They will take a holistic view of your application's strengths and weaknesses; they will use the information the funder has provided to them and consider the project compared to others. This may result in comments they make to the program manager for the next assessment level, and their judgement is also reflected in the score.

For example, it might be a weak application because one critical element was missing across the project. The assessors may include comments that recommend your application on the condition that due diligence is undertaken, or where the funder permits that you provide further information on that element.

If they've identified a project weakness, such as a project that is clearly missing an important target group, this will reflect in their scores in your answers related to need, target groups and co-design.

Strategic assessment

The last step is a strategic assessment.

All short-listed applications from level 2 will be ranked according to the assessment criteria, and they'll be compared against each other using a decision matrix. This will be based on the assessment criteria.

The assessors' scores are sorted by the highest to lowest total scores awarded to applications. If there were priority areas, short-listed applications may be listed in the order of priority. So, for example, if an age group was defined in the guidelines as a priority, the applications with projects that primarily benefit the age group may be listed in the short list first. Some guidelines have a number of priorities, and in this case weighted criteria might be used to determine the short list. (See 'Weighted assessment criteria', later in this step, for more on this.)

In this level, the short list is assessed based on a more complex assessment matrix. This process marks you on how well your project meets the funder's objectives, strategies and priorities. Other assessment criteria may even be used, which they sometimes share with you in the guidelines (either called 'assessment or evaluation criteria'). All applications are ranked against this criteria. Similar to the assessment scoring outlined earlier, scores will be applied based on this criteria. **When you're searching for assessment criteria, one of these three methods will apply:**

1. The funder shares the assessment criteria, and the application has questions asking you to share how you align to these criteria.
2. The funder shares the assessment criteria; however, no corresponding questions are included. This means you need to weave your points into answers across your application.
3. You don't know the assessment criteria.

You'll take different approaches to each of these in your application. Assessment criteria is scored and sometimes you'll know what this score is (weighted criteria), or not (unweighted criteria). Let's look at what this is and then I'll review the three options and how to approach them.

Unweighted assessment criteria

Unweighted criteria means you aren't told what each criteria is worth. Assessment criteria are always weighted at the decision table, even if you don't know what these are.

An example of unweighted assessment criteria is when you find a list of dot points, with no weightings attached. A Western Australian grant for community sport and recreation facilities, for example, included that assessments have been based on criteria. **Some of these include:**

- justifying the project
- planning the project
- asset management planning
- consulting with the community
- access and inclusion
- financial viability
- increase of physical activity.

When all you have is a list like this, it's either a random list, an alphabetical list, or a numbered list. Sometimes this gives you an insight. If it's a random list, such as the example just given, then it could be in order of importance, or not. The only way to identify this is to critically assess the guidelines to identify the key messages. For example, if the guidelines and application seem to focus on the planning and management more than community consultation, then these are likely ranked higher than those listed under community consultation.

If the list is in alphabetical order, it tells me the funder doesn't want to give you any hint of the priority order. If it's numbered and not alphabetical order, that may tell you the funder has listed by most important to least important.

Sometimes criteria are equal, but sometimes one might be worth more points than others. If the funder hasn't shared how much each of these is valued at, which is weighting, you can't identify if certain questions in the application are likely to be more important than others. If they've only given you a list of points and the documents don't say or hint at priorities then it's a guess that each point could be as important as the others or those at the top are worth more than those on the bottom.

I'll make an estimation based on strategic and risk factors from the funder's perspective. For example, if the first three areas aren't planned well, there's a risk the project may not continue - remember that sporting facilities example discussed in step 1c? Now for access and inclusion, this sounds like it's there to align to a state accessibility and inclusion strategy. I'd need to validate that, but it's a good assumption that the last two points are less strategic.

Weighted assessment criteria

Where assessment criteria are listed in grant guidelines, some have points or percentages next to them. This tells you what the weighting is for the criteria. The more each criteria is worth, the more important it is for you to show how you address its components.

You'll receive points against these criteria, and also be compared against other applicants. This is why competitiveness, which I mentioned in step 2b, is important to consider.

At iClick2Learn, we researched 28 business and community grants that publicly stated their assessment criteria, with a total of

284 criteria mentioned. **The following list provides example assessment criteria from this research and their weighting:**

- Project plan is clear and achievable: 15%.
- Budget is comprehensive and provides value for money: 15%.
- Demonstrated need for the project: 15%.
- Demonstrated ability to engage the community: 10%.
- Clear plan to address identified need: 10%.
- Project outcomes are realistic and measurable: 10%.
- Demonstrated alignment with funder's goals and objectives: 10%.
- Clear evaluation measures and methods: 10%.
- Demonstrated financial need: 5%.

If this was in grant guidelines, knowing this weighting can help you identify which key messages are more important to repeat, or reinforce in your application.

Factoring assessment criteria into your application

Now you understand the difference between unweighted and weighted criteria, let's review the three methods grant funders use to handle assessment criteria and how you can use this strategically in your answers.

You know the criteria and questions relate to that criteria

An example of this would be a grant program that stated three weighted assessment criteria would be used - for example, capacity (35%), need (35%) and delivery (30%). The application then had three questions addressing these criteria. This is the best-case situation. You know the criteria and you know the weighting so you know where to focus most of your time (on the criteria worth more). Importantly, you can share information in your answers that helps assessors make their decision in level 3 of the assessment process.

You know the criteria but no clear question relates to some, or all

This is challenging because you need to determine how to communicate your alignment to the criteria. You need to consider where it's appropriate to share this information in your application. If you know the criteria is weighted and one is more important than the other, what are the different ways you can share information to support these criteria? One should therefore be more supported as a key message in your application than the other.

One grant program included value for money as a criteria; however, there wasn't a question asking how the project was value for money.

So, if none of the questions ask about value for money, how might you demonstrate this? Basically, you need to think about how your project offers value for money – perhaps through a partnership with the local energy foundation or co-op that has provided better value for money when negotiating with suppliers, for example, or through the number of people volunteering. You then need to highlight that value for money into the relevant answers.

One way I approached this on a competitive business service grant was to highlight the organisation had existing partnerships and relationships with stakeholders in the service area. I said, 'Unlike new providers to the area who can take months to establish relationships and negotiate conditions, [*Organisation name*] is able to commence the [*name of program being funded*] outreach service three weeks from the signing of contracts.'

You don't know the criteria

The final situation is more difficult and you can approach it in a couple of ways. This is where the work you've done to date and will continue to do in the next step to understand the funder is vital.

You need to take a lot more ownership in this approach. How can the funder make a judgement when comparing your application against another unless you give them the information they need? Simply put, your job is to uncover what the likely criteria are and then provide the right information for their discussion.

Firstly, I check the objectives, outcomes and priorities. I reflect on the motivation for funding. I check the TagCrowd results (refer to step 2b) to identify key themes coming through – 'inclusion' could be one for example.

An example of TagCrowd results providing a strong indication was when I was writing an agricultural funding grant a few years ago and in the information sessions the chair said sustainability was a key message. This word was mentioned once in a long application form full of multi-part questions – from memory, it was at around question 20, part b. However, when I assessed the TagCrowd results, 'sustainability' was the word most repeated. So, I addressed sustainability in relevant questions throughout the application.

Secondly, I check the guidelines and search for sentences that give indications, such as 'robust governance processes' or 'business viability'. I make a list of these and review the application. When a specific question isn't related to those points, I consider where it would be appropriate to include a sentence or two covering those aspects.

I also uncover what the funder has said the application needs to do. For example, the guidelines for another grant stated you had to clearly demonstrate all of the criteria in your application, and then listed four items – including community-led and effectiveness of outcomes. They didn't state these were the assessment criteria, and the application didn't have questions specifically asking about these items. However, given they have phrased the statement this way you could reasonably assume that these were the assessment criteria and make sure you weave in information about them in your application.

Thirdly, I use a method I've developed called the Four Abilities. These are four key things I've found through my research and work over the years that every sponsor and funder want to you demonstrate.

The Four Abilities are:

- **Capability:** How you demonstrate the capacity to complete your proposed project, including the resources and partnerships and the ability shown through your collective skills, knowledge and experience.
- **Sustainability:** Think about this in four categories:
  - organisation sustainability
  - environmental sustainability in meeting projects and targets
  - project sustainability to ensure, if required, it can continue beyond the funding
  - outcome sustainability to ensure the outcomes themselves can be sustained beyond the funding.
- **Viability:** This is about both your organisation's financial viability to manage the grant and deliver the project, and the viability of the project itself. Can you prove, for example, this is the right project to address the need? Will it work?
- **Accountability:** This is about your ability to deliver successful projects and covers governance and your operational structures – including policies and processes, for example.

Once you have a better idea of assessment criteria and (actual or possible) weighting, you can start to think like an assessor – the topic of the next step.

The Four Abilities Framework

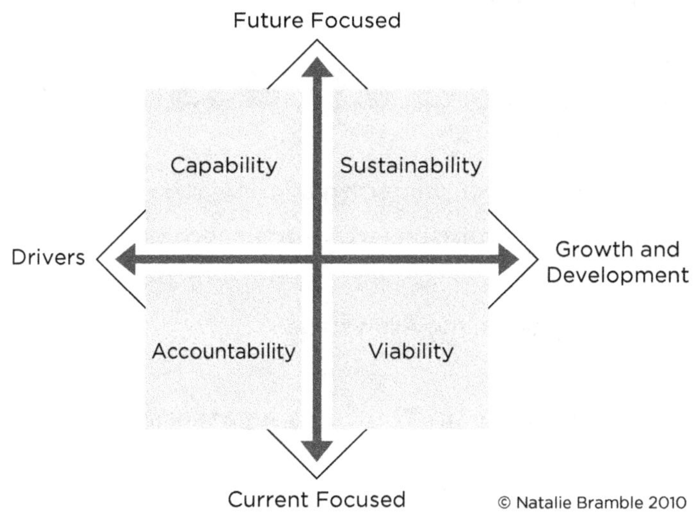

Summary

By understanding how applications are assessed, you should now appreciate how funders think when they mark your application. While you won't always know the assessment criteria for every grant, at least you know what to look for and different ways to approach it. This is where strategy outperforms any AI Assistant.

What can you do now?

To implement the learning from this step you can:

- [ ] Get a past grant application. Look at the guidelines and identify the assessment criteria, or what it could be. Use this to develop an assessment matrix that would be used in level 3. Use this information to identify where the strengths and weaknesses are. What did you learn from this?

Step 3b

Think like an assessor

The previous step got you started on thinking about assessment processes. In this step, let's take that a bit further and put on the assessor's hat so you can think like an assessor. As shown in the following figure, this is the second step in the Align stage.

Stage 3: Align – Step 3b. Think like an assessor

Step 3b. Think like an assessor

3. Align

It's all about the funder's goals.

Practice examples to help you think like an assessor

Now you understand the assessment process, you're going to assess some example answers. Use the grant assessment process outlined in the previous step to judge these answers, particularly the scoring system included in level 2 'Application and project assessment' section. As you go through, also ask yourself which answer you prefer, and why. And then give each answer a score out of five.

Of course, this assessment is difficult because you don't have all the information to check if the answers do align to the funder's requirements; however, as mock answers they provide a good starting point to thinking like an assessor. I've also provided commentary, highlighting key elements from the best example. You'll find some more examples to critique in the online kit, including critiqued examples written by the AI Assistant.

Mock example 1

Here's the first example assessment requirement:

> **Summarise how you will co-contribute to the project**
> **Outline how you plan to raise the funds to contribute matching dollars to the project (30 words)**

And some example answers:

- **Example answer 1a:** We have a plan to raise our income by 25% with key marketing actions, targeting high net worth donors. These milestones are being met and will be achieved by (date). (30 words)
- **Example answer 1b:** Our fundraising strategy highlights opportunities to increase individual giving. Our marketing plan focuses on campaign funding. Donations received to-date, per attached budget, show our 25% contribution is achievable by (date). (30 words)

Which answer did you give the higher score to?

The changes made in the second example demonstrate a proactive fundraising approach. This is important because the grant I've based this on will commit to advancing you a set amount towards an art project as long as you raise your contribution by the deadline.

With the second answer, your funder now understands the following:

- You have a fundraising strategy, indicating you scan your environment and identify opportunities.
- You have goals and are monitoring those goals. You can report on these goals and provide evidence.

- You're being strategic by focusing on a key fundraising donor segment.
- Your donation campaign is delivering the targeted income.

Mock example 2

Now for our second example. The question is:

> **Brief description of the project:**
>
> **Provide a short description of your project. (60 words)**

And the example answers:

- **Example answer 2a:** This project will create training resources to build capability within the 350 Incorporated Associations member committees. A series of short videos, which include interviews with volunteers in their heritage languages and captioned in English, will address the fundamentals of setting up and governing an incorporated association. We will caption these videos in five emerging community languages, including Dari and Tibetan. (60 words)
- **Example answer 2b:** This project builds leadership and best practice governance skills for community leaders. Across 12 local government areas, 350 language schools will access:
    - four in-person workshops (with interpreters)
    - interviews with community leaders sharing experiences and they've successfully used.
    - seven micro-videos to extend learning outcomes (topics include managing and leading an association)
    - videos captioned in five emerging languages. (57 words)

Which answer did you give the higher score to?

The second example uses bullet points to break up what could be a wall of statistics, and highlights the following:

- The project's purpose to develop community leaders, which aligns to the funder's strategy.
- The geographical reach of the schools, which demonstrates to a funder how far the project extends. This indicates value for money across 12 local government areas, which is good for state funding.
- Engagement with existing members, which shows demand and successful implementation.
- The use of interpreters, which justifies their cost in the budget. This also justifies the need for this cost if there's a discussion about a comparable project.

A sidenote: I would use number e.g. 7 rather than the word seven for character restricted answers.

Mock example 3

For this example we're going to look at a compliance question:

> **Licenses, insurance and accreditation.**
> **Describe how you manage and update compliance to maintain documents listed in the last question. (100 words)**

Example answers:

- **Example answer 3a:** We recognise the importance of managing and updating records. We take compliance very seriously and are proud of our record in complying with all requirements listed. We identify everything that needs to be met, including documenting all expiry dates for these and check that they have been reissued when due and update our records. Our compliance manager trains staff to maintain these records and they have never missed one in the last three years. We approve the team to work on projects and double-check these records are updated. Subcontractors provide copies of current records. We have developed comprehensive procedures. (99 words)

- **Example answer 3b:** We have a quality management system that incorporates supplier and contractor due diligence, expiry management, and monitoring registration due dates on the mentioned documents. The compliance manager has developed a robust internal training program to embed these practices across the organisation. Our annual audit demonstrates 100% compliance achieved in the previous three years. Monthly reporting ensures regular monitoring for a proactive and timely approach. The compliance calendar submitted at meetings reduces risks for any non-compliant matters. We validate and approve any updated records internally and with clients across all projects, prior to staff being approved to work on site. (99 words)

What was your score, and why? Let's review these answers.

The first answer has a lot of claims and statements with no clear understanding of how these claims are implemented. The second answer is a lot stronger. It provides the assessor with a clear understanding that systems and policies are in place and the practices are audited to ensure quality and targets are maintained.

Mock example 4

The next assessment requirement has two parts:

> **Project description**
> **Provide a clear description of what the funds will be used for, including how the project is based on evidence that mental health or social and emotional wellbeing will be supported or improved (100 words)**

Two possible answers are as follows:

- **Example answer 4a:** The funds deliver a mental health and well-being program, 'Healthy Minds, Healthy Teams'. The funds will pay for program development, trainers, catering and outcome monitoring.

  "*[The applying organisation]* has a proven track record of delivering annual wellbeing and mental health training for junior and adult players and coaches for the last three years, an initiative of the club as there is no state club training or support. Our workshops consistently show improved mental health and resilience, with a 30% average increase in self-reported well-being scores as demonstrated in our Logic Model. Our series of workshops embed lifelong strategies for positive mental health, wellbeing, and resilience, fostering sustainable outcomes. Educational expert and Metacognitive-Activated learning PhD candidate Anna Ferry will design the stakeholder-informed, evidence-based program and evaluation. (100 words)
- **Example answer 4b:** *[The applicant]* will use the funds to pay for five trainers, venue hire, catering for 20 people per workshop, flyers and program design and evaluation.

  [The applicant] has a responsive approach to increasing wellbeing and mental health, having responded to the lack of specific sports-targeted wellbeing initiatives by establishing their own wellbeing program and appointing a wellbeing officer, paramedic Sam Faraday. Sam has witnessed firsthand the increased incidents because of poor mental health in young people and adults.

  Past program outcomes have achieved positive mental health and wellbeing, with participants recognising trigger signs in self and others to access support. (100 words)

Which answer did you give the higher score to?

Because the question is in two parts, with the second part of the question being the most complex to demonstrate, it's appropriate that the word count is greater for this part of the question.

The first answer in this example is stronger, providing enough details to clearly demonstrate what the funding is being used for. It focuses on the key strengths to the project and having a proven track record with a Logic Model developed. It identifies a lack of other opportunities through a state sports association, which highlights a gap. The answer states that a series of workshops will improve sustainable outcomes, and the final paragraph focuses on demonstrating evidence-based approaches.

Mock example 5

For this example, I've used one organisation to look at how an answer can be improved.

The assessment requirement is as follows:

Demonstrate your agency's capacity to engage Aboriginal families and families from culturally and linguistically diverse backgrounds. (150 words)

- **Example answer 5a:** We have specialist processes to work with local Aboriginal and CALD communities, including developing partners who service and support Aboriginal communities and CALD organisations.

  Our housing and case management policies inform service delivery, which includes provision of culturally specific information. This is readily available and provided at first appointment. Staff undertake mandatory cultural awareness training. We have also developed a Reconciliation Action Plan.

We have a workforce of three locals and partnership arrangements with 13 service providers who support the community.

We have a proven and effective service model. Our space is friendly and a place where women meet to conduct Women's Business, participate in groups, programs and yarn ups, and access information, support and referral. We conduct fortnightly Elders Shopping Trips, in order to better engage with Elder women at risk. We continue to support clients who have exited and returned home via a range of outreach supports. (149 words)

- **Example answer 5b:** SafeHouse Central has proven strategies to engage Aboriginal and CALD people. Our workforce reflects and understands the community, with staff living in the region - one identifies as CALD and two identify as Aboriginal.

  In consultation with local Elders and 13 stakeholder organisations, we co-designed a Reconciliation Action Plan. This plan, as evidenced in attachment, sets and monitors goals specifically designed to enhance engagement. This incorporates actions we undertake to ensure our model of care is community informed and that our team, our policies and practices enable greater engagement. Evidence of actions to date include mandatory cultural awareness training (Aboriginal, CALD and migrant specific), designing culturally appropriate spaces, appropriate team member allocation where able and provision of information in first-language.

  'Women Staying at SafeHouse Central tell me they feel more comfortable and supported, which has increased appointments to access our health clinic.' Genny Almed RN, Town Health Clinic. (147 words)

Let's discuss each answer. First, let's revisit the requirement:

Demonstrate your agency's capacity to engage Aboriginal families and families from culturally and linguistically diverse backgrounds. (150 words)

- **Example 5a:** This is an example of an answer that's gone off track. While the answer can be improved, the focus of the answer is currently on service delivery. The assessment requirement, however, is about engagement, not service delivery. The reason the funder is asking the question is to test if you are able to achieve results through funded services. Funders know organisations that are already engaged with target groups are better able to deliver, rather than those who have none, or limited relationships with the target group. Some interesting elements are included that needed to be expanded on.
- **Example 5b:** While a few statements can be improved, such as 'proven strategies', and what 'engagement' actually means, this answer is better. It demonstrates the following:
  - The workforce reflects the community; this has potential to increase community engagement.
  - The focus is on demonstrating existing stakeholder engagement, such as the 'co-design' of the Reconciliation Action Plan. The stakeholders mentioned indicate broad engagement across these target groups.
  - The agency monitors goals.
  - Their model of care is community informed, indicating engagement and willingness to modify if appropriate to suit community need.
  - They know that policies and practices can create barriers and, although they haven't said how, it appears that they've reviewed them at some point to enable engagement.

- They don't just do the basic mandatory Aboriginal cultural awareness training; they also incorporate CALD and migrant cultural awareness. They have delivered initiatives by providing culturally appropriate space and information in first language.
- Women using the facility appear to feel safe and supported enough to access the health clinic.

Summary

With a better understanding of the assessment process, and a taste of how assessors think, you're more likely to consider your answers more seriously. It's helpful to understand the insights they gain from reading a word or two in your answer and how this assists you.

For simple grants with a page or two of guidelines, you can probably skip the next step and go straight to Stage 4: Write - well, as long as you've gone through the guidelines with The Grant Go/No-Go Decision Checklist in step 2b. For more complex grants, I recommend you continue through this step to dig deeper into the guidelines - because a lot of gold can be hidden in the guidelines.

The next Align step is analysing the application documents and being clear on the items you can draw from in the application pack - the next step shows you how.

What can you do now?

To implement the learning from this step you can:

- ▢ Look for opportunities to sit on grant assessment panels. Local council grants or grants in your industry are good ones to start with.
- ▢ Review answers in previous grant applications and critique them. How would you rework the question, or reframe your words?

Step 3c

Analyse the application documents

The better you understand the funder by spending time at this Align step, the more likely you are to submit a complete and compliant application. As the following figure shows, this next step is about analysing the application documents, using The Grant Application Tool. You'll need to go through every document carefully, review the templates provided and write up your notes as you work through them.

Before you continue, I just want to reinforce that this step and tool is really for more complex grant programs. For simple grants, The Grant Go/No-Go Decision Checklist in step 2b will probably be sufficient for what you need.

Stage 3: Align – Step 3c. Analyse the application documents

3. Align

It's all about the funder's goals.

Step 3c. Analyse the application documents

Tool

viii. The Grant Application Tool™

The Grant Writing System: vii. The Grant Application Tool

This stage involves analysing every word in the guidelines and other documents from the application pack, and making notes on what you need to consider. So many people waste time - either because halfway through the application process they find something they'd missed earlier that makes them ineligible, or because they submit a weak application. As I mentioned in step 2b, over 54% of applicants fail to lodge an application because they ran out of time, didn't meet the criteria or realised it wasn't the right grant.

Completing The Grant Application Tool will help you avoid these mistakes. If you've followed this book since I introduced using The Grant Go/No-Go Decision Checklist (also in step 2b), you'll already have started your notes.

The Grant Application Tool guides you to create a summary of grant information, and your submission checklist. When you transfer information from the guidelines to The Grant Application Tool, it's useful to include document and page references (for example, 'application form, question 6'). This makes it easier if you want to go back to the section later and consider the sentence or paragraph it refers to.

Think about this tool as your 'single source of truth' document. Everything you have in this document comes directly from the application documents. Reduce human error by copying and pasting and include all the key statistics and information. This is the document you go to if you want to fact-check something you've included in your application before you submit it. As a triple-check, you can then go back to the guidelines as referenced and make sure if you need to.

Transferring information from grant documents into another document might feel unnecessary. The benefit is the clear structure to make sense of all the important information, and you're consolidating this information from between three and five documents, into one. Also think about how you learn best. I know I need to be active when taking in information. I need to either copy, paste and categorise, or type out important information for my brain to recall it. Reading alone doesn't work for me.

Being more active when retaining information helps your brain remember it when you're writing. Also, because you've gone through each document line by line, you won't miss anything. If you forget to address or attach something, rarely will this be followed up by the grant assessors. You won't be asked for this information and, more than likely, you'll receive a zero score for not meeting requirements. Even if the information isn't mandatory, your score will be negatively impacted. And a lower score can prevent you from receiving an offer.

Keep checking updated documents

A lot of grant programs encourage questions during the application timeline. They accept these questions and then release answers to them as part of their 'FAQs'. So you need to make sure you sign up to receive these and check them when they're released to see if anything else has been clarified or added you need to consider. This tip has been useful over my career.

Last year, for example, I prepared a grant application for a school. I went through the guidelines and made notes based on The Grant Go/No-Go Decision Checklist. I then checked the FAQs on the funder's website. There it said applications with an attached project plan would be assessed more favourably than those without. This little piece of information was not mentioned anywhere in the guidelines and the online application form did not require a project plan to be uploaded before it was accepted. So, no guessing what I provided when I submitted the application – a project plan, of course! This is likely not the only reason the application won, but everything helps!

That's why attention to detail is such an important skill in grant writing.

Remember - guidelines are goldmines

I know you're excited - you want to start working on the application form to get the money! Maybe you don't have a lot of time and feel pressure to start writing as soon as possible. But please don't give into temptation and start answering the questions. You'll likely miss some vital information that is required or can assist.

Reviewing grant guidelines and documents is a skill. I call it 'putting the strategy hat on'. It's about reviewing the information with purpose. You'll better understand what the funder's asking - even in lengthy multi-part questions

The first thing to understand about guidelines is these documents have been carefully crafted; they have been discussed at length and compiled by the grant program managers, their bosses, and sometimes the board members and subject matter experts. Each word has been used deliberately, and the level of information they include has been provided for a reason.

Understanding the reasons for all of this can be hard when you haven't been involved or overheard their discussions. Oh, to be a fly on the wall in those meetings! Well, I'm not going to be able to turn you into a mind-reader; however, I have been in those rooms participating in and guiding the process. I'm going to guide you as you learn how to analyse and understand these guidelines.

A common mistake is to think guidelines are flexible. Despite them being called 'guidelines', I want you to think about them as RULES to follow. Sometimes we can skim over something important and not think much of it, and later find out that's why we didn't Win the Grant! I was talking with a volunteer the other day who applied for a grant thinking their organisation was eligible. However, they received a letter saying the guidelines stated they must be registered on the Australian Charities and Not-for-profits Commission (ACNC) Register. Thinking back, they recalled this requirement being in the guidelines. At the time, however, they weren't sure what it meant and skipped over it. Unfortunately, it meant the group didn't Win the Grant.

I go through a few steps when I analyse guidelines. I like to type things up using the template outlined in this step. Now, as you go through this template, ideally you should assess every sentence in the guidelines and ask where it fits in this list.

If you've gone through The Grant Go/No-Go Decision Checklist from step 2b, you've probably already taken some notes. This is your opportunity to increase your strategic approach and work out what's important to the funder and what you need to share in your application. In the next stage, I take you through how to pull out these elements into The Grant Answer Map and start writing.

Overview

The overview table from The Grant Application Tool is a good one-pager to print out and keep on your wall, whiteboard or desk. It keeps the important information front and centre and acts as a prompt and motivator to stay on track.

The one-pager includes relevant information you'll need to access quickly, including closing time and date and the value of the grant. Once you've reviewed the requirements, consider the resources and time needed to meet the application deadline. The following figure shows an example of the tasks and estimated times needed to complete the grant application. You can add or change tasks as needed, using the time estimates provided as an example only. Be sure to plan for a finish date 24 to 48 hours before the grant close date and time. Something always comes up and this gives you a time buffer.

Example overview table, including time estimates

<table>
<tr><td colspan="2">Grant name</td><td rowspan="2">Closing date and time</td><td rowspan="2">Enter closing date and time.
*Watch for time zones. The funder may be in a different time zone. If so, include both time zones here</td></tr>
<tr><td colspan="2">Enter grant name</td></tr>
<tr><td colspan="2">Instructions on asking questions:</td><td rowspan="2">Value of grant</td><td rowspan="2">Enter estimated or actual $ you expect to be able to apply for
Budget to be (including / Ex.) GST
(delete what doesn't apply)</td></tr>
<tr><td colspan="2">e.g., send to this email and/or call this person with details.</td></tr>
<tr><td>Enter funder / program manager contact details</td><td>Enter Partner / Supplier / Contractor details</td><td>Enter Partner / Supplier / Contractor details</td><td>Enter Partner / Supplier / Contractor details</td></tr>
<tr><td>Enter your team / project manager contact details</td><td>Enter Partner / Supplier / Contractor details</td><td>Enter Partner / Supplier / Contractor details</td><td>Enter Partner / Supplier / Contractor details</td></tr>
<tr><td colspan="4">Writing and submission timeline</td></tr>
<tr><td>Item</td><td>Date</td><td>Who</td><td>Estimate time</td></tr>
<tr><td>Research funder</td><td></td><td></td><td>Estimate 3 hours</td></tr>
<tr><td>Complete The Grant Answer Map™ for each question. Develop rough first draft</td><td></td><td></td><td>Estimate 2 hours per question</td></tr>
<tr><td>Time for additional research / evidence / consultation</td><td></td><td></td><td>Estimate 5 hours</td></tr>
<tr><td>Finalise questions</td><td></td><td></td><td>Estimate 1 hour ea.</td></tr>
<tr><td>Finalise budget</td><td></td><td></td><td>Estimate 5 hours</td></tr>
<tr><td>Finalise attachments</td><td></td><td></td><td>Estimate 3 hours</td></tr>
<tr><td>Final review and edit</td><td></td><td></td><td>Estimate 4 hours</td></tr>
<tr><td>Submit</td><td></td><td></td><td>*24 to 48 hrs prior to close</td></tr>
<tr><td>Funder's website</td><td colspan="3">Enter link here for easy reference</td></tr>
<tr><td>Guidelines</td><td colspan="3">Enter link here for easy reference</td></tr>
<tr><td>Application form</td><td colspan="3">Enter link here for easy reference</td></tr>
</table>

Knowing what to include in your application

After the overview page, The Grant Application Tool next includes space for more specific elements. In the following sections, I take you through each of these elements, starting with the assessors.

Who are the assessors?

As shown in the following figure, the template includes space to document who the assessors are and how this might influence the 'voice' you use in your answers.

Thinking about the assessors and appropriate voice

Assessors	
Who are they / do you think you're talking to	**What 'voice' is appropriate?**

Understanding who you're talking to is important. Your application is going to be assessed by people during an assessment process. Chances are, up to three people will assess your application and another two to three will make the final decision.

Analysing the right 'voice' is about you identifying the kind of language you should use in your application and the tone you reflect. For example, is it academic, professional or a general, semi-casual tone? What cultural language or schooling level would you expect assessors to have? It helps you think about the assessor, and modify your language, style and tone as needed.

This also helps you to reflect on the language the funders use.

For example, a technically focused application is full of logic, evidence and statistics, but where's the passion, emotion and connection to the people you're supporting? Some assessors love logic, but others want the connection. Likewise, if the application is full of emotion but lacks the facts, it's only connecting with those assessors who are sold on the story.

Let's go over an example project title, presented in different ways. This was for a language school association with over 26 multicultural groups. The funder was a government multicultural agency. Here's a potential title for the project:

Online training for committee members in community language schools

This is a good explanatory title and would work perfectly if the application was for a local government grant, or the assessors were peers from the language school program. But it doesn't speak to multicultural government department staff who have strategic objectives to meet.

A more detailed analysis of the strategic plan and guidelines highlighted that the funder wanted us to talk about building capacity, collaborations and governance. So, we changed our original title as follows to include these aspects:

Building capacity for greater governance and collaborative leadership in the *[state]* Community Languages Schools Program (CLSP)

However, we also needed to think about who the assessors might be. There would be staff, of course, and perhaps consultants. Community members were also likely to be involved. We reflected on what the project delivered. After considering all these elements, we amended the final project title as follows:

Online training for greater governance and collaborative leadership in the *[state]* Community Languages Schools Program (CLSP)

This example demonstrates how important it is to identify who the assessors might be and the voice and tone you should use.

Objectives, scope and requirements

The next part of the template looks at objectives, scope and requirements from the guidelines and application documents.

Funder's objectives and how you plan to meet them

Objectives, scope and requirements	
What they are	How you plan to meet them

Essentially, you should put each point on a separate line – for example, 'Creating jobs' – and then copy and paste the relevant wording from the guidelines. This can be useful to reflect on and refer to later in your answer. Also make a note on how you'll meet this objective – for example, 'Project creates 2 × 25-hr jobs'.

Be clear on the number of objectives you need to meet.

Another tip is to break complex statements up. For example, a community grant stated their objective was to fund 'community-led, local projects that connect individuals and communities to improve mental health and wellbeing'. List each of these objectives separately and make notes against each stating how you'll demonstrate their achievement.

The separate objectives are:

- community led
- local project
- connect individuals
- connect communities
- improve mental health
- improve wellbeing.

Outcomes

Next, list the outcomes – based on what the funders want to achieve and how you can assist them (see following figure).

Listing outcomes based on what funders want to achieve

Outcomes expected	
What do they want to achieve?	**How can you help them?**

This is a similar approach to listing funder's objectives. List the outcomes the funder wants to achieve, remembering to break up more complex outcomes, similar to the example in the previous section. Then, for each outcome, list how you assist the funder to achieve it.

At this point, it's useful to reflect critically on your project. Go back to The Grant Project Plan and Logic Model (refer to step 1c). Are you missing any outcomes? Is it appropriate to integrate these in your project?

If you want to change your project to meet funding guidelines, do it intentionally and carefully. It has to be an authentic integration, not just an add-on.

Priorities

Next note down any identified priority areas and how your project aligns with these (see following figure).

How your project aligns to the funder's priority areas

Priorities	
Do they have any identified priority areas	**How do you align to this?**

This section is particularly important with targeted funding rounds identifying more than one priority area. If the funder does list priorities in order of importance, you should work out how you align to those priorities higher in the list. Sometimes instead of needing to submit an answer you'll just find a tick box and it builds a stronger answer to reiterate alignment of what you ticked, elsewhere in your application.

If the funder doesn't list their priorities, you may not need to make any notes in this section. However, think about this a bit more deeply before moving on. The funder probably still has priorities, and you may be able to make an educated guess after you research them. Check the TagCrowd results of main terms (refer to step 2b). Do any words stand out that could indicate a priority area, such as 'supporting young children' or 'to support flood affected areas'?

Key messages

Next consider key messages and, again, how your project aligns with them.

Key messages

Key messages	
What messages are strong?	**How do you align to this?**

You can identify a funder's key message in a few ways. Sometimes you can sense a recurring 'theme' from the guidelines or application form. For example, one funder only asked governance and accountability questions, and clearly needed to validate that applying organisations had sound governance and operational policies, practices and compliance in place. In this case, you would identify this theme and those messages, and consider why they're important and how you can address them.

Again, TagCrowd results will demonstrate the key words that are repeated consistently. For example, 'measuring' might be one. Go back to the guidelines and get a sense for why this word is repeated so often. What do you think the funder is trying to tell you?

The other tip is to scan for any words in a different format – for example, in bold or italic. **As an example, the guidelines for one of the Australia Post Community Grants highlighted the following (bolding as per original):**

- The project will **help people meaningfully connect** in their local community for improved mental health and mental wellbeing outcomes.

- The project is a **locally led and locally delivered** project that aims to improve mental health and mental wellbeing outcomes of a community.

I hold regular online grant writing Q&A sessions and we talked about this emphasis when the grant was announced. One attendee asked me what 'meaningfully connect' means. I told them, whatever their project was, the way it was delivered would have to be meaningful to the people being involved. And to know what is meaningful to them, you would need to ask them, and they should therefore be involved in the co-design of the project. For example, if the project is a workshop for traditional owners, they may prefer to hold the event on Country, in a space that has meaning to them, rather than in a community hall.

When funders emphasise certain areas using bold or italics, you may find a question related to this area in the application form. If you don't, check the questions in the grant application and find where you can include information to demonstrate relevant information. (I explore writing your answers in much more detail in the next stage.)

Another way you can dig deeper is to find a copy of the last grant application form and compare it to the current one. Now, this only works if nothing has changed in the guidelines and the funder's focus hasn't shifted significantly. So, for example, if it's a multi-year program with the same objectives, outcomes and priorities as the last round, looking at the previous form can provide useful information. But if you notice a change of focus - for example, from youth to families - then this tip is less relevant.

When comparing past and current forms, look for differences in the questions and level of detail required. For example, they may have changed a question from requesting a summary to asking for a detailed answer. From the way the question is now asked, you may sense an increased focus on monitoring and evaluation. They may mention outcomes, where before they were talking about success measures. All these changes indicate tweaks to what is considered most important, and this increases your understanding of how you can maximise points at the decision table.

Assessment criteria

Now you can look at the assessment criteria your project will be evaluated on, to maximise your points (see following figure).

Noting assessment criteria to maximise points

Assessment criteria	
What will they evaluate us on?	How can you maximise points?

I covered identifying the assessment criteria and any weightings in the guidelines, if they're shared, in step 3a.

At this stage, also start to identify opportunities to strengthen your submission and maximise points. One example is an application for a local council grant that allowed additional supporting material. If you were preparing an application for a music festival, including an event management plan would be a good way to strengthen your competitive position and maximise points. Reinforce your capacity to deliver by providing a risk management plan. You can include engagement strategies or marketing plans relevant to the activity you're delivering. You'll find other ways to maximise points as you start writing and work through the guidelines. What's important to think about at this step is what you might be able to gather together in preparation.

Compliance requirements

You need to list any mandatory compliance requirements and how you will meet them (see the following figure).

Compliance requirements and your ability to meet them

Compliance requirements	
What are the mandatory compliance requirements?	**How do you meet these / prove you meet these?**

In the grant application pack, you'll likely find a range of items you'll be asked to comply with - everything from insurance to providing copies of financial documents. Sometimes these documents take time to gather or get from someone else. If you list any requirements here and at this stage, you can prepare in advance and save time later.

I was talking with a friend the other day who is the bookkeeper for a not-for-profit. Tracy said she was frustrated when she arrived at work and 'out of the blue' another staff member asked her to provide a significant number of documents for a grant, immediately. The grant was due that afternoon. She had other urgent work to do that she had to put aside, and the lack of notice increased her workload and stress.

The other challenge in this sort of situation is, if gathering this kind of information is rushed, you don't have time to assess it and tailor it. So, completing this template is not only about preparation. It also means your team will get notified in advance, giving you all time to analyse the information.

Strategies, policies, standards and frameworks

Next, note down relevant plans and how your project meets or aligns with them (see following figure).

Relevant frameworks and your ability to align

Strategies, policies, standards and frameworks	
What relevant industry or funder plans are important / apply	**How do you meet these / prove you meet these?**

We covered these plans in The Grant Project Plan, focused on your project. This approach expands this to focus on the specific funder you've identified and their plans. Put simply, you should understand the money trail. The funder's strategy is the logical motivation for giving; it's the process that surrounds the program and how the funder feels the grant will achieve the impact they wish to make. If you don't put the time in and do this work, you're at a high risk of missing out because your application wasn't aligned to the strategic purpose.

For individual funders, their granting strategy is generally connected to their values or an experience they've had. They can be a bit more flexible in terms of compliance, and emotive impact pitches and user stories connect with these funders.

Organisations offering funding have specific strategic outcomes they want to achieve, and these have performance indicators and reporting requirements. They've gone through a whole process to determine the approach they'll take. They've invested a lot of energy, reviewing how they communicate and assess applications. They need to do their best to ask the right questions, so they get the right information they need.

Businesses and corporates may have marketing, strategic planning or Corporate Social Responsibility goals they want to achieve. There are layers of approval processes to understand.

Philanthropists review communities and issues holistically. Their funding is often driven by their theory of change or an identified gap. Often philanthropic organisations, by nature of their financing flexibility, are the 'first-responders' on community-based issues. They then establish the evidence base to influence government to make policy and funding changes.

Finally, for government bodies, the process is guided by a strategy and/or funding policy document. For example, the Commonwealth government has 'grant-connected policies'. These are policies that have identified grants as a pathway for achieving the outcomes. The money comes from Treasury, which is one reason 'value for money' is usually a key assessment criteria.

Other strategies, frameworks and policies to identify are those mentioned in the guidelines, or policies that are standard in the funder's procurement or contracting processes. For example, the procurement policies may prohibit contracting organisations that don't have policies addressing modern slavery, inclusion or environmental sustainability. This means a funder can only provide grants to organisations that meet their internal policies – if you can't, or won't, comply with these, you won't receive funding. You'll see this noted in the guidelines if it's required. If you're successful, there may also be additional requirements asked at contract signing stage.

I've had a few projects where we've had to bring some creativity into the process and strengthen our position. One of these was the funding request for airport infrastructure I mention in step 1c. This project required a strong business case because, unlike other projects from other communities, it wasn't strong on all the criteria.

So I researched every relevant local, regional, state and federal policy and identified the policy objectives met by this funding.

Now, some funding agencies act alone, but this funding came from transport and tourism bodies, so demonstrating how the project aligned to various department policies was key. Transport policy included aspects such as funding strategies for ageing infrastructure and public transport. I delivered a four-and-a-half-page document in the business case showing how the project helped the state department meet other agency policies. This was certainly not the reason the funding was secured (I also covered many other aspects in the submission); however, it did build a strong, competitive business case.

Statistics and stories

As you review all your documents, you'll find hints on the types of statistics and stories you'll need to support your application. Make a note of these and where you found the information in this section of the template (see following figure).

Noting possible statistics and stories, and their source

Statistics and stories		
Theme / topic	**Key statistic / story**	**Reference / notes**
e.g., Industry, state disability statistics; stories of change etc.	The key statement or statistic from that source.	Where the source is, link etc. for future reference.

You'll need to undertake research relevant for the funders, their objectives and the grant program. You likely also have statistics and stories in The Grant Ready Kit (refer to step 1a). For example, the topic could be 'Disability – national versus local statistics'. The second column could then include the statistic '1 in 6 (18%) Australians have a disability'. Our community strategic plan shows a higher-than-average proportion of disability faced by 22% of residents.' Then in the last column, you could reference the relevant source, departments and links.

This will become your 'single source of truth' document. When you're writing your application, you can use this to check you're using the right statistics. This will save you making mistakes and contradicting yourself.

Actions and follow-up research

As shown in the following figure, the final rows in The Grant Application Tool are for you to take notes on actions and follow-up research. These are useful to plan and budget, and use as a final checklist before you hit submit.

Noting final actions and follow-up research

Actions, follow-up / research		
Questions to ask	**List of tasks to do**	**Research to do**
Questions that come to mind as you read the documents, that you need to find the answer to, or ask.	Above you listed things you need to do to address needs / gaps. These are other things that come up as you read the tender document.	e.g., their policies; their values etc.
Things to cost in	**Our documents you need to check / read / review**	**Documents to attach**
Note down any costings that come to mind as you read the documents.	Note down any internal documents you need to check or read.	List of documents you need to attach as evidence etc. to support your application.

The six headings in this section are:

1. *Questions to ask:* As you review the documents, note down any questions you need to ask about. For example, you might note something you need to ask the funder or a project partner.
2. *List of tasks to do:* Critically assess what you've learnt and work out what you need to do. You might need to get copies of a particular document, for example.
3. *Research to do:* You can make a list of any additional research on statistics, economic impact or the funder's policies or outcomes framework.
4. *Things to cost in:* Note down things you think of or come across in the documents – such as who's paying for the acquittal if it's required. These notes will be useful when you're developing your budget.
5. *Documents to check/read/review:* Examples might be the funder has referenced working with children is an area they want you to comply with. Now is the time to check your team have up-to-date clear checks.
6. *Documents to attach:* Keep a list of the documents you need to attach. Check the funder's requirements for this and the considerations for attachments. (I discuss attachments more in step 4c.)

Before you ask the funder a question, carefully review the guidelines. In one grant program I followed, the funder answered nine different questions with a copy and paste answer from the guidelines. No new information was provided – it was all in the guidelines. Can you imagine being asked nine times to answer something you've already said? I know from conversations I've had with funders they do get frustrated. One funder had a list in their office they were adding to as the grant round progressed called 'My pet peeves' and it was full of basic questions such as 'How much money is there?'

When asking a question of the funder, show a base of knowledge about them. For example, instead of asking, 'Can I do this?', you'd say, 'Referring to guideline 3.4, *x* is stated. I understand this means *abc*. Can I confirm if this includes *xyz*?'

Keep in mind that this is often an open question and answer process, which means any question you submit will be reviewed by your competitors - so check you aren't giving away too much information.

Summary

Now you've used The Grant Application Tool, you should have a deeper understanding of the grant requirements. Hopefully you've done this as soon as you've identified a grant and you've now got time to research answers before writing a strong application. You'll see in the next stage how information from this step will be referenced in your answers.

What can you do now?

- [ ] Search for a grant application that you or someone else in your organisation has completed before. Make sure you have the relevant guidelines for the grant that was applied for.
- [ ] Use The Grant Application Tool to identify those key areas. Now consider your answers - what would you change or improve, knowing what you do now? Make a list of improvements.
- [ ] Check the other application documents, including the application form, sample contracts and addendum. Sometimes different information is included in these documents that can assist you. For example, the application form may have areas to upload documents that haven't been requested in the guidelines.

Summary of Stage 3: Align

Now you understand how you should analyse the key documents in your application kit using The Grant Application Tool. While I might take short cuts in some areas in some application processes, this is one step I always check and, for complex programs, complete.

As you get more familiar with the process, you could create a draft template by simply cutting and pasting statements from the guidelines. When you've addressed a specific point, you can delete it from the template, or keep it in the document but highlight it as complete in some way. My trick is to change the text colour to light grey to identify the task is done. (I like keeping the text in the template so I can go back at any time and check the language and what I've done.)

Doing this work to better understand the funder is worth it. It's clear to program managers when they receive an application aligned to their guidelines and priorities that meets their expectations – versus those applications that have missed these critical points.

When you put a grant application form in, you're putting your hand up to say you can deliver to the funder's requirements, be it outcomes or compliance. So, you should know what you're fully committing to, why you're doing it and the consequences that come with the agreement.

Understanding this is going to assist you to write a stronger application because it'll be evident to the assessor and program manager when they review the depth and key points you've covered in your answers.

You now have a greater understanding of what the commitments are, the promises you need to make when fulfilling the grant requirements and the cost of your involvement. This will support your decision to go ahead with an application, or not. If you decide to go ahead, you can use this process to compare where your promises have fallen short of the funder's expectations, identifying areas you can strengthen in your application.

Stage 4: Write

The Grant Writing System™

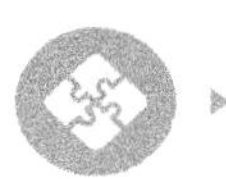
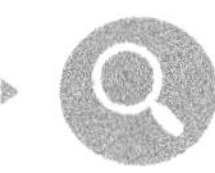

1. Plan 2. Find 3. Align **4. Write** 5. Submit 6. Manage 7. Report

Write a strong application

You've done all the hard work and now it's time to finally start writing. You're up to the fourth stage in The Grant Writing Cycle - Write (see the following figure).

Write: Stage 4 in The Grant Writing System

Write a strong application

4. Write

Communicate clearly and strategically

Steps in this stage

a. Understand the question.
b. Communicate strategically.
c. Refine your answer

Tools to guide you

ix. The Grant Answer Map™

Winning grants isn't about writing skills. Sure, a clear structure and a good edit will assist, but it's not grammar and spelling that wins the grant. It's about the content you put into your answers based on strategic approaches we have covered so far through The Grant Writing System.

The steps in this stage guide you through The Grant Answer Map so you analyse the question and plan, bringing strategy in to write a strong answer. I then discuss how to bring your answer together, with structure and formatting to communicate your evidence. I run through some common questions and how to approach them and provide information on budgets and attachments. Along the way, you'll find examples to demonstrate these points. Again, as you go through these chapters, always remember:

> *Grants are 80% strategy and 20% writing.*

Now I want to pause here. If you've jumped straight to this step, wanting all the gold because you think grant writing is about writing, please stop. Yes, you'll pick up information to build a strong answer; however, you'll be missing a lot of the information I've shared in earlier steps - in particular, step 1c, where you'll find The Grant Project Plan, step 2b where you can find strategic ways to improve your chances using The Grant Go/No-Go Decision Tool, and step 3c, where you can review your project alignment to the funder using The Grant Application Tool. Also, the examples in step 3b help you understand how assessors think when they're reading answers.

If you have gone through those steps, you'll now experience how the work we've done previously comes together to start writing your answer.

The Grant Writing System: ix. The Grant Answer Map

The Grant Answer Map involves three elements. Firstly, you need to analyse each question to understand what the question is asking (step 4a). Second, you need to include crucial elements from the grant guidelines and other strategic elements (step 4b). And, finally, you put it all together in a strong answer (step 4c).

The following figure shows The Grant Answer Map I explore in these steps.

The Grant Answer Map

What they've asked for	**Character, word or page limit**	**Your answer should include**
Strategic points to include from The Grant Application Tool: objectives, scope and requirements; outcomes; priorities; key messages; assessment criteria; compliance requirements; strategies, policies, standards and frameworks		
What stories can you tell, so the funder understands the key points you want them to hear?		
What statistics address the question, and support your information?		

The first four rows are a simple version of The Grant Answer Map (step 4a). This is the minimum you should be using to answer application questions. The last three rows is an advanced approach that brings the power of strategy to your application. We will be reviewing the simple and the advanced version in this stage.

Step 4a

Understand the question

It's time to work out what content you need to respond to the question, as shown in the following figure.

Stage 4: Write – Step 4a. Understand the question

4. Write

Communicate clearly and strategically.

Step 4a. Understand the question

Tool

ix. The Grant Answer Map™

In this step, I introduce The Grant Answer Map, and how you can use it to 'map' the information you'll include. I often call this first phase a 'brain-dump' because we're bringing together everything we've learnt about the funder, the program and our project.

First, however, let's run through some of the common mistakes people make when answering grant application questions so you can understand how this process helps you avoid them!

Avoiding common errors

I've been on so many panels, led panels of judges and had conversations with other assessors, and one of the common frustrations they all have is applications that don't address the questions. Too many times we have to say or write, 'They haven't addressed the question.'

In too many cases, people go off track. They start addressing the question or give us some background information and, suddenly, they go off on a different tangent completely. The other mistake is they have information they want to tell the funder, and what was background information has now turned into two-thirds of their word count. This is such a waste because none of it directly addresses what the question is asking.

Assessors can identify the gold in your proposed project, and we value the commitment and passion you all bring, but we simply can't support a submission that doesn't give us the required information the questions ask for. To be honest, being an assessor and having to say no to a project can be a bit soul crushing. One of the reasons we sit on panels is we want to give back to our businesses and communities.

I kept being asked in workshops, 'Why do assessors say no?' or 'What are the reasons I didn't Win the Grant?' In the assessment stage where you receive points for your answers, assessors generally say things like:

> Applicants did not demonstrate need, including evidence it exits. They did not consult with stakeholders. The application lacked detail and evidence of the organisation's ability to deliver the project.
>
> Grant Assessor's Feedback

So, my answer to these kinds of questions is simple: You didn't give the assessor the content they need to say YES!

Funders are trying their best to support you within the constraints they have and we all understand that when they can't give you detailed feedback on your application, it's difficult to know where you can improve. So, in the following list, I outline the common mistakes that appear on 90% of the feedback I give on weak and unsuccessful applications. As a chair of assessment panels, I also read feedback from other assessors and it's consistent across the board.

Put simply, the seven common mistakes people are making in their application forms are:

1. Not knowing how to address the question because they haven't critically analysed it.
2. Not addressing all parts of the question, and therefore losing points. Often questions are only partly answered and if an applicant has done this in one question, it's highly likely to be a common mistake made across the whole application. This reduces the number of points received overall.
3. Going off on a completely different tangent with background information or completely irrelevant details.
4. Thinking the question is being repeated and either writing 'I've answered this already' or repeating the previous answer almost word for word. Don't do this! Even if it is the exact word-for-word question repeated in the application form, it still requires a different answer!
5. Not providing enough information, or providing far more detail than what's asked for. (This then connects with the next mistake.)
6. Not allocating the character, word or page count strategically. This means the answers they've started with first often have a lot of information, while the ones they've left till last clearly show where they ran out of steam because they don't provide enough detail. I've seen one-line answers in the last few questions in some applications.
7. Failing to use your answers to show how strongly you align to the grant guidelines.

In this and the following steps, I guide you to solve all of these problems.

Analyse the question

The three types of questions you'll find in grant applications are as follows:

1. questions asking for information about your organisation
2. questions relating to compliance and due diligence
3. questions you need to develop written answers for.

The first two types are straightforward. Often, you just need to cut and paste information in – organisation address, contact details and insurance information, for example. The third type of question is the one we'll be focusing on in this step.

To answer this type of question, you first need to analyse it. You need to:

1. break the question up
2. identify the subject
3. understand the action you need to take
4. allocate character, word or page limits.

You then use the first two columns in the top half of The Grant Answer Map to document this.

Top half of The Grant Answer Map

What they've asked for	Character, word or page limit	Your answer should include

Break the question up

First, break the question up. Breaking the question up means you won't miss answering any part of the question – and, simply by answering the question, you're already going to be beating a number of other people and getting more points!

I was delivering some training for an arts organisation, and training a new staff member, Frieda. I was sharing tips and strategies to support her to understand the grant writing process and how Frieda could apply existing skills. I asked for some past grant applications from this organisation that we could use to critique and make the training relevant for the role Frieda was doing. The regional arts development officer at the organisation said, 'I've got one I want feedback on. It was for such a valuable project – teaching artists how to run a business. It should have been funded and wasn't. I want to know why.'

As soon as Frieda and I started assessing the application, I could see what one of the key problems was, just by skimming the answers of the first four questions. They only answered part of the question being asked. For example, the first question had four parts, with a two-page limit. The answer only addressed one part of the question – over two pages. And the question would have been an eight- or a 10-point question. The most that the assessor could have awarded the answer provided would have been one-quarter of the marks allocated. Only perhaps two out of 10 or, at the most, maybe three!

Your job as writer is to get up into the top 10 to 15% of applications discussed in the final strategic review. To do this, your scores must be as high as possible. The main way to achieve this is to address the question, and every part of the question.

Sure, applications can make it through this process if the assessor is emotive about it, has a bias towards the project and advocates for it. However, the final discussion with other assessors, or marking the application on the decision matrix, would identify many gaps, preventing the funding decision being a yes.

Even if the arts business training application scored well and was short-listed because an assessor connected with the project, it would have been knocked out of the competition when compared to other applications. I highly doubt it even got to the discussion table, and if it did the many gaps in the application would have been identified.

Such a shame.

Okay, so how do you break a question down? It's simple – just identify the use of full stops, semicolons, commas, the word 'and', or dot points. I'm going to show you how this applies across three example questions – from a simple, straightforward one, to questions with multiple parts, through to a complex question. I use the 'need' part of a grant application as an example because it's the one question that's common and has been asked in 98% of applications I've responded to, assessed or written.

Let's review a simple, straightforward question:

How did you identify the need?

Now this question doesn't have any additional parts to it. It's a simple one-part question – YAY! These questions are wonderfully straightforward and easy to understand.

The next question appears to be simple but has multiple parts:

Describe your organisation's vision, goals and achievements in 500 words or less.

So, to break the question up and identify its multiple parts, ask what the funder has asked for. You've been asked to describe your organisation's:

- vision
- goals
- achievements.

The following figure shows how it looks when transferred into The Grant Answer Map.

Transferring the broken up question into The Grant Answer Map

What they've asked for	Word limit (500)	Your answer should include
Describe vision		
Describe goals		
Describe achievements		

Use this process with all questions in your application form. You'll use the first column in the first part of The Grant Answer Map to list each of the points mentioned in a new line.

Here's another multi-part question example:

Please explain how your organisation has the appropriate skills and expertise to deliver the project, including prior experience delivering similar project activities and outcomes. (500 words)

This question has many parts. For these types of questions, I firstly break the question up in to subheadings covering what the funder has asked for.

In this example, the funder has asked you to explain how your organisation has:

- the appropriate skills for the project
- the required expertise to deliver the project
- prior experience delivering similar project activities
- prior experience delivering similar project outcomes.

Again, here's how it looks when transferred into The Grant Answer Map.

Transferring a question with many parts into The Grant Answer Map

What they've asked for	Word limit (500)	Your answer should include
the appropriate skills for the project		
the required expertise to deliver the project		
prior experience delivering similar project activities		
prior experience delivering similar project outcomes		

The following example is another complex question, with question hints:

> **Clearly state the need you will address and, if relevant, the particular communities/region(s) or target group that you will work in/with. What gap will you be filling? How do you know that this is a gap? Demonstrate evidence of this need. (500 words)**

The funder has asked you to clearly state:

- the need you will address
- the particular communities/region(s) you will work in/with (if relevant)
- the target group that you will work in/with
- the gap you will be filling
- how you know this is a gap
- evidence of this need, and to demonstrate this evidence.

The following figure shows how this questions looks when transferred into The Grant Answer Map.

Transferring a complex question into The Grant Answer Map

What they've asked for	Word limit (500)	Your answer should include
the need you will address		
the particular communites / region(s) you will work win / with (if relevant)		
the target group that you will work in / with		
the gap you will be filling		
how you know this is a gap		
demonstrate evidence of this need		

Identify the subject

In this part, you need to define what subject the question is focusing on. This is key to preventing you from making the mistake of going off track in your answer.

One important note to make here is there can be different subjects in the question. When reviewing the following example, I bolded the focus of each part of the question. This assists when you address the question because you're focusing on the key subject to communicate.

Let's go through the third example question from the last section. **In this question, the funder has asked you to 'Explain how your organisation has:**

- the **appropriate skills** for the project
- the required **expertise to deliver** the project
- **prior experience** delivering **similar** project **activities**
- **prior experience** delivering **similar** project **outcomes**.

This is a good example because you can now understand how the question has different subjects. In the first part of the question, you're being asked about your appropriate skills and expertise, so your focus here is on your organisation's and team's current capacity. But the second part of the question is asking about your prior experience with these activities and outcomes. The difference in subject focus is slight, but important.

For a more obvious subject focus change in the question, let's review the fourth example question from the previous section. Here's the question again:

> **Clearly state the need you will address and, if relevant, the particular communities/region(s) or target group that you will work in/with. What gap will you be filling? How do you know that this is a gap? Demonstrate evidence of this need.**

This question has two clearly distinct subjects. It's asking about the need in the first part of the question, while the last sentence is asking you to demonstrate evidence of the need. The two middle sentences, though, are focused on the gap and how you know there is one. These are two different things. Many of us can demonstrate and evidence need by now, but having to demonstrate the gap and evidence the gap exists is a different subject focus. **An example of what I mean would be as follows:**

- A need is the local community has demonstrated a need for a First Nations traditional healing and medicine health service.
- A gap is undertaking a competitive analysis or a systems mapping exercise, demonstrating no such service is available, or no accessible or culturally appropriate health service is offering these services for the community.

I've assessed so many applications that miss identifying when the question is asking for more than one thing. This reduces their scores and weakens their competitiveness.

Understand the action words

You might call them verbs, but to keep it simple so people don't have to stress about what verbs and nouns are, I call them action words. These are the words usually at the start of each part of the question. They give you instruction on what level of information funders want you to include.

For example, action words such as 'demonstrate', 'describe', 'summarise' and 'outline' tell you how much information you're expected to provide. Some questions have two parts with two action words – for example, '*Outline* the need for the project and *describe* how the need was identified.' The two parts to the question can be identified by the two action words. They each require different information, and the level of information you must provide also differs.

This is important because if you are asked to provide detail but you only provide a summary, it limits how many points the assessor can give you. Remember - they're assessing a lot of other applications. They have a good idea of what a strong answer is, versus a weak one. And even if you make it past the level 2 assessment stage to the final strategic review, your application will be weak when compared against the other short-listed applications.

Here are some examples of action words used in grant questions, and the level of detail they require:

- A **'How'** question is a process question, so a question that starts with 'How' means assessors are expecting to see an answer that shows a process or the steps. For example, how did you identify the need? From your answer, the assessor expects to fully understand the process you went through or what happened that led you to saying, 'This is a need, and we have to address it.' The need could have been identified through community consultation, a client survey or repeat offending because no education pathway existed, but this needs to be clear in your answer.
- When the funder asks you to **'Explain'**, you need to tell them how things work, or how they came to be the way they are. It's a bit like having to justify something to someone. You need to walk them through the sequence of events and the thinking behind your approach.
- When **'What'** is used, you're being asked a descriptor. An example might be, 'What will you do to address the need?' When answering a 'What' question, you need to provide enough information so the person can understand it. Funders need to be able to paint a visual picture or diagram in their head. Use descriptive words and storytelling here. One final point here is to use what's called

straight talking. A 'What' question is asking for you to simply say exactly what it is and be direct and to the point.

- A **'Demonstrate'** question means you need to back up what you're saying with evidence and proof, showing how it works in practice. You need to give a practical example, visual or visual descriptor, so the assessor can understand how you'll do something, have done something or that your process works.
- When **'Clearly state'** is used, it means you shouldn't use any jargon or acronyms; instead, use plain English and short sentences. You need to include readability strategies here, such as short sentences of 10 words. Don't use multi-syllable words or words most people outside your organisation and industry wouldn't know. Using jargon and complicated language can increase cognitive load on the assessor, and they can get confused and mark you down as a result. It happens regularly; in fact, it happened on a panel just this week as I write this.

A lot of other action words are commonly used in grant applications, and this provides a starting point for you. The key is to find the action word to understand how much information funders need from you.

Allocate character, word or page constraints

Okay, next we are breaking down an example question from earlier in this step. This question is broken down in the first column of the following table of The Grant Answer Map. The next column in the table is where you can allocate character, word or page counts to each question part. (I cover filling out the final column in step 4c.)

Let's say for this question the limit is 500 words. You need to decide how much of this word count you'll allocate to each part of the question. The four parts focus on two main areas – current and past expertise - and you may feel they're equally important. However, while history can be a predictor of future outcomes, we all know organisational capacity can change. So, I would increase your word count allocation on the first two parts, which focus on current capacity.

The following table shows my suggested allocation. The table also shows the action word underlined and the subject in bold from earlier sections.

The Grant Answer Map showing question parts and allocated word limits

What they've asked for	**Word limit (500)**	Your answer should include
Explain how your organisation has:		
The **appropriate skills** for the project	140	
The required **expertise to deliver** the project	140	
Prior experience delivering **similar** project **activities**	100	
Prior experience delivering **similar** project **outcomes**	120	

Keep in mind this is a guide. You may mix these word limits up a little, but it's intended to help you get realistic about the word limit, and where you're allocating it.

Let's consider one more example from this step and my suggested word count allocation. The question is:

Describe your organisation's vision, goals and achievements in 500 words or less.

The following table shows how this question can be broken up and my suggested word count allocations for each part.

What they've asked for	Word limit (500)	Your answer should include
Describe vision	70	
Describe goals	120	
Describe achievements	310	

Note how I've transferred the action word 'describe' into each of the rows? This helps you stay focused on the level of information you need to provide.

I've allocated the word limits this way because you should be able to describe your vision in 70 words, and probably 50. Your goals should only be short statements - even if they are long, for clarity, shorten them if you can. The majority of the words are dedicated to describing achievements (also called outcomes). This is the opportunity to describe achievements that align to the grant program objective and outcomes.

You're now ready to use your understanding of the questions to communicate strategically.

Summary

You now have a better understanding of how to analyse a question to make sure the information you're providing actually answers it. You get points for the information you provide and the degree that it answers the question strongly. Remember the level 2 assessment matrix in step 3b? So many points are lost because the applicant didn't answer the question. Now, this is only one part of it. We're going to move on and show you how the strategic points from the work in the Align stage will be integrated into relevant answers.

What can you do now?

- ☐ Find a past grant application. Choose a question or two and take it through The Grant Answer Map. Did you miss anything? What have you learnt from this exercise?
- ☐ If you're working on a grant application currently, start analysing the question using The Grant Answer Map.

Step 4b

Communicate strategically

Okay, you've broken the question up, analysed it to understand what you need to provide and allocated some guiding word counts. Now, we're going to bring in the big power strategy (see following figure).

Stage 4: Write - Step 4b. Communicate strategically

4. Write
Communicate clearly and strategically.

Step 4b. Communicate strategically

Tool

ix. The Grant Answer Map™

The Grant Writing System: ix. The Grant Answer Map

Once you've broken each question down (refer to the previous step), you can start noting down things you should include in your answer to each of those parts in The Grant Answer Map. I generally keep the parts separate for now, combining information from The Grant Ready Kit (refer to step 1a) and The Grant Project Plan (step 1c).

Be critical here. Don't include information if it doesn't answer the question or support your answer strategically. You'll end up going off track and wasting valuable words on information that won't score you any points!

Let's revisit one of the example questions from the previous step:

Describe your organisation's vision, goals and achievements in 500 words or less.

The following table provides an example of The Grant Answer Map for the separate parts of this question, with notes on what the answer should include from The Grant Application Tool (refer to step 3c). It also considers the funder's outcomes of culture, environment and community.

What they've asked for	**Word limit (500)**	**Your answer should include**
Describe vision	70	Include vision statement. Expand on the cultural / environmental and community aspects of our vision.
Describe goals	120	Include our four goals.
Describe achievements (outcomes)	310	List achievements focused on points listed (in the last three rows of The Grant Answer Map).

Deciding what information to share

This is where all the work you've done earlier shines through. The second half of The Grant Answer Map basically transfers everything you've written in The Grant Application Tool (step 3c) to the right question, so you can share the information. As you get more advanced, you probably won't include much detail in The Grant Application Tool; instead, you'll use it as a checklist and just transfer information from the application pack straight into The Grant Answer

Map. For now, though, until you get used to doing it, I advise gathering and then transferring this information for complex grants.

Let's continue the same example question:

Describe your organisation's vision, goals and achievements in 500 words or less.

The three additional rows in The Grant Answer Map are:

1. What strategic points need to be referenced or included?
2. What stories can you tell the funder to support the key points you want them to hear.
3. What statistics address the question, and support your statements?

To complete the first row, you can use a combination of the information already gathered in the following areas, **either with The Grant Application Tool or the notes you made when going through The Grant Go/No-Go Decision Checklist:**

1. objectives, scope and requirements
2. outcomes
3. priorities
4. key messages
5. assessment criteria
6. compliance requirements
7. strategies, policies, standards and frameworks.

Note that for a more complex grant, I tend to take each of these and put them on a separate row, so I'm making sure I don't miss them. However, for simple grants, you could combine them.

Now you're going to complete the advanced part of The Grant Answer Map. The following table provides an example.

What they've asked for	Word limit (500)	Your answer should include
Describe vision	70	Include vision statement. Expand on the cultural / environmental and community aspects of our vision.
Describe goals	120	Include our four goals.
Describe achievements (outcomes)	310	List achievements focused on points below.
Strategic points to include from The Grant Application Tool: objectives, scope and requirements; outcomes; priorities; key messages; assessment criteria; compliance requirements; strategies, policies, standards and frameworks.		*For example:* • *demonstrates knowledge of key environmental and cultural elements associated with the project* • *illustrates understanding of proposed activities that clearly target the expected outcomes* • *highlights community involvement and understanding of how this will be achieved* • *shows past performance.*
What stories can you tell, so the funder understands the key points you want them to hear?		*Remember funders invest in the impact, so how can you assist them understand this and 'hear' the voices of those you support?* *Align your stories to funder's strategic points.*
What statistics address the question, and support your information?		*Include relevant research here.* *Align your statistics to support the statements and funder's strategic points.*

In the second part of The Grant Answer Map, I've taken the key points from the information related to this question. This helps me write the answer - particularly to the last part of the question, which is 'describe achievements' - because I know the funder wants me to demonstrate these things. This means out of everything the organisation does, I'll select the achievements that best align the funder's key messages - which in this example is 'key environmental and cultural outcomes and community involvement'.

You should also note specific language, and any words or phrases the grant documents use. For example, if you're used to saying, 'designed by stakeholders', but the funder uses the term 'co-designed by community', you would replace your phrase with theirs.

The last two rows in The Grant Answer Map are there to remind you to include both stories and statistics to support your statements.

Now you can go through the application and outline points in The Grant Answer Map for every question you develop an answer to.

When you're expressing alignment to the grant program objectives and other funder objectives, you have to clearly spell this out. Often, the issue is the answers in applications are too broad, and they don't clearly, or specifically, address alignment. The detail is lost in subject-matter content that is heavy to absorb when assessing, or the answer mentions the areas but hasn't highlighted it. The applicant no doubt knows what areas align and they expect the assessor to also be able to see this. However, this isn't always the case, so you need to be clear.

You can approach this in a range of ways. For example, you can use subheadings or a table format to highlight how you're aligning, or you can simply reference the relevant objective. The best thing to keep in mind is it's not the assessor's job to identify alignment to objectives. It's your job to make it clear so they don't miss it!

Structuring your answer

With The Grant Answer Map completed for each question, it's time to start thinking how you'll format your answer. Continuing the earlier example question, a table structure may be the best way to communicate your information (as shown in the following table).

Vision: *Add vision here.*	
Goals	Achievements
List goal 1 here.	*List achievements to meet goal 1 here.*
List goal 2 here.	*List achievements to meet goal 2 here.*

If you can't include a table, you could use subheadings and structure your answer as follows:

> **Describe your organisation's vision, goals and achievements in 500 words or less.**
>
> **Vision**
>
> Add vision here.
>
> **Goal 1**
>
> List goal 1 here.
>
> **Achievements**
>
> List achievements to meet goal 1 here.
>
> **Goal 2**
>
> List goal 2 here.
>
> **Achievements**
>
> List achievements to meet goal 2 here.

Your choice of structure can confuse your assessor or make it easier for them. For example, the key to this question is they want to know why you exist, what your goals are and if you're achieving them. So, if you listed all your goals and then your achievements, you're asking the assessor to work out which achievement belongs to which goal. This can make it confusing. While it's obvious to you, it's not to them. They aren't mind-readers, either. So, you make it easier by grouping achievements under the related goal.

> *Clearly structured answers are easier to read and understand - which can win you more points at the assessment table.*

Communicating your evidence

Once you've gathered and analysed your evidence, you need to review the questions and what they're asking of you. Completing The Grant Answer Map will guide you to identify specific information to include in your answers.

If you've jumped to this section and want some ideas on what statistics and stories you can gather, go to the online kit I've provided to review some up-to-date resources or brainstorm with your AI Assistant.

At this point in The Grant Writing Cycle, you need to focus your evidence. You need to include the most appropriate evidence that not only supports your statements, but also convinces the funder they're making a good investment.

For example, say you're applying for state funding for a tourism project. The strategy you identified in your research shows a state goal for destinations to 'increase visitation by 20% in five years'. So, if you were forecasting increased visitation, you would compare it to your tourism statistics and identify how that supports the funder in achieving their goal. Here's an example:

> **Visitation projections provided in the attachments demonstrate a minimum increase of 13.5% for overnight visitation. This is projected to be achieved from month six. This 13.5% increase contributes to achieving the *[state]* goal *[name of plan or strategy]*, for destinations to increase visitation by 20% in five years.**

The first sentence merely shows the forecast increase using the town's visitation statistics. The second sentence demonstrates to the funder how quickly this can be achieved. The third sentence shows the funder how their support is a good decision and provides them with a return on investment to achieve their goals. (You would, of course, also have this statistic as one you monitor and measure during the project and include in your acquittal.)

Once you have your evidence, you then need to communicate those statistics and stories in your application. Following is an example answer to a question asking you to outline your need for the funding. This answer includes statistics and stories.

I've used a service-based project suitable for an organisation delivering health services. Note the statistics I've included are not entirely correct – for the purposes of these examples, I've made some up.

Service-based example

The internal patient data and population growth data for this example project provides **the following statistics for the related question in The Grant Answer Map:**

- Maitland is the fifth-fastest growing town in Australia, with average population growth of 3.7% over the last five years. Maitland accounts for 62% of the population in the Hunter region.

- The 2022 population projections for Maitland indicate the population is estimated to increase by 2.6% annually – or 12,393 people (from 476,654 to 489,047).
- 15.3% of people identify as Aboriginal and Torres Strait Islander. This is the largest proportion in the Hunter region.
- Maitland is a regional health service area, with the new hospital catering to a regional population.
- Patients are currently waiting an average of 13 weeks (over three months) to get an appointment. The state average wait is four weeks (one month).
- An additional need for 127 patient consultations per month across three clinics is projected.
- The PHN (Primary Health Network) needs analysis *[note years of plan]* has identified Health & Wellbeing of First Nations Peoples as one of their top priorities. Aboriginal people have higher rates of suicide than non-Indigenous people, and for Aboriginal youth aged 15–24, these rates are nearly double (411 Aboriginal people self-harm, compared to 222 non-Indigenous; 17.7 Aboriginal people suicide, compared to 10.5 non-Indigenous).
- We need four more permanent part-time staff to create a flexible workforce to meet projected future demand.

Relevant stories and quotes from the people who will benefit from the service have also been gathered.

The need question these statistics relate to is 'Why is this project needed? (300 words)' Let's review an example answer for this question using relevant statistics and stories:

> **As a regional health service area, the existing healthcare system is struggling to meet the growing demand. At-risk youth currently endure lengthy appointment waiting times**

of approximately 13 weeks, compared to the state average of four weeks. To address this, 127 patient consultations are needed urgently per month, across the three clinics.

'I want my children to access support. They're teenagers. I worry as a mum. I've heard from other mums how hard it is to get appointments. It's such a long wait and it hasn't been quick enough for some youth who have passed.' Mum X

'The service really helped me. I was having bad thoughts, but I now understand how to manage these.' Client, 16.

The PHN needs analysis [reference] identified mental health needs of Aboriginal people to be a priority, with Health & Wellbeing of First Nations Peoples as one of their top priorities.

The population of Maitland, as the fifth-fastest growing town in Australia, is projected to increase by 12,393 people (2.6%) in the next financial year. 15.3% identify as Aboriginal and Torres Strait Islander [reference source]. This rapid growth necessitates proactive measures to ensure essential services can keep pace with the rising demands.

> **To help save lives, it's critical to service this unmet need and position the organisation to scale and meet future demand.**
>
> **The additional First Nations Wellbeing team of four permanent part-time roles will create a flexible workforce solution. This will service current need to provide timely healthcare and contribute to improved health outcome, meeting projected need over the next three years to [year].**

A note here is if the question was asking 'What is the project and why is it needed?', you'd take the last paragraph and put it first.

Does every question need a story and a statistic?

No, they don't. What your whole application needs is a mix of stories and statistics. Some questions are better told in story, while others are better structured as logical statistic-based answers. Keep in mind, though, that those statistic-heavy answers shouldn't be any longer than 60 to 70 words, and it would reflect a quantitative question, such as 'What will you deliver?', rather than a more qualitative question, such as 'What are the project benefits?'

When preparing my answers, I review the application and identify where my statistic-heavy and story-heavy answers are. The goal is to get the 'flow' right through the application. So, you wouldn't have 100 words of straight statistics; instead, you would find somewhere to break this up and include a 15- to 20-word statement from someone, or a story. Similarly, you wouldn't have a story-based answer over 60 to 70 words without a statistic. In the example we just reviewed, the first paragraph is 52 words. The third is 30 words. Note how they're broken up with a quote in between.

When checking for balance, ask yourself if one answer has to be statistic-based, can the next one be story-based? Or do you have a mix across all answers? Is your statistic-to-story ratio well balanced across the application?

Attributing evidence

One question I do get asked a lot is, 'Do I need to reference evidence?' You can use informal and formal referencing, depending on the funder. For example, in the last example answer, I've referenced in an informal way because it's specifically for a service grant from an organisation called the PHN (Primary Health Network). So, if you're demonstrating to a funder how you align to their statistics, you don't need to expand on this informal referencing.

However, if you're referencing data from another source, you should expand on it as much as needed to identify the report and the source – for example, 'HNECC PHN Needs Analysis (year) ...' Formal referencing is an absolute must if your grant has any question or focus on evidence-based, research or academic needs analysis or delivery.

Summary

This step should have brought the last stage, Align, and the previous steps in this stage to life for you. By now you've strategically analysed the question and brought information in from the guidelines, strategies and other strategic elements you identified when you did your research.

You identified which question you integrated assessment criteria into, if they weren't asked separately. You understood the depth of information the answer asked you to provide.

What can you do now?

- [ ] Now it's time to write your answers. Yes, now! Finally, that's what you've been waiting for, and your answer is going to be so much better than it would have been if you hadn't done the work to get here. Well done! In the next step we'll work on refining your answer.

Step 4c

Refine your answer

In the previous two steps, I've outlined breaking a question down and then collating the information you need to include to answer it. As the following figure shows, you're now at the step of refining your answer.

Stage 4: Write – Step 4c. Refine your answer

Step 4c. Refine your answer

4. Write
Communicate clearly and strategically.

In this step, I run through some of the common issues and questions that arise during this refining process, starting with modifying your need statement.

Modifying your need statement for the application

In step 1c, I took you through developing your need statement as part of The Grant Project Plan, and introduced a framework you can use to address questions about need.

Examples of need-focused questions in a grant application form include:

- 'Tell us why you need this.'
- 'What is the need for the project?'
- 'How did you identify the need, and what is it?'
- 'Why do you need this project?'
- 'Why is this project important?'

The key difference between developing your overall need statement in your project plan and writing a need statement for an application is that, for the application, you focus on talking about the needs the funder cares about. These needs should reflect the funder's objectives. The benefits of your project should relate to the outcomes.

The other information from your more general need statement may be interesting, but it won't win you points. Focus on demonstrating how your need assists the funder to meet their objectives.

Also keep in mind the following:

Your need statement is a benchmark question.

Everything you say after your need statement will be measured against that. The flow of information should be consistent through your application. If you go on to state outcomes, the assessor will refer back to your need statement and ask whether these outcomes align to the identified need, as well as the funder's objectives and outcomes.

Assessors will also ask other questions, such as:

- 'In our experience, is this the right project to address the need?'
- 'Have they included the right measures to monitor if they're addressing the need?'
- 'Are the project partners and participants suitable to the target group identified in the need statement?'
- 'Are they missing any key stakeholders that should be included?'
- 'Do the stated activities align to the need statement?'

As the following figure shows, all these elements should consistently map and make logical sense without any gaps.

All elements in your application should flow from your need statement

For example, it would be a gap if you stated a need to manufacture a new product to meet demand and to increase financial sustainability, but then you didn't include increased profit as an outcome, and sales and revenue as a measure.

Reducing the word count of your need statement

Perhaps your general need statement is a page or more. (Typically, need statements that are longer than half a page are for larger projects - generally infrastructure or services for state or federal government funding.) You may need to reduce your word count for specific applications - for example, if you're submitting an application with a 150-word limit for the need question. Focusing your need on the grant objectives will assist you in addressing these within the word limit. Use The Grant Answer Map to guide you.

If you've identified one need that aligns to one of the funder's objectives, then this is the focus. If the funder wants you to address all of the objectives, then your need statement would relate to all of these objectives.

If you're facing this, group similar themes in your need statement. So, for example, if you want to demonstrate needs in community for early intervention services, you will group these together. You would have one topic per paragraph, or per group of paragraphs telling the story. A good way to reinforce the grant objectives and outcomes is to then finish each group with a statement that demonstrates how the solution addresses the need and the funder's goals.

Here's an example, noting that this example was for a grant to a state health department, so it includes health-specific language:

> ***[Your region]* Local Health District has the shortest life expectancy at birth in South Australia (males 66.5 years; females 71.9 years). The highest causes of premature mortality include cancer and cardiovascular disease, with *[your Region]* experiencing a 5% higher premature mortality rate than the combined state Local Health District rates.**
>
> **These two primary causes of premature mortality can be reduced with access to early intervention treatment. This will result in increased health outcomes and decreased dependence on state funding for more expensive complex treatments.**
>
> **Even though *[neighbouring town]* hospital manages a comprehensive range of health conditions, they transfer all high needs patients, maternity and paediatric inpatients and emergency surgery to *[your town]* hospital. This results in an additional intake of *[number]* per month. Some of these medical services could be conducted in-home; however, patients are out of their community, sometimes their region. The lack of short-term patient accommodation further restricts in-home service.**

> **Six patients per day access renal dialysis. One renal dialysis patient needed accommodation while being trained in peritoneal dialysis routines, before going home. This stay was two weeks. Out-of-town residents admitted are occupying acute care beds.**
>
> **If short-term accommodation were available, a community nurse could provide service at the patient's accommodation, or at the Ambulatory Care Clinic at significantly reduced cost. *[Your region]* Local Health District statistics demonstrate an average of 133.50 annual bed-night inpatient admissions are only required because there is no short-term patient accommodation available. The Local Health District reports admission costs are $5,800 for patients without complications. This is a minimum of $774,300 saved with provision of short-term accommodation.**
>
> **In addition, this would free up a further 133.5 bed nights for acute care, which further reduces additional ambulance transport required for patients who cannot be admitted in *[your town]* hospital.**

You'll also find some editing tips in the next step to help you reframe your statement and reduce the word count.

No such thing as a perfect application

Now, applications are never, ever 100% complete or as perfect as you'd like. There's always something you wanted to put in but couldn't. I recognise you might not be 100% ready to submit but ask if it's still worth applying. On smaller grants, particularly local grants focused for community groups, a bonus benefit of applying is assessors become aware of your organisation and project. This means it's better to submit your application if you feel it's 60 to 75% ready, than lose a potential opportunity.

Remember - some grant programs don't have enough applicants. Also, you've already increased your chance to score well from this book, because you've understood the content you need to include and how to address all parts of the question!

An example of this is local Crown Land Managers I worked with for a grant related to their committee hall. They were applying for a local council grant for assistance with costs towards repairs at the hall and tennis court resurfacing. I did a brief review of their grant application and gave them some pointers. I advised them that they were asking for too much, given the total program funds, but that going through the process would be worthwhile as a learning experience, because it was their first grant. They couldn't reduce the ask and it wasn't a lengthy application, so they submitted it.

While they missed out on receiving the grant, their community engagement they discussed in their application impressed one of the assessors and he made contact with them after they'd received their rejection letter. This assessor was a staff member for a federal member of parliament. They directed the Crown Land Managers towards a different funding round and encouraged them to apply for more funds. The Crown Land Managers applied for this round and secured funding to resurface the tennis courts. So, while they missed out on the council application for $3,000, they received $7,500 in funding for the tennis courts. They then went on to secure many more grants for the roof, fans, kitchen and floor sanding. Just one story of so many examples I have of similar situations.

So, you have a few legitimate reasons to submit your application, even if you don't feel it's 100% perfect. So many projects are funded with imperfect applications - yes, even mine. I'm not perfect either (just don't tell my husband I said that LOL). The bottom line is if your heart and your logic say it's worth a shot, do it.

Should you use artificial intelligence writing programs?

If you're using this book to dip in and out of areas that interest you, you may have missed the section on using AI to write your grant answers. I have mentioned areas though the book where your AI Assistant can support your work. I covered pros and cons in the overview of grants section earlier in this book.

In summary, your AI Assistant is useful as a brainstorming tool. I've included some more information, including AI prompts in the online kit. If you want to explore this further, I've provided more information and video walk throughs on how to use some of the programs, including additional prompts in the online kit.

Answering common questions – a quick Q&A

In this section, I've included a couple of common questions that often appear in grant applications, and provided some tips for answering them; however, so many questions are possible that I could write another book! So, you can also join my regular grant writing Q&A online sessions and ask if you're not sure how to answer a question.

'How will your project be sustainable beyond the funding?'

Focus your answer on how you're delivering sustainable project outcomes. Talk about what you've put in place to leverage or enable these outcomes to continue without any additional funding beyond this grant. We all know funded projects simply can't happen again without the funds to pay the people or resources to do the work. However, this approach is about finding simple affordable ways you can plan to extend the life of the outcomes.

For example, if you were running a youth career development program, one aspect of sustainability might be a volunteer mentoring program that extends beyond the funded program period. Let's say the program runs for 12 months and the volunteer mentoring program runs for another six months. This is something you're designing to give the youth additional opportunities to put their learnings into practice and get support and feedback from mentors. This extends the outcomes of the project.

If you're a new organisation, discuss how your partnerships support sustainability of your organisation beyond the funding.

'How will your project create jobs, increase tourism or economic opportunities?'

The key to questions like this is to focus on data and evidence. You'll need to know averages - such as, on average for every building project, how many jobs does this create? You'll also need to know other industry benchmarks - such as, on average, how many tourists do similar events attract in the region? Are they day-trippers? If not, how many nights on average do they stay?

Also look at returns. For example, how many dollars are, or what percentage of funding is, being spent within the community? For every $1 spend in the community, how much economic return does it achieve? What's their average spend per day?

You'll then be able to use this data to sell your story.

As an example, when I was submitting a tourism proposal for a cycling tour, one piece of data I used to demonstrate economic impact was the average economic spend of cycling tourists.

To work this out, you have to know the projected number of tourists expected and how many nights they will likely stay with you (projected length of stay). From that, you can calculate economic spend, as follows:

> **Number of tourists × spend per day × number of nights = projected economic impact**

Based on the data I had, I was able to work out an estimated $77,000 of economic impact would be created by the cycle tour.

Your regional development and local councils have access to certain systems and programs as well, so ask them if they can support you to evidence jobs, tourism and economic impact.

You can explore more examples in the online kit.

Why does the application ask the same question, twice?

While working your way through an application form, have you ever thought, *I've already answered this question*? I was in Brisbane delivering a general grants workshop and had someone ask about the application for a Perpetual Limited grant. Often these similar questions have some differences in how they're worded. In this case, however, word for word they were exactly the same question.

So, how would you strategise your answer in this situation? Again, think about this from the funder's perspective. They have gone through the application so they can make strategic decisions based on the information and data they need to support their decision. They have started at the beginning and gone through to the end, developing their questions. Having been a trainer for SmartyGrants, training funders on how to develop these application forms and working with funders to establish grant programs, I know how many approach the development of application forms.

From the funder's perspective, what you have is an application form with questions that flow, one after the other. For example, question one might be around need, and question two might be a question about the gap. They would have structured the application in this way because, once they understand what the need is, they then want to understand if it's being addressed by someone else, or where your need fits in with the work already being done. In this example, you wouldn't put information about the gap in question one, because it fits in question two.

Now take this kind of thinking back to the example of two questions being worded the same. (This also works where you feel a similar question is being asked, just in a slightly different way.) Review the environment surrounding the question. For example, the question I was shown was, 'What's your capacity to deliver the project?' The first time the question was asked, let's call it 'question B', the previous question A and the following question C were all related to information about the *organisation*. The second time in the application this question appeared, let's call it 'question F', the previous question E and the following question G were all related to questions about the *project*.

So, after considering the context, you know one question is focused on the organisation's capacity and one question is focused on the project capacity. Can you understand how they are two different things?

For 'question B' you would focus on responding about the organisation's capacity to deliver the project, covering topics such as governance, admin and management knowledge, skills and resources. For 'question F', you would focus on answers relating to the project team's knowledge, skills and resources.

Milestones and timelines

I include milestones and timelines in The Grant Project Plan (refer to step 1c) and provide a few tips to outline these in the application.

The key things I want to reinforce here for when you finalise your project timeline in the application are:

- It's sometimes better to use weeks and months in the timeline and indicative dates - for example, Week 6 (eta date) - than only dates. This shows the funder that you aren't 'locked' into a date and if a delay occurs on their end, they won't doubt you can deliver.
- Make sure your milestones align to the activities described in the application.
- Show monitoring and reporting in your timeline.
- Your plan should show the project starting one month to six weeks after securing the funding, which allows for contract signing and administration. Alternatively show the number of weeks to start from the contract signing miletone.
- If the funding is based on milestone deliverables, make sure there's ample time between the finish of one milestone and the start of another. You'll need to allow for a reporting and payment delay between each milestone.

In the timeline, remember that you need to include time for your acquittal and final report. The project isn't finished until this is submitted.

Application budget

When you developed your project plan (refer to step 1c), you drafted a budget for your organisation. Now you can use that information to draft a budget for the funder. Meeting the guidelines for different grants involves many variables. Your basic budget will give you a baseline to guide each grant application you make for the project.

In The Grant Go/No-Go Decision Tool (step 2b) or The Grant Application Tool (step 3c), you should have noted down what the funder won't fund and what they will fund. This is important because you can't ask for something they've already said no to! If you do, your application might not make it past the first assessment level, and it will likely be rejected.

The story of your project should be represented through your cost breakdown. This provides you with a measuring and monitoring tool to run your project and report to your stakeholders. But you don't have to be an accountant to create a budget! When the assessors consider your budget, they're assessing financial transparency and deciding if your financial planning is sufficient for success. They're also making sure you know how to write up a suitable budget for your project.

The budget should be realistic and achievable. It should identify the costs for every activity and provide justification of your workings. This will be useful when you return to it later and update costings as prices change.

Include how your organisation will contribute to the project, even if the funder provides 100% of funding - show them in-kind contributions and your contribution. If you can, tell a story in your budget. For example, instead of putting contribution funds together, show where they came from. If you're including a co-contribution amount of $350, show the details - such as, 'Fundraising 20 hours: $300' as one entry and '10 donations: $50' as the next. Breaking down where your contribution has come from demonstrates the level of commitment and support for your project.

Be realistic about the total amount you're asking for to increase your chance of winning the grant. Is the funding amount specified per project or organisation? For example, will the $200,000 be allocated with an expected $20,000 maximum funding ask? That's only 10 organisations across a whole state. Are you going to ask for $20,000 or less than $20,000? Is your application strong? If not, it's better to plan for a project that sits between 65 and 75% of the funding allocation. This will increase your chance to Win the Grant. It can be hard to achieve 100% of the funding allocation. This is because of the way funders look at their distribution strategy and, honestly, a lot of the time, some budgets seem inflated in an attempt to get 100% of the funding available. Remember:

> *Grants are a help-up, not a handout.*

While I did discuss income and costs in step 1c as part of The Grant Project Plan, some differences emerge when you're developing a budget for a grant application. Here are some good general points to keep in mind when you're developing your budget:

- **Ask for quotes based on the timeline for when you expect to do the work:** If the work isn't being done until February, find out what the projected cost will be after January, when an annual industry price, or CPI increases may occur.
- **Understand your unit costs:** Unit costs are the whole cost of delivering the activity and they will differ depending on the person delivering it. You should involve financial expertise to work this out. As an example, if budgeting for the unit cost of your counsellor, you need to include total costs per hour for the position. Factor in employment rates and on-costs, and other factors such as the cost of the space they use and the materials to do their job. Note some guidelines specify wage costs should be separate from administration costs.

- **Know your fixed and variable costs:** This will be useful when other elements change – for example, if you need to change figures and numbers of attendees for a workshop, this won't affect all costs. It should only affect those costs and income areas related to the change, which are variable. Fixed costs are things like the venue hire fee. You can't change that. This is useful because if the funder offers you less than what you've asked for, you will work out how much you can deliver after taking off the fixed costs. For example, say your fixed costs are $2,500 and variable costs are $20 per person. If you receive $3,000 of the $4,000 you asked for then you can only support 25 people, not the 75 you applied for ($3,000 minus $2,500 divided by $20 = 25).
- **Include every contribution:** Your organisation will receive support from stakeholders. This can be non-financial support and it's important it's recorded in the budget, as much as financial support is. Make sure you factor in the market price for non-financial support. For example, if the local printing shop is going to donate the printing of flyers, note this down at the cost you would otherwise have paid.
- **Follow instructions:** The documents in the guidelines and application pack are specific about what the funders will pay for and what they won't pay for. If you put something in the wrong column, asking them to pay for something they have said they won't or putting in more money than they have said they'll allow, then you may be deemed ineligible. Use the same costings stated by the funder.
- **Take note of the in-kind labour amounts:** For businesses, the extra time you're committing above what you're being paid for is volunteering in-kind as much as it is for a community organisation with volunteers who contribute their time. The key difference for businesses is you can accurately calculate the hourly rate plus on-costs (such as superannuation). Volunteering, however, is slightly different because it is based on what the funder will accept.

- **Check what the funder has stipulated about volunteers:** If they have stipulations about volunteers, it will either be an hourly rate or a fixed maximum – for example 'Volunteer contributions cannot exceed $2,000'.

You can use three different ways to cost in volunteers, depending on the expertise required for the job. The first two are as follows:

1. **Unskilled:** This is when a particular skill set isn't required – for example, digging a garden bed or assisting to deliver meals. The majority of funders state their calculation of volunteer unskilled labour is between $15 and $25 per person, per hour.
2. **Skilled:** This is where you require a skill, but they don't have to be an expert. For example, a driver delivering the meals requires a driver's license. An experienced project manager requires project management skills. You should charge this out at a similar hourly wage. I generally use around $35 to $40 an hour for skilled labour. It shouldn't be any less than the minimum national wage or any more than the funder permits.

Note that the Australian Bureau of Statistics calculates the hours of volunteering and the value of volunteering labour using a calculation method from the United Nations Statistical Commission.* This method outlines volunteer labour costs should be based on what it would cost you to replace the volunteer with paid labour.

So, you could enter your volunteer roles in your budget by job task and assign the appropriate wage for the task, or for general tasks use the minimum national wage as a benchmark. This is the calculation

* See www.abs.gov.au/statistics/detailed-methodology-information/concepts-sources-methods/australian-system-national-accounts-concepts-sources-and-methods/2020-21/chapter-23-satellite-accounts/household-satellite-account-and-unpaid-work/unpaid-work for more information.

method used by state-based volunteering agencies in their 'Value of Volunteering' online calculators.

Some funders still use the old measure, which is dividing the number of volunteering hours by the value of volunteering, so in the most recent statistics this is:

$8.9 billion ÷ 588 million hours = $15.14

So, the methodology from the Australian Bureau of Statistics or the minimum wage for unskilled and skilled labour is preferable over $15.14.

If the funder hasn't said, I use the appropriate wage level or the Australian Bureau of Statistics method, referencing the source if necessary.

3. **The third costing group for volunteers is professional.** Depending on the funder, sometimes professional costing is captured in the skilled category (point 2 in the previous list). However, the level of professional costing I'm talking about here is the contractor and consultant level. So, for example, if your accountant is giving you five hours of their time, you cost them in as 'Accountant, in-kind five hours at $250 per hour = $1,250 total in-kind contribution'. If a funder does not stipulate their professional in-kind calculation, use this method to demonstrate the true commercial value of this support. If you aren't sure, ask the funder.

Budget check

Sound financials and evidence supporting everything you've said you'll do are essential. Check through the application and, wherever you've stated costs, check these costs are reflected in the budget. Consider what might be ordinary expenses items and costs of delivering what you're doing. Check the budget. Are cost items communicated or does it appear as if you haven't thought about something because you've missed it in the budget?

Don't leave the assessor with a view you haven't considered all costs. I recall an arts organisation that wanted to deliver training and mentioned their marketing campaign in their answers, but completely forgot to recognise marketing as a cost of the project in their budget. This cost wasn't identified in the in-kind column either and this did reduce the scores the assessors gave them – which resulted in another organisation receiving funding over their organisation. This might seem like such a simple thing, but the challenge is if this makes it the weaker application, the stronger one does win.

The other thing to watch is for your costs to be fair market value. If they're not, you need to explain. Perhaps the amount includes transport for a remote area, or the contractor you're bringing in is a specialist skill from out of state. List these separately if you can. Also make sure any quotes reflect this.

You can't assume the assessor knows why it's necessary to pay more than market value. I can think of one regional event team who shared feedback from a funder with me. This funder had rejected their application based on excessive costs in the budget they submitted. It turned out they had listed an item and included its expensive transport in the price – making it look like they were trying to claim around 1.5 times more than the retail cost for that item. They should have separated the item cost from the transport cost.

Understanding how the budget also helps you

A well-made budget provides more benefits than only meeting the funder's guidelines; it's going to assist you, too. The budget will give you a way to monitor and measure the success and viability of your project. Assuming you're awarded the grant, it's essential you track the money in and out, and plan for any last-minute changes to the budget.

Your funder will require an acquittal before the end of their financial year. Grants vary on their deadlines but, essentially, you'll be required to explain how well your project stuck to the budget and provided the deliverables. It's best to start planning how you'll monitor and measure the financials of your project early. This should also be recognised as a cost in your budget, because this will take time from someone - your bookkeeper, staff or volunteers.

What financial reports do I need to submit?

Most funders ask for audited financial statements or, if you're new, they may allow your balance sheet and profit and loss statement instead. Funders will assess your financials with a risk and viability lens. They'll be searching for signs of financial management systems and processes.

Financial indicators they may assess include:

- **Ratios:** The solvency ratio is a typical one. In other words, is there more debt than income? They may assess the ratio of fundraising to grants income as a percentage of overall income and review single or group expenses, as a percentage of total expenses.
- **The type of debt and amount of debt you are carrying:** Funders may look at whether it's unusual for your organisation to have a certain type of debt, particularly if it is a large debt. Having larger than expected debts might be considered risky, and funders may doubt if you can meet these obligations long-term given your income history. Funders will look at this particularly if the grant is being paid after the work is done.

- **What line items are in your financials:** Consider the names you use. I saw one financial statement recently that had tens of thousands of dollars in funding listed under 'Retained capital' (other statements might list funds under 'Miscellaneous' or 'Surplus'). If your financials indicate you can afford to fund the project yourself, you may not get the funding. If those funds are actually allocated to other areas, such as employee obligations or another project, separate them out and label them as such. Funders are assessing how effective and efficient you're being with funds, and how well you're demonstrating good financial governance.
- **Financial model analysis:** For larger projects, government funders may align to the financial models used by state or federal Treasury, such as the internal rate of return or a cost-benefit analysis. If you're applying for government funding, it's useful to research the calculations the related Treasury department uses and include these in any financial data you provide - even a reference to the models can strengthen your answer.

Some projects will require these calculations in your application.

Answering questions about risks

A common mistake in grant applications is being overly positive everything will work out perfectly. Being too positive is as bad as being too negative. Assessors know risks exist - most of them are experienced in project management, after all - and they want to check if you've anticipated problems and have a plan to deal with them.

In the grant application, you'll generally be asked to share your key risks. Some funders will give you a minimum number they expect. I discuss listing your key risks in step 1c as part of The Grant Project Plan template, so if you've already completed this work, you can just cut and paste content from this list. Also remember nothing says, 'We have thought about this and planned for it' than sharing your risk management process and attaching your plan (or referencing the plan if you can't attach it in full).

When refining your key risks, think about regular risks – for example, risks you would expect if you were hiring a contractor. Consider key person risk, such as losing a key team member in charge of leading the project. Often not including fundamental critical risks is a weakness.

Also keep in mind funders don't just consider risks in a physical, task or resource sense. They consider aspects such as risks to quality and standards as well. For example, the federal government's Department of Social Services shared the following:

> [For] grant based programmes and service providers, risks are assessed across the following factors: governance; financial management; service delivery performance; issues management; and sustainability.

In step 1c, I discuss risks in The Grant Project Plan and gave examples of a range of risks across the STEEPLE categories. Providing risks across the three levels and seven categories related to your application demonstrates the depth of your risk planning I include a minimum of 10 risks across strategic, operational and project risks from the STEEPLE categories, to showcase the approach to risk management.

You'll likely have to include your risks in a table format. When completing this table, keep in mind these tips to think through what to include:

- **Identify the key risks the funder cares about:** Consider the grant documents and ask yourself, what key messages are there and what are the risks of these? Considering the industry, what key compliance areas exist? For example, if there's a strong focus on monitoring and reporting, then including risks that address this key message gives funders confidence you're considering it.
- **Don't reinvent the wheel:** Use your risk management documents or best practice templates from state regulators. Use the information you've already developed and include extracts from your plans. Reference the plans in relevant questions.
- **Consider the size of your organisation, your resources and partnerships:** If you were contracting a similar organisation to deliver the project, what risks would you consider? How can you remove those risks as objections funders might have to saying 'Yes'. For example, if you haven't received funding before or you're a small organisation with a limited budget, a funder may doubt your ability to manage and acquit grant funds. To address this, you could list it as a risk and in your mitigation notes say something like the following:

  ***[Your club]* has financial policies and procedures in place. *[Your club]* has successfully managed and acquitted an annual budget of $200,000 in sponsorship.**

Structuring the risk answer

If you have to include information about risks in your application, you should think about the structure to use. Of course, it depends on what the question is as to how you will structure the answer; however, the following framework is useful to demonstrate a logical approach to risk management:

- **Standards:** Set the scene by highlighting the standards, accreditation, policy and risk management framework you have in place.
- **Processes:** Mention key processes you have implemented. Things such as business, financial and customer satisfaction processes, on-time delivery, error rate tracking, days without accident, sustainability and community support.
- **Goals:** If appropriate, mention the key goals the funder cares about and relate the risk to the achievement of that goal.
- **Progress and achievements:** Highlight any relevant progress and achievements you've already made.

This framework reduces an assessor's cognitive load by logically structuring your answer from strategic to operational.

Let's review an example answer:

> **Our risk management system and policies comply with industry best practice. We have provided a summary of the risk register, identifying the top 12 rated risks. Our comprehensive risk register identifies and mitigates over 65 strategic, operational and project risks. For two years we have achieved our goal of 97% incident free, in an industry where the average is 67%.**

The following figure shows another example, which uses this framework as a visual.

Risk management framework

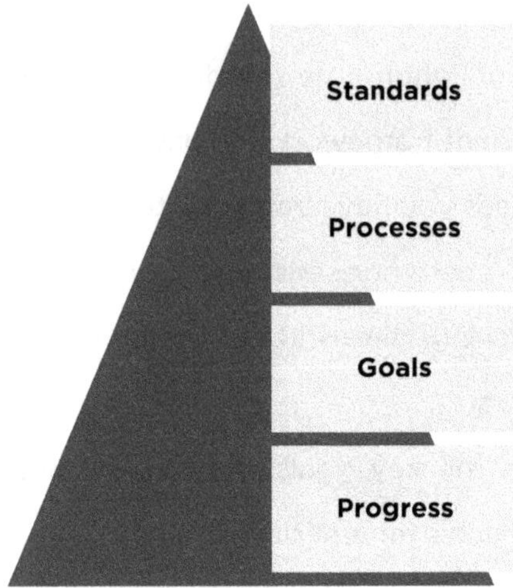

Our workplace health and safety standards comply with industry best practice and legislative safety requirements.

Daily site checklists proactively identify potential event risks.

Our safety goals are 0 requiring hospitalisation and 5% seeking first aid. This has been achieved in the last 5 years.

First aid assistance should reduce by 2% with additional drinking stations, seating and quiet areas; and improved event signage.

Attachments

The three simple rules for attachments are:

1. Strategically choose the attachments which offer the strongest support of your application, rather than simply validate your statements.
2. Attach exactly what they ask for, and only that - sometimes no attachments are required.
3. If allowed to attach additional information, attach only what is relevant and only what supports your statements.

Funders will give you a list of attachments they want, and generally these are in compliance areas. The guidelines will share information about what attachments are expected or allowed. Don't only rely on these, though, because you'll also find information in the application form. The first thing is to follow instructions. Include everything they've asked for and exactly what they want. If they want two years of audited financials, don't just give them the last financial year. If they want a current insurance cover note, check the date is current. If they want an insurance certificate of currency for $20 million, that's exactly what you give them. You risk being rejected in the first assessment level if you don't provide the documents requested, compliant to their requirements.

If you get the opportunity to include additional documents or evidence, don't include irrelevant attachments. Funders don't want a 20-page document when you only want them to review one paragraph in the document. You can take screenshots or copy the information into one page.

The next thing is to identify opportunities to strengthen your submission. Consider only including other information that supports the key messages. For example, if a key message is to demonstrate your organisation has the skills, experience, knowledge, networks and performance of similar outcomes to deliver this work then include information that supports this.

One example was a council grant I recently worked on where they allowed supporting material. The organisation was applying for funding for a community festival, and they attached an event management plan with a site map, a traffic management plan and a risk management plan to support their funding request. That's not the only reason they received a significant investment from council, but it certainly helped.

Check your cross-referencing to ensure how you've numbered appendices and the attachments corresponds with the numbers used in your answers. If an attachment supports a specific question, it can be useful to give it an extended document name that includes the corresponding question number. If your appendices and attachments are considerable, add a table of contents page listing the documents and corresponding answers they support.

Letters of support and referees

You may be asked to include letters of support or referee details. So many people think letters of support have to be provided by a well-known person or a person in a public role, such as a mayor or politician. **What is far better, and provides your application with real strength, is attaching a letter of support from:**

- someone who has been positively impacted by your projects in the past and can detail the benefits of these projects to their organisation and the people they support
- a professional who can state the project is well designed with a high chance of achieving the listed outcomes, based on their expertise
- your project partner who can expand on why they have chosen to support your organisation to deliver the project and how it assists them, their members and their community.

The problem is that support letters can take a long time to secure, and the writer may not know what you want said. So, provide a briefing template or write it for them. To do this, you'll have to write a few variations or provide some options for them to select from.

Here are a few tips to consider when you're developing a draft or running through what you want them to include in the letter of support:

- The letter of support should be relevant to the grant and the grant objectives.
- The writer should reinforce that you're the best organisation or person for the grant.
- The letter can fill any gaps and strengthen those areas you weren't able to expand on in your application.

- You should focus on grant outcomes and demonstrating any of those outcomes, including knowledge of similar projects delivered with similar outcomes.
- The writer should share why they are supporting you. This should strengthen your evidence of your capacity to deliver.
- The letter should include specifics of any in-kind or financial support they're contributing to the project. If it's from a project partner, it's also useful for it to have some detail of their role in the project.
- Your partners/supporters should share the benefits their organisation, or people connected with them, receive as a result of their involvement with you.
- Stories of need and demand from the writers perspective should also be included to support your statements.

Follow the same rules above for referees. If you have to provide contact details of referees, provide them with a one-page overview of the project, highlighting the key messages you'd like them to reinforce when the funder calls.

What if I'm not getting the information I need?

I've added this section for those grant writers who weren't involved in creating the project and who need to gather information from others to write the grant. If this is you, your path is going to be different because others will do the planning and budgets, and you'll communicate their work. So, the previous steps would have helped you understand what to ask from them.

The key challenge with this role is that you have to wait for other people and manage them so you can meet the writing deadline. Tension develops because they don't understand what your role is and how critical it is to get the information to you as soon as possible. Sometimes roles and tasks are misunderstood and not clear.

The following sections offer two pieces of advice.

Have a clear delineation between who is doing what, and to what degree

For example, if it's about research, are you finding it, consolidating it or both?

I had a client once who two hours before the deadline then asked me to load up an application. It wasn't stated as a request - it was stated as an expectation. I had in my email provided all the documents and mentioned they were ready for them to load up. Before that email, we'd had verbal conversations that they needed to lodge the application under their account, which I didn't have access to. Goalposts move sometimes because people are busy or there is so much going on they forget. I was delivering a workshop that day so I couldn't help out. They submitted it and it worked out, but it didn't feel great having to reinforce this at the time.

Don't be soft on deadlines other people have to meet

I used to be a lot softer than I am now - a bit of a pushover really - because I didn't set boundaries. When people would miss deadlines to give me information, I'd gently ask, and ask, and ask. I used to think, *That's okay. I'll get it done. I'll just have to work late or on the weekend.*

Being too soft on other people when they missed deadlines is the biggest mistake I have made as a grant writer.

As an example, I was working for an organisation a few years ago. We had a few applications to submit, collectively worth over

$13.5 million. I was far too soft. I kept telling people what I needed, and not getting it. One simple thing I needed was their budget and costings to demonstrate value for money. I also needed their service model and information from the partners they wanted to work with.

On top of this, there were a few technical challenges and then, three weeks before the grant was due, my main contact went on a two-week international holiday that I hadn't been told about! There were still so many gaps and all I could do was wait and chase up their project partners for information, which was outside the scope of my engagement. My requests were piling up.

A week before the application deadline, the contact returned but this was the week I had planned to start my holiday. I did my job and wrote all the applications with the information I had, including designing their service model, which wasn't my agreed role. I worked about 10 hours a day for a full week – on my holidays.

It was intense and I learnt my lesson. I don't allow people to miss their deadlines anymore. Long story short, don't be too nice. You have to be hard on their deadlines. Work out your timeline and keep them to it. Tell them the consequences of not proving the information you need.

Work out the point where you say, 'Submit *xyz* list of items by *x* date or I can't write the grant for you.' It's better to walk away earlier, than put yourself in a stressful situation. A luxury I know if you're a contracted writer and not a staff member; however, it's important that everyone knows the consequences. If you're a staff member, then explain how much extra they'll have to pay overtime to get it submitted if you have to work late. Hold people accountable for their promises.

Summary

These tips should have helped you refine your application. At this stage, you should be up to your second or third draft. In the next step, I go through how to review the application and edit your answers. I provide some great tips on reducing word count, which is always a challenge.

What can you do now?

- [ ] Make sure your need statement directly targets the funder and the relevant specifics, such as outcome or target group from the guidelines.
- [ ] Check your application. Does the content flow and is it consistent from need to target group to project to activities to outcomes and measures?
- [ ] Make sure you've identified reporting milestones in your timeline, such as your acquittal.
- [ ] Check your budget factors in everything you're doing and everything your partners are bringing to the project to demonstrate the true value of commitment.
- [ ] Check your financial reports are clear. Does it seem that there's money that could be used to pay for the project because of the ledger name? Make sure you include notes to financials, so they know these funds are already committed.
- [ ] Review your risk management plan. Is there an adequate range of risks and categories? Have you included risks the funder will care about?

Summary of Stage 4: Write

We've covered quite a lot of information in the steps in this stage. In summary you've learnt how to:

1. understand the questions
2. communicate strategically
3. refine your answer.

What can you do now?

Up to now I've focused on answering those questions that you need to craft answers to. There are going to be answers that you think, *That's fine. I have that, it's easy* and you'll skim over them. The one thing that I'd suggest you do is to make sure those simple questions are answered no later than a few days before the grant is due. A typical one is the budget, risk management plan or timeline. If you've developed it in the planning stage, or on another document ready to cut and paste into the application, then the thinking is done.

The big trap for these questions in the application forms is where there are multiple lines and cells for answers. In this case, completing those cells means that takes a lot longer than you think. So do it sooner than later. You'll need some thinking time between answering the other questions anyway, which will give your brain time to rest. Better yet, if you have support and a sharable application form, ask someone else to complete this information and other standard questions.

Stage 5: Submit

The Grant Writing System™

© Natalie Bramble

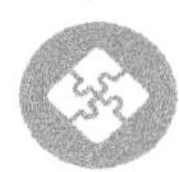

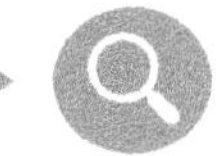

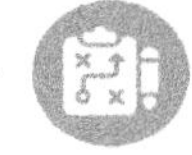

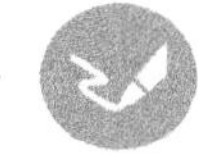

1. Plan
2. Find
3. Align
4. Write
5. Submit
6. Manage
7. Report

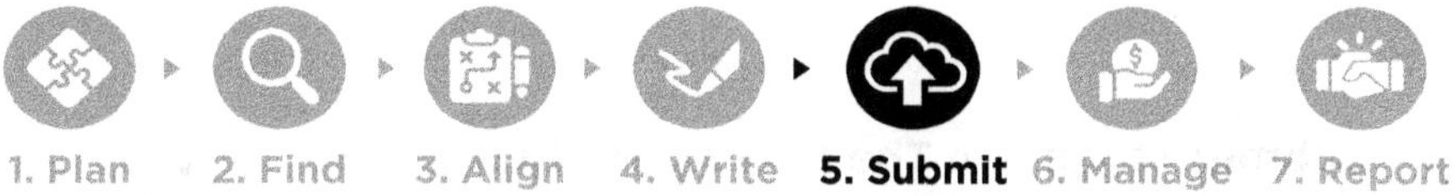

Submit without regret

The final part of preparing your answers is editing your drafts and compiling your documents for a review. This stage is all about getting you ready to confidently submit without regret (see the following figure).

Submit: Stage 5 in The Grant Writing System

Submit without regret!

5. Submit ▶ **Steps in this stage** ▶ **Tools to guide you**

Confidently submit without regret!

a. Review and edit.

b. Avoid submission mistakes.

x. The Grant Submission Checklist™

At this point, you'll go through your answers to identify your strengths, your weaknesses and any missed opportunities where you can add value.

Remember – assessors are under pressure. They have limited time to assess documents, and they must consider, absorb and understand information as effectively and efficiently as possible. Luckily, you can take steps to help assessors with this.

The steps in this stage will guide you so you can press submit, without regret. Nothing is worse than realising you forgot to attach a document, or you've included contradictory statistics after pressing the submit button.

I discuss how to do a strategic quality review of your application, edit your answer, check for consistency of terminology, style and grammar, and use persuasive writing. I also run you through checking your list of attachments and using The Grant Submission Checklist to avoid making common mistakes and submit a compliant application and submit a compliant application.

Step 5a

Review and edit

As shown in the following figure, the next step is reviewing and editing your application. Part of the editing process is to undertake three strategic reviews. The first is a strategic quality review, followed by a content and editing review and finishing with an independent mock assessment. All these reviews rely on you having the time. If you don't have time to do all three, you should at minimum do the first and second review, a content and editing review, which I devote most of this step to. First, though, let's have a quick look at an overall review for quality.

Stage 5: Submit – Step 5a. Quality review of the application

Step 5a. Edit and critically analyse

5. Submit

Confidently submit without regret!

First review: Quality review of your application

As shown in the following figure, you can first complete a broad strategic quality review of the application, including your answers and any supporting information. This review critically assesses the key information aligns to the funder's core messages, priorities and values.

Some questions to ask at this stage include the following:

- Have you demonstrated you understand the funder's requirements?
- Have you demonstrated your experience and knowledge?
- Have you reinforced the value your project offers?
- Is your approach and your capability to implement the project clear?
- Do language, tone and style in the application match what you feel the funder expects and will understand?
- Have you included a word or phrase deliberately because that's how it was stated by the funder? (Check your notes from The Grant Answer Map in steps 4a to 4c.)
- Is this application of an acceptable quality?

If you can, take an overnight break and review your application fresh the next day. Your goal is to consider it from the funder's perspective.

Ideally, you would ask someone else to review your work in a 'mock assessment' scenario (the third review, covered later in this chapter). Remember, though, while this person may give feedback on content, you've done the hard work to understand the funder. If they don't think something should be in the answer, or should be replaced with something else, then consider it. Consider, but don't necessarily remove it. If you have a sound reason for including it, leave it in. In some cases, if it's your boss, you may need to take them through The Grant Answer Map so they understand your approach. Also remember to ask specific people to review the sections matched to their skills and experience. For example, if your project manager drafted the budget, ask your bookkeeper to check it.

Second review: Edit format and content

In this review, you need to analyse your format and content, and I cover specifics in the following sections. As you go through these sections, you can make changes as you go or track those changes – for example, using the Track Changes feature in Microsoft Word, or using an online system that automatically saves changes, or version control. This stage is an art-form. So, as with art you can get it right or decide you've overworked the editing and want to go back an edited version or two.

Format

Firstly, if the funder has provided an application template, use it. You may find other templates, such as a spreadsheet template for the budget. Use whatever is provided. Check the format you're submitting hasn't been changed around by someone.

Logical flow

Check your answers are structured logically. Think of the flow of information as a series of steps. Are they in the right order? For example, in a list of ways you'll work with your disability clients to ensure health safe working practices are implemented in their home, your last point wouldn't be about your cleaning staff undertaking a site induction. Site inductions would be one of the first few actions listed.

As always, ensure you're thinking like the funder. Review the way the questions are asked, and the additional tips provided, and ensure your answer style matches.

Check the question and then look at your last paragraph or two. Should they start your answer? Some answers tell a story and the last point is the most important point. Most assessors and funders value 'straight talk' that is to the point and direct.

Consistency of terminology, style and grammar

Check the words you regularly use. For example, if the grant documents use a word like 'success measures' but you're used to saying 'outcomes', check you've used their term consistently.

Check words you've caught yourself capitalising - is this needed? And is it consistent? Also check how you've referenced testimonials is consistent - is it bold and italic, or only italic?

Have you correctly spelt the funder's name? Have you mentioned another organisation because you cut and pasted your answer from another application?

Punctuation is important. That's why it's useful to read the answer out loud or see it in larger font. Where you choose to use a comma or a semicolon can affect your message. Fortunately, online systems such as ProWriting Aid (my favourite) or Grammarly can identify a lot of these errors, and your AI Assistant can be useful.

Visuals

Many grant applications are text only. However, if attachments are allowed you could include visuals.

If you can include visuals in your application, the top tip is to balance them across your answers. In applications, visuals should only be used to visually represent information or reinforce an important message. They are not replacements for explanations or details. You can't answer a question by asking them to look at the visual - and it may not be accessible. So include alternative text on your visuals, an explainer underneath the visual or, if it's an image file, an appropriately explained file name to make it accessible.

To check the image shares the key message, do the 'blink test'. This test is used by web designers as a challenge to see if the website conveys the key message in three to five seconds - the time it takes before most people blink. Let's try it. Close your eyes, open them and look at the image for three to five seconds (or until you need to blink) and then look away. Write down what you recall and go back to the image. Were you able to gather everything important in the one glance before blinking? Does the image convey your key messages? Is anything distracting the viewer? If needed, make the image clearer to pass the 'blink test'.

Write for the assessors

I stress this point throughout this book, but it's worth repeating now. The person assessing your application isn't you. They don't have the same depth of knowledge and information about your organisation. Go back to the notes on voice and tone you made when going through The Grant Application Tool (refer to step 3c). Is this still the voice you want?

One mistake people make is they don't 'layer the learning'. What I mean by this is you shouldn't go into highly technical detail straightaway. You should introduce what you're about to discuss, provide more detail and then start to get into the technical aspects.

Lists: numbers or bullet points?

When we see a numbered list, our brains tell us there's an order - either a sequential order or priority order. So, if you want to highlight an order, use a numbered list. Consider using a maximum of five to seven items on a list. If you want to increase the assessor's ability to remember, have a maximum of three.

When you use dot points, you're identifying these items have a collective purpose, but no order. You can also use different dot point styles. For example, if you want to reinforce benefits, you could use ticks to list all the benefits the funder receives by selecting your application.

Choose the right approach for your lists and what the online form allows. Some online forms don't allow dot points, so use the asterisk (*) or a dash (-) instead.

Persuasive writing

Back in step 1a, I introduced the four modes of persuasion - an expanded version of Aristotle's three modes of persuasion. I call these four modes the head, heart, gut and pocket.

Here's a reminder of how they work:

- **Head:** People make decisions based on logic and are influenced by bias.
- **Heart:** People made decisions based on emotion.
- **Gut:** People make decisions based on gut feelings that tell them the organisation is credible.
- **Pocket:** People make decisions based on the project's benefits and how this gives them a return on investment.

Assessors are your advocates at the decision table. Even if they aren't physically there, their comments and feedback are reviewed by the final decision-makers. So, use the head, heart, gut and pocket method to consider how to persuade the assessors.

Now, review your answers. Are they statistic heavy? Can you break these statistics up with a story? How are you balancing those four modes of persuasion in your answers and across your whole application?

Combatting bias in decision-making

People are people. We all have our strengths and weaknesses and sometimes we do things without thinking them through. Have you ever driven home, thinking you'll stop in and get milk, and the next minute you're parking in your driveway thinking *Oh, I forgot the milk*?

While assessors do undertake training and other checks are in place – either through independent auditors or other people such as panel chairs who do probity checks – they can miss things. They're human. As can happen to all of us at different times, their brain has taken charge and decided what's best. So, it's your job as writer to consider what objections and assumptions people may bring in at the assessment stage. For example, in a recent application I was reviewing, I noted the client partners with a faith-based university. I realise some people have objections to religion and, in many cases, funders won't fund religious or political organisations because they aren't for charitable purposes. So, how do you combat bias in this case?

If you need to introduce something that someone might question or dislike, you immediately need to follow it up with strong logic, such as statistics on outcomes achieved, and an emotive connection, such as a testimonial on the difference the organisation has made to a person. This way bias can be minimised through facts and empathy.

The power of 'so what?'

As you consider your answers, ask, 'So what? What does this mean? How does this support the client?' Asking 'So what?' can help ensure you're not sharing information without contextualising and demonstrating the result. 'So what?' also helps you cut the filler words and fluff and get straight to the point in plainer English.

Consistent references

If you provided relevant references such as a source of data in one question, include these same references in other related answers. An example would be if you've mentioned a risk management policy in one question. Check it's referenced in any later related answer - such as a specific question or example about workplace health and safety. Remember - sometimes applications are divided between assessors and you don't want them noting you've missed something they feel is obvious.

Check the appendix and attachment numbering and referencing through the document. Go through each mention of an appendix or attachment and the reference number - for example, 'Appendix A' - and check this is the correct reference.

Contradictions and missing information

Check if any contradictions have emerged through the application and attachments. For example, perhaps you've stated in an answer you have identified a risk and you give an overview of your mitigation strategy. You then need to check what you've said in this answer matches what you have in your risk management plan.

Check every mention of a number or statistic. Particularly review the statistics you included in your single source of truth document, The Grant Application Tool (step 3c). Make sure these are consistent across your application.

Confirm additional information you're providing doesn't contradict the first statistic, or you haven't used a different number for the same thing - for example, you've stated 15 volunteers are gardening in one answer, and then stated 12 in another. It might be 12 volunteers are gardening, while the other three are project volunteers managing paperwork and process, not gardening. But is it clear, or does it appear to be a contradiction?

Paragraph length

Long paragraphs don't give the brain time to stop and absorb. For submissions, paragraphs between 50 and 100 words are easier to absorb. The more complex the information, the easier it should be for the brain to absorb.

Where possible, keep paragraphs to one idea or theme. You can bridge between one paragraph and the next by showing the link between the two. For example, at the end of a paragraph you could say, 'Now, we'll move onto step 2.' However, talking about step 1 and step 2 in the one paragraph might be too much information for the assessor to absorb. It makes logical sense to list all the steps and descriptions of those steps in different paragraphs with headings.

If you want a message to stand out, adopt a copywriting approach. Have one to two short sentences in their own paragraph.

Review how you open and close paragraphs. Do your openings make statements, followed by more information, and then come to a summary or a bridge to the next paragraph? These approaches assist information flow and reduce confusion.

Sentence length

Check your sentences: is there a mix of short and long sentences? If you have a series of long sentences, can you break a few up into shorter sentences? Try to keep your sentences to an average of 15 words. The more complex the information, the shorter your sentences should be. Short sentences increase readability and reduce filler words. This increases the brain's ability to absorb new information and reduces your word count.

For sentences longer than 15 words, critically assess if you can shorten them or break into two sentences. Sometimes a longer sentence is needed to keep the reader's interest, and too many short sentences in a row can start to feel disjointed. However, at least by assessing your sentence length, you're more likely to produce a clearer answer.

If you're listing more than three things, use dot points. This works if you're restricted by words because it cuts out the 'filler' words. Dot points also increase negative space, which gives the assessor's brain time to pause and absorb.

Strip out filler words

If you've reviewed your answers and kept to shorter sentences, you'll start to identify the regular filler words you use. I used to be a prolific user of the word 'that', for example. I now know how unnecessary it often is, and to edit it out – well, mostly. It saves so many characters. I originally also included filler words 'very' and 'actually' in this draft, which I removed right after I typed them! It takes practice, but you'll pick up on filler words when you're more conscious. Most software systems identify filler words you can remove to increase clarity. This will assist you to develop an active voice.

A quick way to check for your filler words is to use TagCrowd (which I discuss in step 2b). Copy and paste any form of your writing, from a grant application to a report. Find the words you use the most and assess if they're needed. Take them out of a sentence and see if this makes any difference. Often, the sentence is a lot clearer without them. Sometimes you can replace three words with one.

Also watch out for words like 'aim' and 'want' that weaken your answers. Don't say 'we aim'. Say 'we will' or make it stronger with a statement like, 'Our 2024 Strategic Plan demonstrates'.

Search for the following words and assess if you can remove them to strengthen your message, and save characters and words:

Actually	Really	Very
Aim	Should	Want
Also	That	We
Are	There/There is	Will
Believe	There are	Wish
Currently	To	

Search for words that end in *-ing*. Reframe them to use active language. For example:

'We're focused on strengthening the department's ...'

changes to...

'This approach strengthens ...'

Search for the words 'of', 'in', 'to', 'for', and 'was'. Can you remove those words or words following? For example, 'In order to' becomes 'to' – two words and nine characters saved.

Search for the word 'and'. You can often replace 'and' with a dot point, breaking up a long sentence into two. Remember – reducing the words in your sentences reduces cognitive load.

Be specific

Check if your language is specific enough. We all use words to generalise our statements and dilute the strength of our message. For example, a statement like, 'We've used our systems a few times for projects' is subjective and vague. As an assessor, it doesn't give me confidence you know what you're doing. However, saying, 'Our project management process has delivered six successful funded projects' is stronger by offering the assessors some insight into your practices. You could then provide more specific detail, such as what type of projects and the financial value to strengthen this statement further.

Spelling and grammar

STOP. Don't scan over this. I know this is something you'd expect to find in a writing tip list, but don't assume you won't make this mistake. I've seen substantial errors made that change the context of the answer. One memorable example was when someone wrote in an answer to a workplace health and safety question they were 'complacent'. I'm sure they meant to say compliant, but their answer didn't score well!! When something like this happens in an application, you generally find additional errors throughout.

One thing I'd recommend is to read your answers out loud to someone. Ask them to sit in front of you, close their eyes, and listen closely to your application answers. You'll pick up more errors this way than you would if you only skimmed the highlights. Stop when the information is confusing. Make a note of the area to review.

Or you can read them aloud to yourself or read the words in your head, although sometimes that doesn't work because your brain tells you it makes sense - it's like checking for your own spelling errors!

Third review: Taking advantage of an independent mock assessor

Ideally, you would have a few people critically reviewing your application. Ask them to score your questions out of five. If the funder has shared the assessment criteria, ask them to use these to rank you on the listed factors.

Ask them to review the document and note:

- any areas they were confused

- information that was hard to absorb
- moments when they thought 'what does that mean?'
- terminology they didn't understand
- the five key points they understood and remembered from the application.

Reflect on their notes and your approach. As mentioned earlier in this step, this isn't about saying you should immediately change things. Perhaps there's a clear reason the reviewer doesn't understand the terminology, but the funder will because you noted to use these terms in The Grant Application Tool or The Grant Answer Map. This is about reflecting on the feedback and asking what should be improved. For example, perhaps the reviewer was confused because your sentences were too long. Consider their feedback, and then make your own choices.

Summary

You've now completed the three main reviews, but you're not quite ready to hit 'Submit' yet. The next step takes you through some common submission mistakes, and how to avoid them.

What can you do now?

- ☐ Understand your filler words by using TagCrowd to identify those regular words you repeat far too much and that don't add value to your sentences.
- ☐ Do the three reviews. If you're short on time, at minimum, you should complete the second review.

Step 5b

Avoid submission mistakes

Even after all your work and time spent reviewing your grant application, some mistakes and oversights can still slip through. In this step, I outline some of the more common ones, and take you through my checklist for avoiding them.

The Grant Writing System: xi. The Grant Submission Checklist

As shown in the following figure, to guide you to avoid submission mistakes at this step, I've put together a final template checklist for before you hit 'Submit'.

Stage 5: Submit - Step 5b. Avoid submission mistakes

5. Submit

Confidently submit without regret!

Step 5b. Avoid submission mistakes

Tool

x. The Grant Submission Checklist™

The Grant Submission Checklist includes the common mistakes but, of course, it may not cover every single situation. You can use this checklist as a basis for developing your own checklist - including the skills you want to strengthen, or areas you often find yourself missing. Some funders provide a submission checklist and, if they do, check that also.

Check the following before submission:

- **Project title and description:**
  - Do these reflect the type of project and outcomes the funder wants to achieve?
- **Need:**
  - Is the need for the project well described?
  - Have you clearly demonstrated the demand for the project?
  - Does the need reflect the objectives of the grant program?
- **Stakeholders:**
  - Have you clearly described the target groups who will benefit?
  - Have you included quotes or testimonials in language the target groups use, so the funder can connect with them?
  - Is it clear the target group has been engaged and/or co-designed the project?
- **Capability** (resources and experience):
  - Have you demonstrated your resources and partnerships to deliver the project?
  - Have you positioned your organisation and people as being knowledgeable about similar projects?
- **Budget:**
  - Are you sure you've only asked the funder to pay for eligible costs?
  - Is the budget within the minimum and maximum amounts?
  - Are you asking a reasonable amount out of the funding bucket, and an amount you feel is appropriate and competitive?
  - Have you costed indirect costs in the budget – for example, administration, bookkeeper or rent costs?
  - Does your budget add up to the total project budget?

  - Is the total funding amount being requested clear?
  - Have you reviewed your application and checked all activities are costed?
- **Timelines:**
  - Are your project start and end dates within the funding period?
  - Does your timeline reference action to monitor outcomes?
  - Are your timelines realistic and achievable?
- **Risk:**
  - Have you included a range of risks across the three levels and seven categories of STEEPLE?
  - Does your risk management plan indicate key themes funders have expressed in the application pack?
  - Have you considered all the licenses and insurances required?
- **Financial viability:**
  - With co-contribution, is it clear how your organisation will pay?
  - If the financial reports show a lot of funds in accounts, is it clear these are committed elsewhere, or does it appear you should use your own money to deliver the project?
  - Does your financial statement make you look too healthy, with potential funds the funder may think you could use? If so, make it clear these are already committed with notes to the financials at minimum. Ideally you would adjust the reports to make it clear for everyone.
- **Sustainability:**
  - Have you indicated how the project outcomes will be sustainable, and how you've considered this in the project?
- **Implementation and outcomes:**
  - Can you demonstrate sound project management practices to deliver the project?

   - Have you indicated how you'll monitor, evaluate, report and improve during the project to achieve the outcomes?
- **Structure:**
   - Are your answers well-structured and easy to follow?
   - For long answers, can the assessors easily identify sections of your text?
   - Have you broken up chunks of statistics with lighter content?
- **Content:**
   - Have you started answering the question in the first paragraph?
   - Have you checked any statistics mentioned are correct, and don't contradict each other?
   - Are your terms consistent, particularly if you've used a funder's term – for example, 'success measures', rather than 'outcomes'?
   - If the question had tips indicating what you should include, have you done this if appropriate?
   - Can you reduce your sentence and paragraph length to make the content easier to absorb and remember?
   - Have you used industry terminology you haven't explained?
   - Have you made any assumptions of knowledge?
   - If your application is information rich, have you structured it to layer the learning and reduce cognitive load?
- **Attachments:**
   - Have you only attached the necessary, required information asked by the funder?
   - If you're able to attach additional supporting information, have you only included specific extracts or information, not whole documents?

Summary

You've gotten this far in the journey and now it's time to hit submit if you're satisfied the application is as ready as it will ever be. Remember, no application is perfect. It's better to submit it if you're satisfied you've put as much strength into it as possible, and you are confident you've hit the key points the funder cares about, than not submit it at all. Yes, no doubt you'd change some things, but note down these as lessons learnt and consider what you can do next time to reduce the mistakes.

A big congrats. Hit submit - it's time to celebrate! - but don't walk away just yet. You can do some things after you hit submit that can help you, which we'll explore in the next stage.

What can you do now?

- [ ] Develop your own submission checklist, complete with areas you know you need to strengthen, and things like reminders to remove your filler words.

Summary of Stage 5: Submit

The steps in this stage have taken you to the point where you've reviewed your application, edited as required and are now ready to submit. After you submit your application, update The Grant Ready Toolkit with any new information you've found or updated during the application, such as new testimonials, statistics or case studies.

What can you do now?

Have another look at the completed application form you reviewed at the end of stage 3. How would you change the answers now? Would you structure them differently? What about editing – what might you remove? Do you notice the prolific use of a particular filler word?

Check the application against the submission checklist in step 5b. Can you note down any areas for future improvement?

Stage 6: Manage

The Grant Writing System™

© Natalie Bramble

1. Plan 2. Find 3. Align 4. Write 5. Submit **6. Manage** 7. Report

Manage the outcome, win or lose

You've submitted your application and - after likely an anxious wait - you've now learnt if you won or lost. You're now up to the Manage stage in The Grant Writing System (see following figure).

Manage: Stage 6 in The Grant Writing System

Manage the outcome, win or lose

6. Manage
What to do if you win or lose.

Steps in this stage
a. Manage the project.
b. Monitor and evaluate outcomes.

Tools to guide you
xi. The Grant Evaulation Plan™

Writing successful grants is a learned skill. You improve your skills when you focus on developing them.

The way I think about funders and grant funding is that they're similar to project partners - they've invested in you, but now you need to work to keep them, and the cash. Even if you aren't funded, you're on the funder's radar and next year's grant round may be your turn to receive funds. You don't want your funders saying the following:

> They committed to the funding and then pulled out two months before the acquittal was due, saying they hadn't even

> started the project. They should have told us sooner. It was an eight-month project.

or

> Well, they apparently delivered the project, we've seen photos, but we couldn't get any information from them about what they did and what the outcomes were.
>
> Grant Funder's Feedback

Regardless of the outcome, you should continue to share your project idea with stakeholders, influencers and potential funders. You never know who is ready to support a project and you could receive a nice surprise - be it support or money. One community trying to raise funds for a tourism art silo project experienced this when they received a $200,000 donation from a local. They hadn't approached this person for support, and they had no idea they were interested in their project. The only way the donor knew about the project was because of the promotion and word of mouth. So, it's worth doing.

In the steps in this stage, I guide you on what to do if you win, or if you lose. If you win, I discuss what's included in a contract, your legal responsibilities, and how to create an evaluation plan to keep the money you've been given.

Step 6a

Manage the project

Waiting to find out whether you've been successful with a grant application is often an anxious time. While you wait, think about those items you mentioned in your application. Consider the following:

- Do any policies or documents need updating?
- Should your website be updated?
- Did you gather any testimonials or case studies you could add to The Grant Ready Toolkit?

What you do with the project itself depends on whether you win or lose with your application (see the following figure). In this step, I take you through both possibilities, and what you need to (or can) do in response.

The Win-or-Lose flowchart

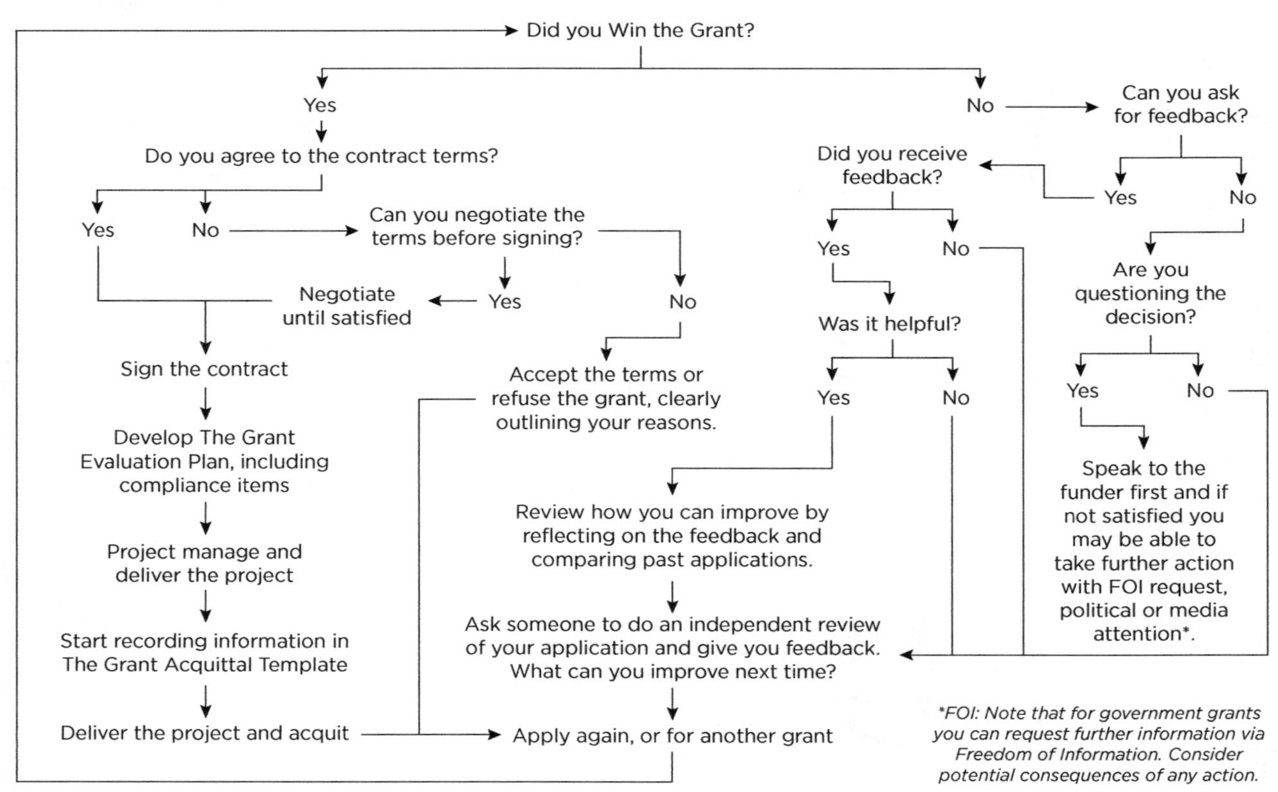

Managing the project if you win

As shown in the following figure, once you receive the fantastic news that your funding application has been successful, your main focus then needs to be managing the project so you keep your funding.

Stage 6: Manage – Step 6a. Manage your project so you keep your funding

6. Manage

What to do if you win or lose.

Step 6a. Manage your project so you keep your funding

One word of warning before you put the music on and celebrate. For now, keep the news quiet. Most funding announcements are embargoed, which means the news can't be publicly shared or promoted until a date the funder determines. Funders are generally keen to share the message first because it maximises their exposure. This means you should wait until your funder announces the grant recipients.

Now, I know it's tempting to say, 'Yes, just give me the money.' However, think about this first stage as an offer, not acceptance. Check the conditions the funder wants you to agree with, work for your organisation.

In the following section, I review a couple of things to consider before signing.

Has the funder offered less than you wanted?

If the funder hasn't offered the full funding you've asked for, can you fill the funding gap before accepting the offer? It's okay to negotiate at this stage, telling the funder you can't do the project for the offered amount, or telling them you can, but you need more time to fundraise and fill the gap.

The other thing you should negotiate on is the numbers and outcomes. You may not be able to deliver the same project with the same number of beneficiaries, for example, for the reduced amount. Are you clear on the fixed and variable costs and how this reduced funding offer affects the budget? You can use this information to negotiate - for example, you could ask the funder to cover the fixed costs and negotiate on the variable costs.

Say you're running a grant writing workshop for 60 people. The trainer and the venue are fixed costs the grant is being asked to cover and you included a lunch on the day for networking. However, they've only offered you half what you applied for. Does this mean you'll reduce the lunch to sandwich platters, or are the number of attendees and room size being reduced? Maybe you can ask for a co-contribution from attendees?

These are all things to consider before you accept the reduced funding offer.

Has the funding offer been delayed?

Funding delays are common. The impact on your project plan delivery timeline could be affected. For example, at iClick2Learn, we submitted a grant request in partnership with a not-for-profit association to deliver online training for volunteers across a state. The decision was due in October, but at the end of January the following year, we were still waiting on the determination. We knew, even if we were successful, we'd have to review the project and/or contract our deadlines to get it acquitted by the end of the required period. This isn't unusual and we generally plan for funding delays in our milestones. These delays then have minimal impact on our delivery schedule because we're using existing internal resources and can expand as required.

However, some projects must wait for contractors and supplies. So, if there's a longer delay than expected, how does this impact your project deadlines?

Consider the impact on stretching your resources. For example, you might be able to fill casual jobs or increase volunteer hours, but is this going to burn everyone out? If you're the business owner and you invest a lot of your time, what's the impact on your business? Will this mean you'll be more operational and less strategic? And will your sales fall as a result?

Examining the funding contract

Once you're told you did Win the Grant, your organisation will be provided with a contract, and you may not be given a lot of time to sign. One sporting grant I won gave a sports club 48 hours to return the signed contract - and the funds were in their bank account two days after the signed contract was returned. This kind of speed is generally due to pressure from either their finance or strategy team to show on their records the money has been spent, particularly before the end of financial year. Government agencies must convince the Treasury department to give them money. Like us, these agencies are always putting in grant requests, business cases and funding submissions. So, if there's time pressure, have adequately experienced and skilled people review the contract requirements.

Verify the contract includes things you expected. Contracts do generally repeat what you've included in your grant application; however, you may have put dates in your application based on receiving the grant earlier.

A few things to check include:

- What are the payment arrangements? Have they said payment is dependent on any reports?
- What conditions, if any, in the contract allow the funder to pull out of the agreement, and any stated future funding?
- For what reasons might the funder ask for the money back, and can they ask for the full amount, or only unspent funds?
- Do you pay for things first, and then report to get the milestone payment? If so, how will you manage this?
- Have they included GST or not? Is this what you expected, and what you put in your application?
- When are the reports due, and what information do they want from you?
- Have they asked for any additional reporting or measurement?
- What has been included around deadlines and commitments? Consider the wording here carefully – for example, does it say reports are due 'by' or 'from' a date? The word 'by' is different to the word 'from'.
- Are any additional administration requirements listed?
- What requirements are there for using the funder's logo and any media contact? How long do approvals take?
- Do any clauses restrict your ability to advocate for your cause? (These are commonly called 'gag-clauses'.)
- What legal compliance obligations exist? Can you meet these?
- How can you change the agreement?
- If there's a dispute, how will this be managed?
- How is intellectual property managed? Who owns it? Does this mean you'll have to give away intellectual property?

Note any obligations that survive beyond the funding period. A typical one is asset related. If the funding has been used to purchase an asset, what's required to replace it or sell it? Has the funder said you have to ask for permission, or to inform them before the sale? If so, you need to add this information to your asset register so others know if you're not there to ask.

Another one to watch for is what logo and brand acknowledgements survive beyond the funding period. For example, say you receive funding for resurfacing a tennis court and 10 years later it needs to be done again. What's the impact of having to keep the previous political party's logo on signage when another party is now in power? All logo and brand acknowledgements should have a maximum sunset clause on them. This gives you an ability to then go out and seek funding and be able to recognise the new funder.

Once you've considered the previous list and other areas in the contract, you'll be able to make an informed decision. If you need to query anything, ensure you clearly understand what the contract is saying, and then reach out to your contact in the funding organisation and have a discussion.

You may want to negotiate changes in the clauses. Keep in mind most funders have standardised contracts, so getting things changed may be difficult, but it's worth a conversation if you're unhappy about a clause. The best way to do this is to first understand why the funder requires the clause in the contract and then share with them the impact this has on your organisation. This is not about bartering for the best deal. It's about both sides understanding the purpose and impact of the clause.

Remember to always focus on the relationship and an outcome that's best for all parties.

You may have to set a 'walk-away' limit before you start negotiating. In other words, know the point at which you agree to proceed, or walk away from the opportunity. At this stage, go back and review your project plan and budget. Talk with partners and check you can deliver the work. Make adjustments and plans for any gaps.

Complying with the contract

You'll often have a bit of time between signing it off and receiving the money. You can use this time to get prepared and ready for the project - either as soon as you've been notified, or after the contracts have been signed and the money is in your bank account. Either way, you should get prepared.

I develop a table. (You can also include the same information in two lists, but I find tables in a spreadsheet easier to create a list of jobs to do and track.) The Grant Evaluation Plan, covered in the next step, includes compliance items. I then use this information to develop our final work plan that goes into our project management system, spreadsheet or calendar. Sometimes, for example, you're the project manager and other people in the team take care of compliance information. Creating The Grant Evaluation Plan early means you can provide them with the information to fulfil the contract.

The work plan includes actions to ensure compliance with the contract and your promised deliverables and outcomes. In one project we delayed developing this plan, and this was the one project where we missed delivering on an activity. Fortunately, this didn't have an impact on the project deliverables or outcomes because it wasn't listed as a performance indicator - we'd offered it as a bonus. However, that's just luck. It could have been an issue. We still delivered the bonus, of course, a little later than planned. So, what do we always do now? We start with The Grant Evaluation Plan before we start working on the grant and we haven't missed a compliance item since then. (See the following step for much more detail on what to include in your evaluation and work plan.)

What if things change?

No-one lives in a perfect world and things are guaranteed to go a different way than you first planned and promised the funder. So, if delays or changes that affect your project emerge, reach out to the funder early. You may be able to get a variation to the contract that considers any delays or shifts.

What if you lose?

If you don't Win the Grant, don't get disheartened. Winning grants is a process. In the same way as we don't get a yes to every job application - and we often don't know why we didn't get it - we don't always get funding approved. I know you're probably frustrated and, yes, maybe a little angry. So, let off some steam. A former colleague of mine, Dr Lee Summers, told me she'd do 'the two-finger dance' around the room and it still makes me laugh thinking about it. If you need to do something similar, go right ahead.

When you're ready, make a list of what you've learnt from the experience. What are the key things you now want to do for your next grant? If you've adopted any of the tools I've shared, what would you update or change?

In the following sections, I outline some other aspects to consider.

Will funders give you feedback?

A lot of funders offer generic feedback. This is sometimes hard to relate to your application - for example, if it says applications didn't clearly demonstrate how they align to the grant objectives, you might think, *But I did that* and then disregard the comment. Please think about this as an opportunity, though. They aren't being critical of your application directly, so don't disregard what they've said.

Use this opportunity to review your application with fresh eyes. Pretend you're the assessor. Critically review what you've submitted. Find those areas where you can improve. Then, think about the application from your organisation's perspective. What can you do better next time? What improvements could you make to your application? If the content doesn't seem to be the issue, perhaps you could improve the structure?

You can ask funders for individual feedback, but keep in mind they aren't obligated to do this. In some cases, particularly government bodies, they may have policies to prohibit them from providing feedback. Sometimes, though, you'll hit gold. Someone will be helpful and may go through points in your application, showing you where it can be strengthened.

One of our iClick2Learn community learning members, Nicholas, does this all the time. Mostly, he gets a 'No, we can't tell you anything', but when he gets a yes, he says it's worth all the rejection he's had. So, it's worth a try.

If the funder publishes information on who's been funded, check the list of recipients and the types of projects funded. You can learn the types of projects the funder feels are suitable, and an average amount of funding given for those types of projects.

The other reason you might want to connect with the funder is more of a logical reason. For example, one Parents & Community (P&C) Committee wasn't successful in their grant application for a school garden. When the list of successful applicants was published, they saw other schools had received funding for a school garden. They enquired with the funder only to find out a major glitch in the system had resulted in around 200 applications being lost and not showing up in the database. This led to a review of their application because they had taken the initiative to enquire, and their project ended up being funded. So sometimes it's worth calling.

Can you challenge the decision?

The majority of funders always say the decision is final, even if you might think they're in the wrong. So don't go in all fired up ready to argue. Keep your enquiry friendly and professional. You could note another similar organisation was funded but you weren't and ask for specific feedback on this. You could ask if they'd accept an application from you in the future. If you've received a rejection letter identifying why you weren't successful and you disagree with this, you could ask questions about this. The best way to approach this is with a curious, learning mindset. You want to learn so you can Win the Grant next time.

For example, a filmmakers group I've supported applied for a grant that was open to not-for-profit organisations and charities. The funder's eligibility included a requirement for all applicants to be registered on the Australian Charities and Not-for-profits Commission (ACNC) register. The applicant remembered this but didn't make note of it. (You won't do this because you've got The Grant Application Tool from step 3c!) Anyway, when they were told they were rejected because they weren't registered and were, therefore ineligible, they went to the ACNC website to register, ready for the next round of funding.

After some research and discussions with the ACNC, the filmmakers realised they weren't eligible for registration because the ACNC register is only for charities. They went back to the funder and advised them of this. The funder said, 'Thanks, we'll note this for the next round of funding.' Note they didn't state they were wrong. They probably weren't aware of this change because organisations used to be able to self-register if they didn't have a charity status. Ultimately, the funder didn't change their decision. Now, the filmmakers did reapply in the next round and were successful. So, as long as you keep your enquiry respectful, you'll likely be accepted in the future if you meet requirements.

If you do have a valid reason to push back, you can. You could take it further if you're able to – for example, by submitting a Freedom of Information request (this is called different things in different states and territories). A homelessness organisation I worked with missed out on national funding, and their competitor was awarded the funds. They queried the decision based on value for money because their competitor only delivered one-third of the housing stock the homelessness organisation had committed to in their unsuccessful application. They didn't have any success with the federal agency. They advocated to their federal member of parliament, who couldn't get an answer either. They submitted a Freedom of Information request and didn't receive any information to support a claim. So, they couldn't take it any further, because there wasn't a federal anti-corruption commission at that time.

However, the funding agency is now aware of their position, and this can mean one of two things:

1. The funder will be sensitive to this organisation's applications in the future and may give them some favour.
2. The organisation is now on the funder's 'handle with care' list, which might restrict them getting a yes in the future.

It's for this second reason a lot of organisations and people who are connected to those organisations don't often speak out, for fear of retribution. So, seriously consider if it's worth taking a complaint further.

But it's not all doom and gloom. Another example is one I challenged. The federal agency involved had provided a formatted template. We had written two grant applications and used the same application form. Applications needed to be downloaded, completed offline and then submitted. We submitted the last at 2 pm on Friday. They closed at 5 pm. Half an hour after our submission, I received an email saying the last application was rejected. I tried again, and I received the same auto-response email. It was now around 3.30 pm and I was getting a bit stressed!

I called the office, and was told every applicant was required to download a new application form for every project, because each application had a unique number for every project. I now had 45 minutes left and they weren't extending the deadline. I checked the wording in the guidelines, which clearly said, 'Applications are numbered when you download them' – not what it should have said based on what I was told which was, 'You must download an application form for every project you apply for. Every time an application form is downloaded, a unique number is created. You can only use one application form per project. Do not duplicate application forms. Duplicate application forms will not be accepted.' It's a lot more words, but it's much clearer.

It was now 6.45 pm and I had escalated my complaint two managers above. I was getting a little short because this was worth fighting for. It didn't matter if it was a no; if I couldn't submit the application, it was going to be a no anyway, so I had nothing to lose. When the program manager again tried to refuse the application, I said, 'It's obviously a common issue because you're on the phone to me at 7 pm on a Friday night, so I'm sure I'm not the only one you've been talking with.' The conversation ended with a 'Yes, we'll accept the application.' Both applications were funded, so in the end it was worth me challenging the misrepresentation in the guidelines.

Can someone review my application?

Yes, I'm a big fan of independent assessments. However, first go through your application with fresh eyes, using this book and the information we've covered to identify areas that can be strengthened.

You can then ask someone else to review the application and identify any areas they felt could be improved.

Just remember, though, it's not your fault. You don't know for certain what the funder's process has been, and you don't know the standard of other entries. I've seen strong applications lose out because the funder felt they had supported enough projects in that region the previous year, or that the organisation had received a lot of support from them already in the past. The money has to be spread around. Some funders have a national footprint, so they assess the funding they give across Australia. Some local funders, such as local councils, have to share grants with different types of organisations, projects and target groups. Political sway, or 'pork-barrelling' as it's called and been reported in a Grattan Institute report, could have been a factor.*

You could have missed out because the timing isn't right and they're committed elsewhere. In the case of government bodies, it can take a few years for policy priorities to align to your need. Keep in mind they have a state- or nation-wide footprint to fund other policy targets.

For one regional medical accommodation project, I secured an initial $3.2 million in funding. The organisation has since been trying to get more units funded. They've been advocating and communicating to every type of funder available. As I write this, the funding's been announced, and they've been awarded a further $2.5 million dollars. Now, it's in a majority party seat, known to swing towards independents in the past. You probably won't be surprised to hear the state election is only a few months away. So, two things here

---

* See the Grattan Institute's *New politics: Preventing pork-barrelling*, available at grattan.edu.au/wp-content/uploads/2022/08/New-politics-Preventing-pork-barrelling-Grattan-Report.pdf, for more.

could have influenced the decision. One, the organisation has been advocating for this project for over six years across the region. There wouldn't be anyone who would be able to say this project isn't deserving. And the second thing is the timing to support the project lined up.

So, don't beat yourself up. The most important thing to recognise is it's not all about your application. Don't let yourself, your boss or others make you feel bad.

Grants are a competition and they're sometimes a game of chance; most importantly, they're a learning experience. Even applications I know are strong, which I know I've done everything I can on to Win the Grant, sometimes slip through.

Chalk it up as a learning experience and, as they say, 'Try, try again'.

I also provide some final tips for improving your chance of success in the conclusion to this book.

Summary

The points in this step have helped you think through what to do if you win or lose. Either way, you can take steps to maximise future success. If you've won, the money is yours and now you need to manage a project to success and evaluate it, which I cover in the remainder of this book.

What can you do now?

- [ ] Use the flow cart diagram earlier in this step to guide you through your next action.

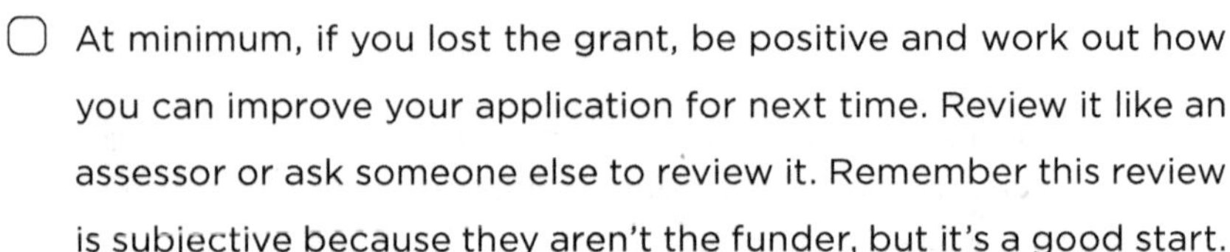

- [ ] At minimum, if you lost the grant, be positive and work out how you can improve your application for next time. Review it like an assessor or ask someone else to review it. Remember this review is subjective because they aren't the funder, but it's a good start.

Step 6b

Monitor and evaluate outcomes

You've won the grant and have gotten started on your project. You likely have staff and volunteers to organise, venues to book and milestones to check off. But you can't forget about the funder and what you've committed to them. They need to be kept informed on your progress and how you're spending their money. In this step, I provide a framework to make that reporting easier.

The Grant Writing System: xii. The Grant Evaluation Plan

As shown in the following figure, part of the Manage stage is also monitoring and evaluating outcomes. The Grant Evaluation Plan gives you a framework to guide you to manage your grant, and make sure you're giving the funder the information they need.

Stage 6: Manage - Step 6b. Monitor and evaluate outcomes

6. Manage

What to do if you win or lose.

Step 6b. Monitor and evaluate outcomes

Tool

xi. The Grant Evaluation Plan™

You've been given the funds because you've committed to do certain things (activities), achieve results (outcomes), and report on the progress (milestones) and the money spent (budget). These are foundational elements to report on, sometimes at different stages during the funding period, and by completing a final report - known as the acquittal.

> *It's fantastic you're cashed up! Your challenge now is to plan the work and get the results, so you can keep it!*

I developed The Grant Evaluation Plan to guide you through this. Gather the funding contract, your application documents and any project plans or Logic Models you've developed for the work that's just been funded. Keep in mind any changes that were made after discussions with your funders. This might mean your project plans and Logic Models need to be updated to reflect the work you've agreed to do.

If you use project management systems, use The Grant Evaluation Plan to assist with your planning, and transfer information straight into your systems. If you don't, The Grant Evaluation Plan template will work for you, if you check and update it regularly (e.g. monthly).

As you work through the template and this step, note the following:

- Because the majority of funding is within a 12-month period, the timeline used in this template factors in seasonal days and time to develop your acquittal report. (I talk more about acquittal reports in step 7b.)
- For the example I've used through this step, I've assumed the grant closed in July and you were awarded the grant contract and funds in full in October. The acquittal is due on 30 June.

Working through the template allows you to outline your plan to monitor, evaluate, review and improve (MERI) your work. This is the MERI Framework, developed by the Australian government for the natural resource management (NRM) space. If you've been involved in any NRM projects, you may recognise it. And if you're experienced in project management, MERI is similar to the PDCA - plan, do, check, act - process.

The MERI Framework guides you to consider the four areas as follows:

- ***M**onitor:* This is when you work out how you'll collect your data.
- ***E**valuate:* This is when you assess what you've been doing and if it is making a difference.
- ***R**eview:* At this stage, you'll reflect on the information you've gathered and consider if you're achieving the intended results, or if something has to change.
- ***I**mprove:* This relates to the steps you take to make improvements.

While MERI was developed for the natural resources sector, I use it for everything. I love the framework and believe it reflects a best practice approach, guiding us to do the right things to achieve our outcomes. At iClick2Learn, we create a MERI Outcomes Plan for every project and program we're working on. The core MERI plan doesn't differ, because we use the same internal frameworks, processes and systems to deliver our outcomes.

Breaking down the Grant Evaluation Plan

In the following sections, I walk through The Grant Evaluation Plan in three phases:

1. **Phase 1:** This is when you make notes about your approach, using the MERI Framework.

2. **Phase 2:** At this stage, you list actions - the things you have to comply with or the goals you'll meet.
3. **Phase 3:** You'll work out how and when you're going to track this information and complete these actions.

You can then put this plan in your calendar or scheduling software to keep on track.

Phase 1: Your approach

You first need to make notes on your approach. I provide a simple walk through here to get you started. Once you understand the kind of notes that are required, you can add more detail. For example, a funder we're working with is strong on compliance with the Privacy Act. So, we've included specific information in the monitoring and evaluating steps to highlight data collection, storage and use.

The following outlines the areas to start making some notes on, and what you might include.

Monitor

Monitor project outcomes based on activities. Use monthly project and budget reports to track progress.

Evaluate

Use a range of evaluation methods, both qualitative and quantitative.

Methods can include:

- surveys
- polls
- focus groups
- interviews
- case studies.

Review

Use monthly project meetings to review up-to-date information to discuss results and any modifications or changes. This will improve responsiveness. Complaints and results that don't meet standards will be escalated and may be actioned before the meeting. Delivery methods, processes and performance will be reviewed.

Improve

Any changes made will be monitored to verify they're delivering required outcomes and goals.

Relationship between MERI and stated grant need, outcomes and measurements

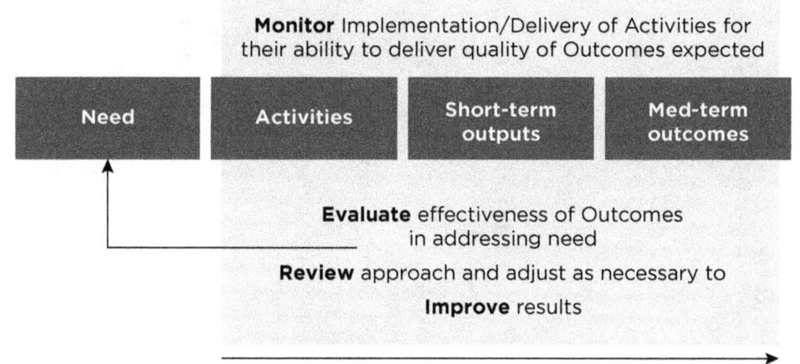

Phase 2: Actions

For this phase, you can start using a table. The following provides an example, and I've included some extra information on the first three elements after the table. (I discuss your work plan in phase 3.)

The example used in The Grant Evaluation Plan following is a half-day job ready skills workshop and, again, I've kept the notes high-level for simplicity.

Milestone, activity or compliance		**Outcomes**	**Monitoring**		**Work plan**	
Type	Description	What are they?	How	When	Who	Where
Activity	Target group attendance	15 attendees who are working fewer than five hours a week; ages 15 to 25	Monitor registrations	Weekly and daily in the last week before cut-off (one week prior to workshop date)	Amy	Report from event system
Compliance	Information privacy	Permission to share data with funder; signed permission given	Must agree to register	On registration	Amy	Event system
Milestone and contract compliance	Post-workshop report on outcomes	Numbers attended Ages of attendees Desire to apply for jobs 25 hours+ has increased by min. 25% 70% indicate interest in different jobs they may not have considered before, and non-traditional jobs 70% feel more confident in an interview setting 70% indicate improved understanding on roles to match their interests 70% indicate improved understanding of employer expectations	Survey pre-workshop and post-workshop Workshop activities and post mock interview discussion *Note: baseline data required	During the workshop	Tamal	Set up survey and provide Take observation notes in workshop

Milestone, activity or compliance

In the first column in The Grant Evaluation Plan, you note down all jobs and tasks. You can do this by project milestone, task or a mix of both - whatever works for you. The key thing is not to miss anything. Consider other actions, such as mid-project reports if they're due, and don't forget compliance items. You will have committed to certain things in your application, and in your contract. Ensure you're fulfilling what you said, and what's contractually required. Make a list of everything and ensure each job is in The Grant Evaluation Plan.

I find it useful to include the type of action I'm noting down - for example, 'activity' or 'compliance'. This way, I can put the details in a spreadsheet and sort by action. Action generally requires more work and planning - for example, setting aside an hour or more in my work plan.

Also factor in regular project timeline and budget tracking to keep you on time and on budget. Things can go off track, so doing this regularly - for example, every four to six weeks - will assist you to identify any issues early on and allow you to respond quickly to keep the project on track.

Your funder will require an acquittal (see step 7b for more on this). For now, remember to factor in the work required to acquit your grant. Work backwards - how long will it take to write a report? What information has to be provided? How long will it take to pull this information together?

Outcomes

Note down the outcomes you've agreed to and provide details on all measurements.

If you have outcomes being reported as comparisons, consider how you're going to establish a baseline. For example, if you're going to say attendees have improved confidence, then you need to measure their confidence level before the activity and after.

Monitoring

This is where you include what method you'll use to capture the information. **Examples include:**

- observations
- discussions
- documents and information started, produced and implemented
- interviews
- video feedback
- focus groups and case studies
- online methods (such as attendee polls, whiteboard interactions, reactions, chat discussion)
- surveys.

You'll notice in the above list, I've left surveys to last. Most people put these first because they feel easy, but they're not always the most effective. Let me explain ...

For some projects, you may want to go into more detail in the notes in The Grant Evaluation Plan and include the survey questions you're asking and why you're asking these. For example, for the Win the Grant workshops iClick2Learn delivers, we map monitoring methods to our learning frameworks and social return on investment methodology. We then factor in any stakeholder expectations, such as those from a funder or a client who has hired us to deliver. This means we ask survey questions only if they have a purpose, such as to measure impact, or align to a reporting requirement.

Say we want to monitor an attendee's engagement and satisfaction level with the face-to-face workshop. We're not going to wait until the end of the workshop to do this. The trainer uses observation and discussions during group activities to check-in and make sure the workshop is supporting attendees, delivering what they expected and engaging them in the learning. We then may ask a survey question at the end - for example, asking them what they enjoyed the most, and what they enjoyed the least.

For online webinars, where trainer to student interaction can be impacted (both visual and spoken), we use polls, annotations, reactions and chat interactions during the webinar. We also look at data on how long on average people stayed, and use a post-workshop survey. These methods are mapped to our social return on investment indicator, and net-promoter scores which puts a value on their degree of satisfaction.

The important thing to remember is this:

Measure what matters.

Regardless of when you're planning to ask questions as part of the monitoring stage, the key thing is to ask questions with intention, and focus on what you want to do with the information and why the question's needed.

When you decide the questions you'd like to ask, check in on the method you've chosen. Is there a better way to ask it? For example, rather than asking people at the end of the workshop to reflect on how much they've learnt, we have a visual scale and ask them to identify where their knowledge of the topic is before the workshop starts. We then ask them to reflect on where they feel their knowledge is before they leave the workshop. This helps attendees reflect on what they've learnt and reinforces key moments. This increases their ability to retain those key elements and combat the 'forgetting curve' (as it's called in the learning world).

Consider the other projects you want funded. Can you ask one question when you're gathering information to demonstrate demand for your other ideas? For example, if you want to run more workshops, you could ask, 'What other information would you like to learn, and why?' You can then use this data in your next grant application.

Phase 3: How and when

Answers to this stage will support you as you develop your work plan or schedule. In the template, I generally map these out based on weeks or months, and then we transfer the plan to our project management system. If we're working with other partners or experts, then we use the most easily shared task management system - a shared spreadsheet! I find it easier to use common tools when you're collaborating, rather than trying to train someone how to use a new system and risk them not reporting.

Timeline

Once you've completed the outcomes table, you should be able to use this information to develop an evaluation timeline, scheduling in the due dates and deliverables in your project management system or calendar.

Considering the impact on others outside your organisation

Until now, I've been talking about what you deliver for others. Let's now talk about what information you should ask your contractors and suppliers to provide, and what they need to commit to.

You've committed to a timeline, so you'll also need to co-ordinate anyone outside of your organisation who is involved in the project. This could be your project partner, local council, media, suppliers or contractors. You're now a middle-manager! You'll be managing expectations of people you report to, and managing the people who report to you, so they meet your expectations!

Go through The Grant Evaluation Plan and note down all the things you expect of others. This should include due dates, activity or milestones, and any reporting you require to track those outcomes. Set some check-in dates with those who are responsible to deliver. For example, if you've hired a builder, you would check in on the builder's progress regularly, so you can make adjustments and advise those people who can't start work until the builder is finished.

Now, consider what this means for any contracts or agreements you make. What should be factored in to protect your organisation? Go through the items listed in the previous step, where I cover examining the funding contract.

Also keep in mind that most contract laws refer to verbal agreements as being legal and binding. **An agreement is anything that includes the following elements:**

- an offer and intention to enter into an agreement
- a discussion and negotiation on the items being agreed to
- a consideration, which is where one or more parties are receiving a benefit in exchange (financial or non-financial)
- all parties having the capacity to enter into the agreement, which covers not only the parties being in a position to provide approvals but also aspects such as mental capacity to agree
- an acceptance of terms.

So, things such as verbal discussions and emails are considered agreements. Best practice is to get everything in writing. If you're having verbal discussions, then confirm the discussion and agreements via email.

Check the contract clauses you must comply with. Should they be included, or recognised in any contract or agreement with others?

For example, say compliance with the Privacy Act is required, and the person you've hired to develop and deliver a survey is the one responsible for managing the data. How will you confirm they comply with this requirement?

Many funders want the results of any intellectual property that's been developed during the course of funding to either remain shared intellectual property, or be their property they can freely share, considering they've paid for it. Consider what this means for you – otherwise, it could cost you time and money, or you could lose an opportunity.

As an example of this, a Landcare group hired a contractor to deliver a research project. They signed a contract agreement – and didn't realise by doing so they signed away their right to any intellectual property that was developed during the project. Yes, a contractor was paid to produce research and their contract said they kept the sole rights to the resulting research.

The group, unfortunately, lost an opportunity, and it was a commercial opportunity. The contractor went out and sold the report and research produced. The Landcare group lost an opportunity to commercialise it, which the contractor could have shared profits on.

For some organisations, releasing research publicly like this could be signing away a commercial advantage. For example, if this was a business instead of a Landcare group, the released research could go on to give competitors insights on their future plans. These are some of the signs I search for when I'm producing a competitive analysis.

Now, if a funder had wanted to claim intellectual property, this contractor agreement would have been non-compliant with the funding contract, and the Landcare group could have lost the whole project by signing this agreement. While it wasn't the case in this example, it could have been.

Summary

Now you've learnt how to design an evaluation plan, make it a regular process you implement as soon as the project funding is announced. I'd even suggest you use this process for projects that you're trialling or piloting to help you get the best results and track the data needed for the next grant application.

What can you do now?

- [ ] An easy action for this step is to complete The Grant Evaluation Plan and put all your milestones, activities or compliance actions across into your planner, diary or project management system.
- [ ] Check and update The Grant Evaluation Plan during regular meetings and discuss those that aren't delivering as expected.

Summary of Stage 6: Manage

You should now have some ideas on what do to if you miss out on a grant, and how to work with the funder if you Win the Grant. The Grant Evaluation Plan will save you stress and time when you work through this template before you start delivering.

Before we move onto talking about your reports, I want you to pause and repeat this next statement:

> *Your acquittal begins when you start work on your project. Not after!*

It's important you start collecting information along the way. As soon as something happens, file the information – when you spend money and get a receipt, when you get data back from a survey, and when you take a photo of the building progress. File it.

This is important because you might not be the person writing the acquittal report and, if you are, you've saved yourself at least a week or two having to track all the information down again!

What can you do now?

Using the information covered in this part, you should now have completed The Grant Evaluation Plan for your project.

- [ ] Work out how you will diarise these deliverables and get these started.
- [ ] Think about easy-to-use systems, such as survey forms with a couple of questions you can use, to gather information from others involved in the project.

Stage 7: Report

The Grant Writing System™

© Natalie Bramble

1. Plan 2. Find 3. Align 4. Write 5. Submit 6. Manage **7. Report**

Report and leverage data for more funding

You won the grant. You've developed your evaluation plan to stay on track and out of trouble. You're now ready to start gathering information so you can report to your funders (see the following figure).

Report: Stage 7 in The Grant Writing System

Report and leverage data for more funding

7. Report

Leverage the data and attract more funding!

Steps in this stage

a. Share good news and manage challenges.

b. Use reports and outcomes as marketing tools.

Tools to guide you

xii. The Grant Acquittal Report™

The steps in this stage discuss when and how you should report back to the funder, how to structure reports, and using The Grant Acquittal Report to save time and stress, particularly if it's not you having to complete the report! I also cover how to use your outcomes to attract more funding.

Most people think reporting to funders only happens when it's scheduled; however, it happens as soon as you start promoting the win, which should be after you receive the agreed payment and the okay to tell the world!

I know I said this in the previous part, but it's worth repeating:

Your acquittal begins when you start work on your project. Not after!

The other thing I'd like to emphasise is the importance of embracing the reporting process. If you've completed The Grant Evaluation Plan (refer to step 6b), you've identified when reports are due to comply with the contract, but have you considered other opportunities? The steps in this stage guide you to think of these other opportunities and using your reporting to take advantage of them.

Step 7a

Share good news and manage challenges

As part of your funding agreement, you're likely to be required to deliver mid-project reports and/or a final acquittal report. But you don't have to wait until the report is due before you share good news with your funders. Imagine if you gave someone money to do something and it took them a year to say thanks. That's not a positive way to build a funding relationship. Imagine hearing them say this about you:

> They were painful to deal with. We never heard from them during the project and getting their acquittal report was like pulling teeth.
>
> Grant Funder's Feedback

We don't want that! So, plan and deliver the due reports and add extras along the way to build a solid relationship. The key is to identify the moments of impact funders will likely care about and share good news when it happens. Let me be clear, don't add them to your newsletter list! This isn't what I mean, and is more likely to put them offside, rather than on your side.

In this step, I take you through using reporting to build and solidify your connection with the funder. I also outline how to share good – and not so good – news.

Use reporting to build your connection to funders

In step 1c, I talk about how stakeholders are influencers. Well, your funders are major influencer opportunities for you to attract more funding - either from them or from other funders. So, invest in your relationship. Funders invest in your work because they care about the work you do and the outcomes you're going to achieve. If you cared about something and invested money in it, wouldn't you want to know how things were going? Of course you would! So, think of your funders as investors and consider ways you can build a connection between them and the people you're supporting.

As an example, I was working on a project for a philanthropic consortium, deciding which three communities they were going to choose to be awarded a share in $5 million. One of the methods I proposed was capturing stories of people in the potential communities to share with the decision-making panel. They decided not to invest the money for a videographer to record and edit videos. However, I know how vital it is to connect funders with the people they're supporting. So, I mentioned the idea to Alli, the program manager, and we decided to produce some raw (let's call them 'authentic') video interviews. I donated pro bono time to edit them into a short video. The panel loved these videos so much they were shown at the boards of the two philanthropic foundations. These stories made an impact on them personally, and increased a sense of ownership the funders had, and continue to have, in the program.

How do I share good news?

Instead of thinking of reporting as dry and boring, a more positive way to think about it is simply sharing good news (see the following figure).

Stage 7: Report - Step 7a. Share good news

Step 7a. Share good news

7. Report

Leverage the data and attract more funding!

Consider what's important to your funders and how to share the messages from the people you're supporting, or the outcome you're achieving.

Here are some example grants and some ways you could share good news related to them:

- **Grant to publish a tourism brochure:** You could produce a video of the tourism officer taking brochures to a local business and showing their reaction and appreciation.
- **Grant for people connecting or learning:** Create videos sharing people's positive comments and learning, and their feelings and emotions on the day of the event.
- **Grant for manufacturing a new product:** Create an unboxing video, showing the business owner's excitement as they receive the prototype, and a video of a client testing the prototype, including the lessons learnt and potential improvements. Then create a follow-up video when the product is ready to go on sale.
- **Grant for mural at a school showcasing the local story of Country:** Create videos of young people (who are the interviewers and film crew) showing the process of developing the design and painting it. Then create a final video showcasing interviews with other students, Elders and community on the day the mural is launched, capturing their feelings and appreciation for this acknowledgement.

Consider the times when significant project milestones are reached. Identify a way to gather information at these times from the people involved on the difference the project is making to them.

What if it's not all good news?

First of all, remember funders are like us. They've made mistakes, or things have gone wrong for them in the past. So, don't stress. Life happens.

You don't need to let them know about all the little things that have been a challenge. The key things they care about being informed on relate to deadlines, outcomes and acquittal. Here are some examples as you think through when it's appropriate to let them know about an issue, or not:

- **Will it delay the acquittal or other reporting deadlines?** If the issue is going to delay the date you're required to acquit or report on the project, then you need to advise them of the change and discuss options. They may approve a contract variation. It's sometimes harder for government to do this because of their budget cycles.
- **Will this delay put the start or completion of the project in jeopardy?** If yes, advise them as soon as you know you won't be able to complete the project. Some funders can be flexible. Philanthropic organisations, for example, may be able to extend the project and the contract finalisation date. Other funders may have to ask for the full amount of funding to be returned, or perhaps only the part you haven't yet spent. There is sensitivity for government funders because of policy and budget reasons and potential public backlash on funded projects.
- **Does this increase cost?** If you can manage the increase by raising funds elsewhere, then other than in your reporting the funder probably doesn't need to know about the extra costs. If you can't manage the increase, think of other options and contact

the funder, letting them know. If it's minor for them, they may help out! It's certainly happened before.

- **Will this decrease your ability to meet the outcomes you'd agreed on?** If yes, then after you consider the options, contact the funder and let them know. They may offer some alternatives or agree to a contract amendment.

The key is to know if the issue is major enough to let the funder know and, if so, let them know as soon as possible. Focus on what the options are. It's best to bring a few options to the table to discuss with the funder to show them you're capable of fixing it. It's also a good idea to ask the funder for their feedback on these. They've likely worked with a lot of different organisations and projects and have witnessed some creative ideas.

Planning your report

Whenever I'm managing a project or an acquittal, I file copies of all relevant documents – including copies of emails and photos – as they happen in The Grant Ready Kit (refer to step 1a). I also have a draft report I add information to as the project progresses, using headings from The Grant Acquittal Report (see step 7b).

Working out how to structure your report

When considering how to structure your reports – and before you do unnecessary work – ask the funder if they can provide a copy of their reporting template. Let them know you're committed to completing your reports and you want to capture information along the way. Review the application form and consider the questions they asked that you feel they may want an update on.

If they can't provide a template or don't yet have an approved one to share, ask them if the headings in The Grant Acquittal Report would suit, or if they have any additional questions they generally ask.

Putting a process in place at the beginning of your project makes it so much easier for you, or someone else, to complete a report during, or at the end of, the project.

Summary

This step should have given you some ideas about how you can communicate and build a relationship with the funder. It's important to consider this as a relationship because they do have a longer term investment. I've known funders visit an organisation three to five years after a funded project because they're interested in the long-term results. So, put your funders down on your communication plan and stay in touch.

What can you do now?

- [ ] Add the funders to your stakeholder list and include them in your organisation's communication and marketing plan. Consider adding a reminder six months to a year after the project is due for acquittal to share a good news story with them. But don't add them to your monthly newsletter list – that's a bit much! Just let them know when there's important information they may appreciate knowing.

Step 7b

Use reports and outcomes as marketing tools

In this step, I outline all the elements in The Grant Acquittal Report. You can use this template for your final acquittal report to your funder, but also use the notes you make it in as the project progresses for any mid-project reports. I also run through some ideas for using project outcomes to attract more funding.

The Grant Writing System: xii. The Grant Acquittal Report

You're now at the stage of writing your final acquittal report for your funder (see following figure). Not only can this report communicate results, but elements from it can also be used as marketing tools.

Stage 7: Report – Step 7b. Use reports and outcomes as marketing tools

7. Report
Leverage the data and attract more funding!

Step 7b. Use reports and outcomes as marketing tools

Tool

xii. The Grant Acquittal Report™

The Grant Acquittal Report guides you to gather all the information you need for your final report. **Here's what you'll need to include:**

1. Project title.
2. Project summary.
    - Describe the activities undertaken with the grant funding.
3. What were the key things you achieved?
    - Align these key achievements to things the funder, your target group and your organisation cares about.
4. Explain the outcomes and impacts your project created.
    - It's useful to include outputs – for example, if you were running a workshop, include how many manuals you produced.
    - You could use your Logic Model to explain this in a clear, structured way.
    - Another framework that's useful is called Results Based Accountability. You could use these three questions to structure your answer:
        - What did we do?
        - How well did we do it? This allows you to evaluate the quality and performance of how you delivered the project.
        - What changes were made? You could focus on the most significant changes (outcomes) directly resulting from the project. Be sure to focus on the target group your project was designed for. You can then discuss other benefits to others.
5. Did your plans change during the project? If so, describe why they occurred and how you managed these changes.
6. Were there any unexpected outcomes in the project?
7. What did your organisation learn from this project?
    - Consider organisational learning, processes and systems, professional development and community engagement.

- Include any learning about your organisation's purpose and future projects. What did you learn about the target group in this project? For example, was there a strong demand for future projects to address a need relating to your purpose?

8. Provide information on the marketing undertaken during the project, including where you displayed the funder's logo or name.
9. Show your actual to budgeted financials. This is a comparison of actual financials to original budgeted financials.
10. Provide your financial reconciliation or acquittal, clearly showing income and expenses for the project.

A note that everything you include in your draft report should reflect the promises you made in the grant application and agreed to in the funding contract.

Using outcomes to attract more funding

The statistics and stories you gather for your report can be used in your marketing. You should be developing marketing materials that highlight all aspects of your project - your outcomes, the beneficiary and stakeholder stories, and stories from the people in your organisation who are involved.

Share these results in your annual reports and develop a story for local media. It's important that you share how fabulous your organisation and team is for delivering a project that made a difference. Of course, give the funder a lot of praise and thanks for the work they did in supporting you. If you don't build your profile, your competitor will and they may be the ones to get the call when a funder has some discretionary cash to give out before the end of financial year.

Market your success

Your organisation needs to maximise the opportunities you have to market your successes so you can attract more supporters and funders. From little to big achievements, they are all worth celebrating and sharing with your fans, followers, friends and funders! Of course, you're not going to bombard them with newsletters and irrelevant emails or tags on social posts. This is about sharing your good news with a planned approach as part of your marketing strategy.

So, consider how you can market your success stories and schedule regular, consistent promotion of everything you're achieving. Success attracts funds and support. Maximise every opportunity you have to share the difference your organisation is making.

But, before you jump right in and start emailing so much you get a spam alert on your email and banned from Facebook, let's take a planned approach to what you're doing and why.

The first thing to consider is the purpose of what you're doing. If you don't have a clear purpose and an audience you want to talk with, you'll end up doing scatter marketing – otherwise known as 'spray and pray' (spray your message out and pray someone notices!).

Instead, do a little planning using my 7Ms of Marketing framework:

1. **Meaning:** You need to be clear on the purpose of your marketing actions. How can you make sure that your marketing is meaningful? A good meaningful marketing goal most likely would be 'We will promote our project successes, demonstrating our capacity to meet the needs of our communities and achieve positive outcomes and impacts that make a difference'. This statement gives you direction. You can then break it up into themes:
   - promote project success
   - demonstrate capacity to meet community needs
   - achieve positive outcomes and impacts.

I explore these themes further as we look into the rest of the 7Ms of Marketing.

2. **Markets:** If you understand who you're talking to, you'll be able to use their language. For example, if you're targeting other funders, donors or partners, you would use the words 'outcomes' and 'impacts'. If you want your local community to support you, you would talk about successes and the differences you've made to local people. It's not a matter of choosing one or the other; it's just about having a range of posts that speak to the key supporter markets you're looking for.
3. **Message:** Using the three themes identified earlier, let's create some marketing messages for two markets – funders/partners and local supporters. Here's how you can focus on the three themes, tailored to these markets:
    a. Promote project success:
        i. Acknowledging the grant funder and program partners at the launch
        ii. Sharing a community story of need and support at the launch
    b. Demonstrate capacity to meet community needs:
        i. Meet the staff, talking about their experience and qualifications
        ii. Interview a staff member on why they love the work they do in the community
    c. Achieve positive outcomes and impacts:
        i. Statistic and testimonial demonstrating achievement or exceeding planned goal
        ii. A story of change – where a program participant shares the difference the program has made to their life (either written or video).

4. **Mediums:** Consider all the marketing options available to you, from your newsletter and website to socials and print media. How will you reach the market and what messages are best shared on that medium?

   For example, the story of change can be shared across socials and in your newsletter. You can also have it sitting on your website and YouTube channel. A 'meet the staff' article is good for socials and your 'about us' page on your website.
5. **Monitor:** The purpose of this step is to remind you that you should monitor your marketing activities to see which ones are working across the different mediums.
6. **Maintain:** Consistency is the key to marketing. You have to maintain the momentum. Also remember that you don't have to create new posts all the time. You can take one marketing item, such as a website article, and create five different social media posts from it. You can then post the same article, with five different posts, one every week. A quick tip is use your AI Assistant to help you create posts. Develop a calendar and schedule them ahead. This saves so much time!
7. **Measure:** Invest your time in what works and don't try to market across every medium out there. Measure engagements and click throughs to identify what's working well. Determine which medium and which stories get the most engagement. Then do more of that.

What can I promote?

Let's look at an example of a community cultural event grant and brainstorm some marketing opportunities using a simple timeline. The scenario is this: it's the second year of the event and you're going to focus your marketing on those three themes I outlined in the previous section. Let's get started!

The following table provides some ideas.

	Grant announcement	**Sponsorship program launch**
Promote project success	Team success securing the grant; thanking supporters and funders	Interview with a sponsor from last year sharing why they believe the event was successful and why they're continuing to support
Demonstrate capacity to meet community needs	Sharing how needed the event is and why it's important to community members	A story from a participant or someone involved in the management of the event talking about the great teamwork and achievements
Achieve positive outcomes and impacts	Stories of people involved in, supporting or attending the previous event, sharing their positive experience	Statistics from last year's events and a comparable measure that shows the event growth - for example, the increase in ticket sales or stallholders

The table shows a very simple example, but from these six ideas, you can create one story, two images and quotes, one video and four social posts for each of these (one short story, two images, one video). You've created 24 posts for your social media. WOWSERS. And, better yet, you could repeat these at least twice over the year. Why can you repeat it? Because not everyone is going to see or remember the first post. Also, marketing is about consistency and repetition so even if they do recall something, they won't remember the specifics of the message you're sharing. They'll just listen to the messages you're repeating and form a perception of who you are and what you're achieving.

Building a relationship with the funder

Building this relationship will provide additional opportunities for you both to identify other ways you can assist each other. For example, if the funder is doing research, involve yourself. Show them you're a reputable source to represent your clients and community. If you're planning a change to your services or searching for additional opportunities to fund your work, reach out and ask funders for their insights and input. (Don't ask for money at this stage! This might happen but it's not a money conversation at this point.) This gets funders interested in your work and they may introduce you to an opportunity they have, or something being shared through their network. Tag funders into your social marketing. When you achieve milestones, send them an update.

Summary

In this step, we explored how you can market and promote your outcomes and successes. Organisations that promote themselves and their impact get support for a reason. I was talking with a CEO the other day who told me their marketing person in the last 12 months has increased their social media presence and engagement. It's no wonder she has a waiting list of 100 volunteers and at least every two days there's a new post about another donation someone has made. Success attracts success.

What can you do now?

- [ ] If you don't already have a marketing and communication plan, develop one.
- [ ] If you do have a marketing and communication plan, make sure you share progress and good news broadly.

Summary of Stage 7: Report

In summary, here's a checklist for you, covering the key highlights in this stage:

1. **Identify the different reports required:** You'll need to provide a final report, and in some cases you'll be asked to provide milestone reports. Be clear on what the differences are between them. Ask the funder when you start the project if they can provide an example acquittal report. If not, ask them if the headings from The Grant Acquittal Report align to their reporting requirements.
2. **Template your reports:** Use The Grant Acquittal Report to set up a template document with headings and dot points for each report you must develop. As your work progresses and things happen you want to share in your reports, you can gather relevant information and use it as a draft report. The headings and dot points on deliverables will be a good reminder and save you thinking work when it's time to finalise your report and acquittal.
3. **Reduce third-party reliance:** If others have to provide information, set up reminders for them or confirm they have the work scheduled on their end, in advance of the deadline. They're best placed to know how long the job will take, which will assist with your planning.
4. **Be clear on your approval process before submitting to funder:** Do you know who approves your report, and how long it will take for the approval process? Important particularly for milestone payments.
5. **Report statistics and stories:** You'll need to include statistics in your report, but don't forget to include the human side of the outcomes of your work. Share the good news. Include a case study or a range of testimonials showing how your work has affected people's abilities, soft skills and knowledge. Include links to videos showcasing what you've done.

6. **Build your relationship:** Focus on building a relationship with your funder - and, again, I don't mean by adding them to your newsletter list without their permission. Send a thank you email, letter or card from your CEO or Chair once the contracts are signed. When something positive happens, share it with funders. If you've heard positive feedback or received a thank you email or card, let them know. Don't let the milestone reports or final acquittal be the only connection with them.

Working through this checklist reduces the stress of reporting periods, and solidifies your connection with funders - perhaps leading to more opportunities.

What can you do now?

If you haven't already, ask the funder for an example acquittal form. Set up The Grant Acquittal Report template. If it's your first time tracking information, set a monthly reminder to note down and capture information as it comes up.

Conclusion
What's next?

I hope this book has helped you identify areas you want to improve in and motivated you to write more grants. I've covered a lot in this book, and there were so many things I would have loved to expand more on in the 'how' side of some of these areas to support your work. I also wanted to make sure this book was relevant as different funding themes changed. This is why there's more information in the online kit you'll find on the website to guide you if you need it.

The biggest recommendation I can offer you as you continue your learning is to get on grant assessment panels – even in your local council or with a local business that offers sponsorship. You will learn so much reading other applications, and seeing how a range of applicants answer the same question, in different ways. Considering how they structure their answers, what content they use and what the strengths and weaknesses are, can help you with your own grant writing.

Writing successful grants is a learned skill. You improve your skills when you focus on developing them.

To help you on your way, the following is a summary checklist of some of the key knowledge and skills shared in this book that grant writers need.

I've grouped them into levels of learning, from beginner to expert. As you go through the checklist, either answer yes, or rate how much you believe you know about each topic. Use this checklist to consider the areas you'd like to learn more about. You can also do this quiz in the online kit and learn more with me and the team, online at iClick-2Learn. Check upcoming sessions at www.winthegrant.com.

	Beginner	Intermediate	Advanced
Types of funders and grants	I know the different types of funders. I understand the different models of grant funding. I know there are other ways to get projects funded.	I've applied to at least two types of funders. I've had experience across these types of funding. I've helped with fundraising and sponsorship.	I've completed numerous applications for all funders. I've regularly written grants across all types of funding and worked in fundraising and sponsorship.
Knowledge of strong grant applications, and common mistakes	I understand what strong grant applications include and what common mistakes are. I know The Grant Writing System will support my work.	I have done an assessment of a grant I've written to identify improvements. I understand what common mistakes I'm making. I use The Grant Writing System to improve.	I rarely make mistakes and only use The Grant Writing System to double-check I'm not missing anything.
1. Plan – getting my organisation grant ready	I have The Grant Ready Checklist and have started to develop The Grant Ready Kit. I have reviewed the types of organisational plans. My organisation is starting to develop our strategic plan and risk management plan. We know what policies we need to develop and have started.	I use The Grant Ready Kit and regularly update our organisation's documents. I've shared this kit with others on the team. My organisation has a strategic plan and a risk management plan, and we either have, or are working on, the other plans we need. We have some policies and are developing others or updating them.	My organisation has developed all the plans and necessary policies. We have a regular schedule to update these plans and policies. We update The Grant Ready Kit regularly.

	Beginner	Intermediate	Advanced
Compliance (e.g., standards, legislation, regulations and accreditation)	We have started to identify what compliance requirements we have and are prioritising those that create the greatest risk situation for our organisation (e.g., working with children and conflicts of interest).	We have started to develop a compliance calendar and are continuing to add to it as we work through compliance requirements. We will be able to add to this calendar as needed to meet funder requirements.	My organisation has a robust compliance calendar addressing strategic, operational and project/service compliance. We can easily demonstrate our compliance systems and processes.
1. Plan - getting my idea grant ready with project plans or business cases and evidence	We are aware that we should start developing simple project plans for our ideas. We have started or implemented a plan to start capturing statistics and stories in our organisation. We are aware of some sources of third-party evidence. We don't just work on the first idea that comes to mind, we ask if it's the right one to meet the need.	My organisation develops project plans. We haven't yet had to develop a business plan; however, I have an understanding about the type of project where I may need this. We are capturing internal data and starting to assess it to make sure it's the data we need. My organisation has a sound list of data sources relevant to us. When we need the data, we search for updated data. I use The Grant RICE Score to prioritise our many ideas and projects.	We develop project plans for all our projects. My organisation is able to or knows how to develop business cases. My organisation has processes to capture information in every stage of its work. We know where to source relevant data. We update The Grant Ready Kit as new third-party evidence is published.

	Beginner	Intermediate	Advanced
For human service-focused projects and organisations: Theory of Change, Logic Model and service model	We are aware that we will need to consider developing these tools to be more competitive. We have started discussing it and expect to commence developing these shortly.	We have started developing these tools or are updating them.	My organisation has a Theory of Change. We develop Logic Models for our work. We have a designed service model.
Need statement	I have just started developing a need statement. I'm trying the framework in The Grant Project Plan.	I have reviewed past applications and can identify where we can improve our need statements. I've used the framework in The Grant Project Plan to develop some drafts and have improved.	I am confident that I'm developing strong need statements. I use the framework in The Grant Project Plan to check occasionally. I can easily modify the need statement to suit the funder's objectives and outcomes.
Stakeholder analysis	We have started developing our stakeholder analysis. We are learning more about stakeholder engagement and co-design.	We have a stakeholder analysis and will be using this in our next project. We understand the different levels of stakeholder engagement. We understand and apply co-design where appropriate.	Stakeholder analysis, engagement and co-design are integral to the way we work.
Pitching our ideas and projects	We share our ideas and ask stakeholders for feedback and input.	We are clear on our ideas and have developed different pitches for various stakeholders using The Grant NDOIS Pitch frameworks.	We have pitch documents ready. Our team can easily discuss the project with potential supporters and funders.

	Beginner	Intermediate	Advanced
Budget and financial indicators	We have someone that can help us develop a budget. I understand how to produce a financial report for the funder.	I can develop a simple project budget and seek help where needed. I can assess a financial report to make sure it presents our organisation's financial capacity and available funding correctly.	I can develop complex budgets for all types of projects. I know what needs to be modified, or where notes need to be provided to explain financial situations to the funder.
2. Finding the right grant with the right funder	I have registered with funding websites and know how to search for funding. We are making sure our website and marketing shows our projects, track record and outcomes. I use The Grant Go/ No-Go Decision Checklist to identify if the grant is right for us. I've created a Grant Calendar.	I use reverse searching techniques to target funders that align to our project outcomes. I have started developing a network and am aware of influencers. I check The Grant Go/No-Go Decision Checklist to identify if the grant is right for us.	I use reverse searching techniques, and review current grants with a creative mindset. I can identify ways to build the project to align to funding or decide when to walk away and not waste my time. I review The Grant Go/No-Go Decision Checklist from time to time.

	Beginner	Intermediate	Advanced
3. Aligning to the funder	I now understand assessment processes and have practised being an assessor. I know how to find the assessment criteria, if published. I have heard about outcomes frameworks but I'm not sure how or where to find them.	I can identify assessment criteria, key terminology and themes. I can research the funder to identify alignment to other strategies or policies. I know what to consider to improve our score at the assessment table. I understand there are different outcomes frameworks that may be useful and can find some.	I can identify assessment criteria, either listed or from key themes coming through the application pack. I know how to look at a project and source relevant strategies or policies to show how the project meets these goals. I can easily find and align to all relevant outcomes frameworks related to the funder or the project.
4. Writing a strong application	I understand how to use the simple version of The Grant Answer Map (step 4a). I'm learning how to craft answers that address the question.	I frame my answers using the complex version of The Grant Answer Map (step 4b), incorporating strategic approaches.	From time to time, I check The Grant Answer Map; however, it's part of my process now. I can confidently craft answers to address relevant points and weave in strategic areas.
5. Submit without regret	I can use online systems to help me edit my answer. I have others read my answers and give feedback on where I can improve. I check The Grant Submission Checklist and the funder's checklist before submitting.	I'm improving my editing and formatting skills. I check The Grant Submission Checklist and any funder checklists before I submit.	I can self-edit and use online systems to check. For more complex grants, I may check or develop a version of The Grant Submission Checklist; otherwise, I'm confident in my work.

	Beginner	Intermediate	Advanced
6. Manage the outcome win or lose	I refer to The Grant Evaluation Plan to help me understand what I need to do next. I have started writing and diarising a list of jobs I need to do to evaluate the grant.	I can support a team member to negotiate with a funder and review a contract. I may ask for help if needed on some clauses. I can develop a simple evaluation plan and project-manage others to deliver.	I can confidently negotiate with the funder and review a contract. I have developed MERI evaluation plans and considered how to design this to capture more data for future projects.
7. Report and leverage data for more funding	I've started a document and folder to capture information ready to be able to deliver a report. I've thanked the funder and shared our media release and launch of the project.	I'm using The Grant Acquittal Report as a template checklist to capture information. Every three months, I make notes on project progress. I've reached out to the funder and let them know about progress. We promote what we do and the outcomes we're delivering.	I have a process and start The Grant Acquittal Report for all funded projects. I'm updating it every few weeks with information. I keep all records on the projects in The Grant Kit, ready for acquittal. I help develop marketing and communication about our work and achievements.

And that's a wrap!

I know. I can't believe it either! This book has been a labour of love and everything I've put in here I have done with the best intention to help you Win the Grant you're applying for. I genuinely want you to succeed and I've held nothing back. Well, that's not quite true - my editor did cut out a few stories, LOL! But, I'm sure you'll hear all about those in the online kit.

You have the desire for and interest in grant writing, and with these two nuggets of gold you will be able to achieve many things. I hope that this book has given you, as one workshop participant put it, 'inspiration and motivation' to go out and apply for those grant opportunities - particularly if you are expanding your grant skills to write larger, more complex grants.

I also hope that you've found this to be a practical, valuable resource you'll use for many, many years to come. My heart will be full if I see shared images online of cracked book spines, well-worn covers and creased page edges that have been thumbed through often!

If we haven't already met, I'd love to connect with you during our free grant writing Q&A sessions, and if you come to one of my workshops, please come up and say hi.

Finally, I'd love to ask just one small thing from you. I'm sure you've felt my true passion for making a difference in the pages of this book. I'm a values- and purpose-driven person and it does my heart good to know I'm making a difference Since I'm not sitting beside you right now, I don't have a sense of the usefulness of The Grant Writing System to your work. **So, a small thing from you (which would mean a *huge* thing for me)** would be if you could please, please share the difference this book has made to your work. I would LOVE to hear when you Win the Grant! I would dearly love for you to tag me into posts about your grant announcements or share those fabulous successes and videos of change. It's easy to find me. My handle is #nfpguide, @nataliebramble or @iclick2learn across all socials.

All the best, and thanks so much for the work you do to make our communities healthy, inclusive and adaptive.

Appendix
Troubleshooting common grant mistakes

The following table shows the common problems that occur consistently across grant applications. I've gathered these common mistakes via my own research and work as a grant writer, working with other grant writers and as an assessor, and from discussions with funders.

In the table, I've also included the steps and tools through the book that can you can use to avoid or correct these mistakes.

Common mistakes made in applications related to Stage 1: Plan to get grant ready!		
Common problems	**Why does this matter?**	**Where do I find more information to help me?**
Weak statistical evidence: Applications are strong on story-based content, but weak on statistics and data-based evidence. **Weak anecdotal evidence:** Applications are strong on statistics and data-based evidence, but weak on stories.	Unsubstantiated statements are only opinions, not fact. Not including evidence weakens your competitiveness and can seed doubt in the assessor's mind. Story-based applications might influence the heart-focused assessor to love who you are and what you want to do, but they'll fail at the third assessment stage when logic-focused assessors highlight the gap. You need a mix of stories and statistics.	Use The Grant Ready Checklist (step 1a) and read about project plans and supporting evidence. Also read the steps in Stage 3: Align. You'll understand what other evidence the funder cares about. If you use The Grant Answer Map (step 4b), you won't forget to include statistics and stories.
Weak answers lacking information: Applicants don't have information to answer the questions.	You can't answer questions without having information. You need strong information that's well thought out and represents the value your project delivers.	You should complete The Grant Project Plan (step 1c) for all your ideas. For larger projects, a business case is useful. These documents will help you respond to the questions.
Project need: Applicants can't demonstrate the need and evidence of the need for the project.	If you can't adequately demonstrate need, the assessors might think your project is a 'want', not a need. They prioritise needs. Need is one of the first questions you're asked in 95% of applications. It's a benchmark question. Your activities and results will be assessed against the need.	Use the need statement framework within The Grant Project Plan (step 1c) to help you address the application question. You also need to craft a need statement to suit each funder's objective - see step 4c.

Common mistakes made in applications related to Stage 1: Plan to get grant ready!		
Common problems	**Why does this matter?**	**Where do I find more information to help me?**
Weak project: Applicant appears to have selected a weak project idea. It doesn't appear to meet the need and the outcomes don't align to the need.	Funders want to fund projects that have a high chance of success to deliver outcomes and have been well thought through. Often organisations work on the first or second idea they thought of and these are similar ideas the funder has seen many times.	The Grant RICE Score (step 1b) will help you assess and prioritise ideas to select the one that is likely to be the strongest project to address need. The Logic Model in The Grant Project Plan (step 1c) will help you work through the project idea to validate it achieves the outcomes to address the need.
Outcomes: Applications aren't able to prove they can achieve results.	Funders need confidence you can do what you've said you will, and deliver the outcomes. Everything you state, you must prove.	You should have a range of case studies and bios of your key people in The Grant Ready Kit (step 1a) or The Grant Project Plan (step 1c). Use examples that align to the funder.
Application timeline: Applicants spend too much time developing or searching for information to include in their answers.	The issue is you're spending too much time getting organised and not enough time focusing on the grant application. It's clear to the funder when you've lacked the time to build a quality application, run out of energy and ended up not answering questions or missing information	Use The Grant Ready Kit (step 1a) to identify and gather information ready to include in your application. Use The Grant Project Plan (step 1c) to identify evidence and information needed in the planning stage. You'll also need to gather evidence during Stage 3: Align (see step 3c).

Common mistakes made in applications related to Stage 2: Find grants and choose the right one

Common problems	Why does this matter?	Where do I find more information to help me?
Alignment to the funder's objectives: Applicants don't demonstrate awareness of or alignment to the funder's grant objectives.	The assessor and funders need to identify in your application where you clearly understand the funder's goals, objectives and desired outcomes. Work out how you can help funders achieve this and tell them.	Use The Grant Go/No-Go Decision Checklist (step 2b) to help you pay attention to these areas. The Grant Application Report (step 3c) can also help you work out how to show this alignment.
Applicant is ineligible: Applicants submit an application that isn't eligible.	If you're not eligible and you've applied, you've wasted time and energy. Over 30% of applicants are ineligible. You need to consider a few factors around eligibility, not just your legal status.	You'll find eligibility in the grant guidelines and other documents. Review the points from The Grant Go/No-Go Decision Checklist (step 2b). This will help you decide if the grant is suitable for you to apply for and identify any weaknesses. The Grant Application Tool (step 3c) will help you work out how to show you're a good fit for the funder's grant program.
Applicant is not a good fit: Applicants waste time on the wrong grant.	Funders won't fund a grant if it doesn't align with the objectives of their funding program.	
Engagement/ partnerships: Lack of engagement and co-design from target group. Lack of understanding of the target group shown.	Some funders have a particular focus on target group engagement or co-design and failing to include evidence of this seeds doubt that you can deliver a project that's needed by the target group.	The Grant Project Plan (step 1c) covers considerations for stakeholder engagement. Understand the funder's requirements around co-design and how you'll show this if needed in your application.

Common mistakes made in applications related to Stage 2: Find grants and choose the right one		
Common problems	**Why does this matter?**	**Where do I find more information to help me?**
Engagement/ partnerships: Application lacks partnerships.	Funders want to know that you have suitable partnerships engaged and supporting your project. This shows broad support for what you're doing.	This can happen because potential partners aren't clear on what you're doing, why and what you'll achieve. Use The Grant NDOIS Pitch frameworks to develop clear, convincing pitches that help motivate and inspire support.
Evaluation and measurements: Application doesn't describe or detail measurements, evaluation and continuous improvement approaches.	Funders want to be confident you'll monitor what you're doing during the project to make sure you're on track. Other applicants will include this and, to be competitive, you'll need to.	You should include evaluation and measurement in The Grant Project Plan (step 1c). Your timeline should identify steps taken to evaluate mid-project. When writing the application, align measurements to the funder's objectives and outcomes. Measurements must align to your needs and outcomes.

Common mistakes made in applications related to Stage 3: Align to the funder's goals		
Common problems	**Why does this matter?**	**Where do I find more information to help me?**
Duplication of services: Application appears to replicate existing programs, services or activities.	Some funders won't fund a project when they feel there is enough of the type of project in the area or funded elsewhere. You need to demonstrate how you're different from others and how you address a gap.	Consider your competitors and review The Grant Application Tool (step 3c) to identify opportunities to showcase your difference. Review the need statement framework (step 1c) to showcase the gap.

Common mistakes made in applications related to Stage 3: Align to the funder's goals		
Common problems	**Why does this matter?**	**Where do I find more information to help me?**
Terminology: Applicant doesn't use the funder's terminology.	The assessors and funders need to understand what you're saying. If you use your terms, not theirs, they may not clearly understand what you're trying to say.	Review The Grant Go/ No-Go Decision Checklist (step 2b). Consider the points in The Grant Application Tool (step 3c) to understand what's important, (e.g., language used in frameworks). Use The Grant Answer Map (step 4b) so you remember to incorporate the right terms in your answer.
Contradictory answers: Applicants include information in one answer that's contradicted elsewhere.	This raises doubt in an assessor's mind. Are you contributing 10% or 28% of the total budget? This occurs generally because people are either changing things as they quickly respond to an application or making things up as they go along.	The Grant Application Tool (step 3c) includes a table to enter information you'll be using in your application. Consider this your 'single source of truth' document you copy all your statements and statistics from, update and check before you submit.
Budget: Applicants ask for the funder to pay for something they have said they won't.	Funders won't give you funds for something they've told you they won't pay for. Sometimes your application will be rejected in the first assessment level if you've done this. Follow and comply with the information in the grant guidelines. If you aren't sure, ask, but never assume.	Check The Grant Application Tool (step 3c) and the application pack provided by the funder. Make sure you haven't made an error (e.g., putting an expense in the wrong area).

Common mistakes made in applications related to Stage 4: Write a strong application		
Common problems	**Why does this matter?**	**Where do I find more information to help me?**
Questions: Applicants don't answer questions in full or they don't address what is being asked.	You've missed an opportunity to achieve as many points as you can. Missing 50% of the question could mean 50% of the points are lost.	Use The Grant Answer Map (step 4b) to check you understand all the parts of the question. Understand how much information you need to include in your answer.
Answer limits: Applicants don't use the word, character or page limits effectively.	Some parts of the question should have more words, characters or pages than other parts of the question. You've missed an opportunity to achieve as many points as you can.	Use The Grant Answer Map (step 4b) to help you strategically assess which parts of the question need more words or characters than others.
Writing: Application is poorly written, confusing, in mixed 'voices' or uses unexplained terminology.	Your answer being hard to read increases cognitive load on the assessor. You may not receive as many points as you could have.	Review all the writing tips in stage 4. Of note, particularly focus on the structure of your answer.
Repetition: When it appears to be a similar question, applicants copy and paste their previous answer.	Funders haven't made a mistake repeating the question. You've made a mistake thinking they have. If there's a similar or even the same question word for word, you need to answer differently.	Check the tips in step 4c to work out how to answer questions when you're in this situation.
Sustainable outcomes: Applicants didn't show how they could continue to deliver outcomes beyond the life of the funding.	If you have a project that the funder knows survives the funding period, or you're asked how you'll ensure sustainability of outcomes, you need to demonstrate this. If you don't you'll lose points in the assessment process.	You should consider this in the project planning stage. Review the Q&A in step 4c, where I discuss sustainability of outcomes. For assets, be aware of the contract conditions that survive beyond the funding period.

Common mistakes made in applications related to Stage 4: Write a strong application		
Common problems	**Why does this matter?**	**Where do I find more information to help me?**
Assumptions: Applicants make assumptions the funder has existing knowledge of them or their project.	Unless you already have a relationship with the funder, you need to remember they don't know you, your capability, your location or your results. Check for any assumptions you've made (e.g., an assumption they understand your industry terminology) and test these or make them clearer.	Have someone independently review your application. This could be a project partner but should be someone who isn't close to the funding application.
Format: Applicants don't use templates provided, or the format asked for.	Funders use templates because it makes their job easier, particularly when comparing short-listed applicants.	If funders ask you to use a template to complete and submit, use the template! You could be deemed non compliant if you don't.
Budget: Applicant's financials show they're able to fund or have funding from similar sources.	Your organisation may be seen to be too financially viable over others. This could come from how you present your budget or existing funding received (e.g., from another department or another program from the same funder), and may be seen as 'double dipping'.	Check your financials. Clearly identify the funds that are committed to other work. If you're already supported by the funder, or another department/program within the same funder, check with the funding program manager. Ask if you're able to apply or not.
Budget: Applicants are successful but realise they haven't asked for enough funds to complete the work.	Some funders will pick up missing items in the budget. This reduces their confidence you know what you're doing. If you or the funder don't pick up the gaps, it could mean a headache for you - now you have to find the extra money!	When you developed The Grant Project Plan (step 1c), you would have used estimates for the budget and activities. Factor every cost in. Be aware of your unit costs and consider how you'll include contingencies in your budget. Also see step 4c.

Common mistakes made in applications related to Stage 4: Write a strong application

Common problems	Why does this matter?	Where do I find more information to help me?
Budget: Applicants build a project to meet the maximum amount of money available in the grant round, or per organisation.	Funders generally want to spread their funding around as much as they can, depending on their risk appetite. Asking for everything might deem your project un-fundable.	Step 4c includes information on what to consider and what the funder might deem appropriate. Be realistic about how much you're asking for.
Budget: Budget is unrealistic. It's above the expected costs for items or includes contingencies and miscellaneous amounts the funder hasn't indicated they'll accept.	Budget doesn't provide value for money when compared with other applications. It might look like a 'slush fund'! The funder is aware of average/ expected expense items and indicative costs and your application might be rejected if its budget goes outside these average costs.	Review the information on budget and contingency allocation in step 4c. Check with the funder if you want to include contingencies. If you need to cover aspects such as transport or travel, include those items separately where you can.
Timelines: Applications outline unrealistic timelines.	Funders are concerned you'll be unable to deliver what you say, in the time you have.	Check The Grant Project Plan timeline (step 1c). Review the timeline in your application. Make sure you've allocated ample time to activities and allowed a buffer. Note seasonal times. These may impact your project so factor in decreased availability for your team, attendees or suppliers.
Timelines: Applications are asking to fund activities that start or finish after the date the grant acquittal is due.	Funders won't accept applications with incorrect dates. Rarely will they ask you to update your application. You'll be rejected.	
Risks: Risks in the application form are basic, or not relevant.	Funders lack confidence you've considered a range of risks, and the key risks that have potential to derail your project. Most application forms ask for a minimum of five risks.	See step 1c and step 4c to review using the STEEPLE tool to consider broad risks across three levels.

Common mistakes made in applications related to Stage 4: Write a strong application

Common problems	Why does this matter?	Where do I find more information to help me?
Implementation/ milestones: Applicants don't provide detailed information, evidence or research on how they'll implement their idea.	Funders need confidence you can deliver what you say, and you have the right people, partnerships and systems in place.	Review the milestones outlined in The Grant Project Plan (step 1c) and see step 4c for more on these concepts. A service model, roadmap or implementation schedule is a good way to demonstrate this.
Instructions: Applicant doesn't follow instructions from the guidelines and other documents. **Attachments:** Attachments are irrelevant and not referenced/related to the answer. Applicants sometimes miss including attachments they've referred to.	If you can't follow instructions, it reduces the funder's confidence you'll be reliable and able to do what's asked of you and what you've agreed to.	The Grant Application Tool (step 3c) is useful to document specific instructions. Use this and The Grant Submission Checklist (step 5b) to make sure you haven't missed anything.
Referees: Referees don't know they've been listed or haven't given permission.	If funders call your referees, they want to validate the letter of support or reference.	Review step 4c for information on letters of support and referees.
Late submission: Application submitted late or the online system timed out and work was lost.	In some special circumstances an application may be accepted late. This generally only includes significant events such as fire and flood. It's rare for funders to provide extensions.	Set your timeline up in the one-page overview of The Grant Application Tool (step 3c). If an issue arises, the earlier you have a conversation with the funder to seek approval for an extension, the better.

Common mistakes made in applications related to Stage 5: Submit without regret!		
Common problems	**Why does this matter?**	**Where do I find more information to help me?**
Spelling and grammar: Applications contain mistakes that change the context or confuse the assessor.	You don't have to be perfect at spelling and grammar. However, check there aren't mistakes or words correctly spelt, but not correct for the context of the sentence. For example, complacent instead of compliant.	Read the application out loud to pick up any words that don't seem right or are confusing. Go through the three-step editing process from stage 5 and The Grant Submission Checklist (step 5b). Use grammar tools to avoid mistakes.

Common mistakes made in applications related to Stage 6: Manage the outcome, win or lose		
Common problems	**Why does this matter?**	**Where do I find more information to help me?**
Due diligence: Information in the application does not appear to align to what they've found about you in their research.	This reduces confidence the funder has in you. It raises the question, 'Did they tell the truth?'	Make sure your public presence supports your application. Review step 6a for more on what to do after you've submitted the application.
Outcome monitoring and evaluation: Applicants have failed to monitor and evaluate outcomes during the project	Funders want to make sure you have timelines and activities scheduled to monitor and evaluate your work.	Complete The Grant Evaluation Plan to make sure you are monitoring, evaluating, reviewing and improving your work to meet or exceed outcomes.

Common mistakes made in applications related to Stage 7: Report and leverage data for more funding		
Common problems	**Why does this matter?**	**Where do I find more information to help me?**
Funder relationship: Successful applicants don't build a relationship with the funder.	Having a relationship with a funder will make it easier when things in your project need to change.	Review step 7a for tips on building the relationship during the project, not just at acquittal time.

Common mistakes made in applications related to Stage 7: Report and leverage data for more funding		
Common problems	**Why does this matter?**	**Where do I find more information to help me?**
Applicant compliance: Applicant has an existing relationship with the funder and did not complete or fund the last funded project.	Funders rarely fund an organisation when they have an outstanding acquittal.	Use The Grant Calendar (step 2a) to keep a record of all funding programs your organisation has applied for. In a situation where your organisation doesn't have a good track record, contact the funder and discuss what needs to be done. Show funders what you've achieved since then.

Glossary

Following is a glossary of terms used in this book. I've also included an up-to-date glossary in your online kit.

acquittal A final report that shows the funder that you have done what you said you would. It includes information about where you have spent the money and reports on the success of what you delivered, and may also include an audited financial report.

addendum/addenda Additional information that may be provided before the application deadline. These documents can include important information, such as answers to questions being asked by prospective applicants or additional information provided to clarify areas.

advocacy Campaigning, usually in public, for a cause.

anecdotal Personal opinions, experience and stories.

applicant The person or organisation applying for the grant.

application forms and templates Standard application forms provided for you to complete. This provides a consistent assessment approach. Additional information may be asked, which could include templated budgets and other documents.

application pack The series of documents you need to download to apply for the grant.

application process The guidelines outline what the process is from application to decision. (Only some funders provide this.)

assessment criteria A list of key points that funders use in the evaluation of your application, compared to other short-listed grants. The majority of funders share assessment criteria.

assessment process How funders will assess the grant, including the assessment criteria, who will assess applications and the assessment timelines. (Not all funders share all these details in the guidelines.)

assessor A person who volunteers, or is employed or contracted by the funder to assess your application.

audited financial reports Financial reports that have been audited by a qualified auditor.

auspice A partnership between two or more organisations where one is the applicant and the others may not be eligible to apply for the grant in their name.

baseline The process of setting a measure before you start something.

benchmark The process of comparing a measure to the same measure in one or more projects or organisations.

business case The next level up from a project plan, covering what you want to do from an investment and return perspective. It involves a lot more desktop and market research and stakeholder involvement than a project plan. A business case is generally developed for larger projects to convince someone their large investment is worth it, and you can deliver it. (*See also* project plan.)

co-contribution A contribution the applicant is asked or required to make. This may be a cash or non-cash contribution, or a mix of both as listed in the guidelines.

contract A legal document containing specific information about what you'll deliver, how and when. Breaching the contract has consequences.

cost–benefit A financial analysis that compares the financial and non-financial cost and benefits of doing something.

demand Evidence that people want and support your project.

desktop research Research you can do with your computer; also called 'secondary research', because it is research that has been done by others.

evaluation Assessment of the effectiveness and impact of the project. Evaluation takes place during and after the project. Evaluation must be planned for before the project starts in order to collect the right data to inform the evaluation.

evaluation criteria *See* assessment criteria.

funder The person, organisation, foundation or government body offering a grant.

funding period The term of funding. The guidelines will tell you when the program closes, and when the acquittal is due, which is the end of the funding period.

grant guidelines Document detailing the grant process, including communication, compliance, assessment criteria (if provided), the assessment process and any legal matters such as conflicts of interest.

human services Programs, projects or services that are delivered to help people.

impact The longer term benefits of your work. These are the benefits of the outcomes you've achieved. For some projects, impacts can be achieved for several years after you have completed your work.

in-kind Something other than money donated to your project (e.g., volunteer labour).

intangible Evidence capturing people's stories, testimonials and feelings; also called 'soft' or 'qualitative' data.

key performance indicators (KPIs) A set of success measures to be included in your application.

letter of support A letter provided by a person or organisation who supports your project. It's intended as a reference but should be strategic, identifying why they support you and how you will deliver what you say.

market research Research that involves the 'market' directly and includes interviewing key stakeholders directly; also known as 'primary research', because it is research you have done.

monitoring Ongoing reflection of the project delivery, performance and outcomes. Monitoring provides useful opportunities to improve during the project and to collect the data needed in order to evaluate the project.

NDOIS Natalie's method to explore a project's need, demand, outcomes, impact and solution.

need Funding is provided to address community needs. The funder may be aware of some of the challenges and opportunities specific to your community; however, it's up to you to show them that you understand what these needs are.

objective A goal or target to achieve; the thing to work towards.

on-costs Employment overheads (e.g., workers compensation and superannuation).

outcome The benefits that are realised during a contract period. The outcomes achieved need to align to the objectives of the grant. Outcomes are achieved within the funding period.

philanthropist A person or foundation investing money to improve society.

pilot A project that is the first and is being delivered to test if the assumptions and plans work, and to deliver data on how to change them if not.

primary research *See* market research.

probity How an organisation ensures that the grant process is ethical, fair, transparent and honest for all parties. This means that the funder will outline what they do to ensure these points, and they will ask you to confirm and validate statements, such as the fact that you either declare any conflicts of interest, or state that you have none.

program A designed series of projects, activities and events. A program addresses outcomes in different ways over a series of projects, and generally has longer term positive impacts. Some projects are run many times over.

project A short-term initiative designed to achieve a small number of focused outcomes. It has a defined start and end and may not be delivered again.

project plan A plan that describes what your project, program or service will achieve, its purpose and information on how you'll achieve the outcomes. This includes information on the skills and ability to deliver the work, specifically how it will be delivered and what the costs and risks are.

qualitative data Data that captures emotions, thoughts and expressions, and uses describing words. This data supports the story that your statistics are telling; also known as 'soft' or 'intangible' data.

quantitative data Data based on numbers, percentages and ratios, and which is easy to translate into a statistic; also known as 'hard' data or 'tangible' data.

secondary research *See* desktop research

service delivery model A visual or written step-by-step description of how all elements of your service are delivered. For example, how people find out about you, how they access what you offer and how you deliver this.

services Something available to help others. For example, delivering meals or providing the elderly with community transport. Services can be once-off or delivered for years. Generally, services are designed to support people in complex areas or with essential needs, so they are usually in place for more than 12 months.

Sometimes a new service is trialled over a short time; this is often called a 'pilot project'.

stakeholder Individuals and organisations that are impacted by or can influence your work. It is important to consider the stakeholders, their engagement and the level of consultation required. Some stakeholders are more important than others.

tangible Evidence related to data and evidence, such as statistics and facts; also known as 'hard' or 'quantitative' data.

target group Identified group of people who the project is being delivered with, for or to.

viability Whether a project can be self-sustaining and is the appropriate thing to achieve the desired objective.

weighted assessment criteria An indication of what assessment criteria are more important than others.

Grant Writers: Unlock Your Grant Writing Success!

The Grant Writing System™ will take your grant writing game to the next level:

Access the FREE Online Kit: Access the online kit absolutely FREE with this book!

Join Natalie and the Team: Participate in our exclusive Grant Q&A sessions. Get direct answers to your burning questions and gain invaluable insights.

Learn at Your Own Pace: Learn 24/7. Over 300 videos, courses, and resources to master program design, planning, risk management, budgeting, and more! Gain access to member-only workshops, events, and expert Q&A sessions. https://www.iclick2learn.com.au/community-not-for-profit-online-training-library/

Shortcut the Learning Process: Don't have time to waste? Book a mentoring session and fast-track your progress.

'The mentoring and guidance ... has been invaluable ... I've seen an increase in successfully winning grants since implementing Natalie's grant writing concepts and approach.'

Jordana Morrison, Grants Writer

Connect, book and find out more at www.winthegrant.com

Upskill your organisation or community

Presenting and speaking: Natalie's passion and excitement for grants will motivate and inspire your attendees and podcast listeners.

Design Tailored Grant Training Programs: Customised grant training programs specifically tailored to your strategic and learning goals. From beginners to advanced practitioners, we've got you covered! Our grant programs regularly achieve 80+ Net Promoter Scores.

Deliver Engaging Practical Workshops: Interactive, hands-on experiences with practical skills and strategies attendees can apply immediately.

Invest in Knowledge: Bulk purchases of *Win the Grant with The Grant Writing System* are available to gift to your community, team or volunteers.

License The Grant Writing System: Harness the power of The Grant Writing System by licensing it to train your community.

'This has been the best grants training I have ever done 👏 and I've done them all.'

'I like that there are really practical tools.'

'I love that there is follow-up Q&As to circle back to reinforce the learning journey.'

'Very enthusiastic and inclusive. Upbeat energy. Amazing trainer.'

'Experienced in what she delivered, down to earth and easy to talk to.'

Connect, book and find out more at www.winthegrant.com

Professional Grant Writers

Are you ready to take your expertise to the next level or start and grow your grant writing business?

Expand your grant writing business or become a licensed trainer of The Grant Writing System™.

Improve or Start Your Grant Writing Business: Take your existing grant writing business to new heights or start one from scratch. Including writing and business skills and strategies to build a thriving business that delivers exceptional results for you and your client.

Join the Professional Grant Writers Network: Network with like-minded professionals and expand your reach by joining our Grant Writers Network. Get referrals, connect with fellow grant writers and exchange insights.

License The Grant Writing System: Harness the power of The Grant Writing System by licensing it to train others. Empower others with this invaluable resource while creating a lucrative opportunity for yourself.

Connect, book and find out more at www.winthegrant.com

About the Author

Natalie Bramble

MBA TAEu

Natalie is a multi-award winning entrepreneur and community development specialist. With a career spent at the intersection of enterprise, community, tourism and economic impact, she's committed to building inclusive, healthy and adaptive communities by driving and supporting social and economic impact initiatives.

Natalie has delved into every topic that's captured her interest and adds value to her work, including asset-based community development; human-centred design; social impact; social return on investment; law; entrepreneurship; governance; community building and critical thinking, to name a few.

Natalie put all this together to create a learning enterprise with a social purpose. iClick2Learn designs and builds training for government, associations, enterprises and community organisations. 100% of our profit is invested right back into education to educate volunteers and staff Govern, Fund and Manage their community organisations. We build the capacity of people in the for-purpose sector by giving them the tools and knowledge they need to create social change. Natalie has been an advisor, consultant, trainer and facilitator over the last 18+ years helping over 10,000 community leaders, and longer than that as a volunteer herself.

As an energetic and motivating facilitator, she captures and leads deep, reflective conversations that build self-awareness and enable abundant mindsets to envision and plan for positive futures. Working across government, corporate and the community sectors, she's a collaborator at heart and firmly supports community self-determination.

Natalie's a big thinker, able to communicate and bring concepts to life and inspire others to vision the future. She's also grounded in results and focuses on practical approaches and enabling systems to make things happen.

These days, you'll find her reading, studying or learning new concepts, theories and software systems, developing ideas or helping someone else with their ideas. While a bit of a long-range planner and dreamer, she's also well-grounded in practicality and strategies to achieve these.

Natalie supports several social and charitable organisations and gives her time as a company and non-profit volunteer director as well as sitting on a few non-profit boards in a voluntary capacity.

Natalie lives in Dubbo with her husband and co-founder of 20 years, and their feline fur-babies. In her downtime, she enjoys recreational cycling and hiking; exploring and experiencing different cultures and food; sewing; and is an avid reader of anything except horror!

www.ingramcontent.com/pod-product-compliance
Lightning Source LLC
Chambersburg PA
CBHW071403050426
42335CB00063B/923